When **KARL MARX** Died

By Philip S. Foner

History of the Labor Movement in the United States (4 vols.)

The Life and Writings of Frederick Douglass (4 vols.)

A History of Cuba and its Relations with the United States, 1492–1895 (2 vols.)

The Spanish-Cuban-American War and the Birth of American Imperialism, 1895–1902 (2 vols.)

The Complete Writings of Thomas Paine (2 vols.)

Business and Slavery: The New York Merchants and the Irrepressible Conflict

W. E. B. Du Bois Speaks (2 vols.)

The Fur and Leather Workers Union

Jack London: American Rebel

Mark Twain: Social Critic

The Jews in American History: 1654–1865

The Voice of Black America: Major Speeches by Negroes in the United States, 1797–1971

The Case of Joe Hill

The Letters of Joe Hill

The Bolshevik Revolution: Its Impact on American Radicals, Liberals, and Labor

American Labor and the War in Indochina

Helen Keller: Her Socialist Years

The Black Panthers Speak

The Basic Writings of Thomas Jefferson

The Selected Writings of George Washington

The Selected Writings of Abraham Lincoln

The Selected Writings of Franklin D. Roosevelt

The Autobiographies of the Haymarket Martyrs

"His name and his work will endure through the ages."

The concluding words of the speech by Frederick Engels at the grave of Karl Marx, who died March 14, 1883

When
KARL
MARX
Died

Comments in 1883

PHILIP S. FONER Editor

INTERNATIONAL PUBLISHERS, New York

ISBN 0–7178–0385–6 (Cloth); 0–7178–0386–4 (Paperback)
Library of Congress Catalog Card Number 73–85995
© 1973 by International Publishers Co., Inc.
First edition 1973
Printed in the United States of America

CONTENTS

5. THE COOPER UNION MEMORIAL MEETING

6. REACTION TO THE DEATH OF KARL MARX IN EUROPE

ENGLAND

HOLLAND

ROMANIA AND SPAIN

ITALY

RUSSIA

7. CONTEMPORARY ESSAYS AND ARTICLES ON KARL MARX

)

APPENDICES

Introduction

Marxism is today the most influential body of thought in the world. Hundreds of millions live in societies whose fundamental principles—socialism—were laid down over a century ago by Karl Marx and his collaborator and friend, Frederick Engels. Both were Germans, but they propounded principles which were and remain universal and international. The universality and internationalism of Marxism have been demonstrated again and again from the moment it came into existence, and one of the manifestations of its international character was evident in the mourning which followed the news that on March 14, 1883, Karl Marx, the father of socialism, had died. Coupled with the grief was the universal respect for the enormous contributions this man made to mankind.

Two weeks after Marx's death, the Zürich *Sozialdemokrat*, organ of the illegal German Social Democratic Party, announced that it would issue a special memorial number to include tributes from the Socialist and labor press of Europe and the United States "to this eternal fighter for the social revolution."[1] This special number never appeared; nor did one scheduled for March 14, 1884, the first anniversary of Marx's death. In time the project was forgotten. To be sure, on anniversaries of Marx's death there were repeated reprints of Engels' moving and brilliant speech at the grave. But beyond this, nothing of the opinion of Marx at the time of his death was collected and published in a single work.

In 1933, on the fiftieth anniversary of Marx's death, the Marx-Engels-Lenin Institute in the Soviet Union issued, in a number of languages, a pamphlet entitled, *The Fourteenth of March—1883: Frederick Engels on the Death of Karl Marx.* (An English-language edition of the pamphlet was published in the United States by International Publishers.)[2] The pamphlet contained Engels' cables and letters announcing Marx's death, his articles on the event in the Zürich *Sozialdemokrat* of May 3, 1883, and, of course, his celebrated speech at Marx's grave. However, the first serious attempt to fulfill the plan envisaged by the *Sozialdemokrat* at the time of Marx's death, occurred with the publication of Gerhard Becker's "Nachrufe auf Karl Marx

1883," in *Zeitschrift für Geschichtswissenschaft* of 1968, issued in the German Democratic Republic.[3] The twenty-two page article contained obituaries and editorials which had been published in the Zürich *Sozialdemokrat, New Yorker Volkszeitung, Kölnische Zeitung,* and *Vossische Zeitung,* and the report—a partial account of the proceedings—of the great memorial meeting in honor of Karl Marx held in New York's Cooper Union, March 20, 1883.

My own interest in collecting and editing reactions to Marx's death was stimulated by my coming upon the account of the Cooper Union meeting in the *Voice of the People,* official organ of the Central Labor Union of Greater New York and Vicinity.[4] Apart from being impressed by the reports of the tremendous outpouring of members of the working class of New York to honor Karl Marx, and the broad spectrum of progressive opinion represented by the speakers, I was curious to see if a similar meeting had occurred in any other country. It had not I discovered, but in the course of my research I came across the issue of the Zürich *Sozialdemokrat* which announced the plan to publish the tributes to Marx at the time of his death. I decided then not only to fulfill this plan, but also to broaden the project to include all opinion of Marx in the contemporary press——laudatory and hostile—during the weeks and months after March 14, 1883 as well as reports of the death and of the proceedings at the grave.

I discovered in the course of my research that there were many countries in which Marx's death was not even noticed, and that newspapers of many cities in countries where some notice was taken of the event, carried not even a brief obituary note. *Pall Mall Gazette* of London had noted with surprise on March 16, 1883 that it was "extraordinary" that Karl Marx's death "should have been allowed to pass almost unnoticed." This was hardly the entire truth, but it did accurately describe the situation in many countries. Perhaps *Pall Mall Gazette's* editor should not have been surprised since Engels' speech at the grave noted that "Marx was the best hated and most calumniated man of his time."

Not only did scores of newspapers in the United States and Europe during the two weeks following Marx's death contain no mention of the event, but even monthly and quarterly journals in these countries devoted no attention to it in the months after March, 1883. Particularly flagrant examples of magazines guilty of such omission are the *Atlantic Monthly*, published in Boston, which carried an article "Academic Socialism" in its August, 1883 issue without a single reference to Marx; the *North American Review*, published in New York, which featured the article, "Communism in the United States" in its May, 1883 issue which neither mentioned Marx nor his death two months earlier, and *The Contemporary Review*, published in London, which had the article, "The Progress of Socialism," in its April, 1883 issue without a single mention of Marx.[5]

I have not had the opportunity to conduct research in the publications issued in 1883 in the Far East. But a study of newspapers published in the Middle East revealed nothing that could be included in this volume.[6] More startling was the absence of any apparent notice of Marx's death or comment on the man in the press of Latin America. Not even *El Ferrocorrel*, the leading liberal daily paper published in Santiago, Chile, or *El Atacomeño*, organ of the liberal-Masonic forces in the northern mining city of Copeapó, Chile, had anything on Marx's death.[7] Fortunately, José Martí's sympathetic account of the Cooper Union Memorial Meeting was published in *La Nación* of Buenos Aires,[8] so that some readers in Spanish America were able to learn of the death of Marx and of the high estimation in which he was held by members of the New York working class and their leaders.

There are, to be sure, copies missing, for March, 1883 of newspapers which may well have commented on Marx's death.[9] It may well be that in the future these missing copies will turn up, and more will be added to our knowledge of opinion of Marx at the time of his death. Furthermore, some papers which might have been expected to comment on Marx's death did not appear at all for several months during 1883.[10] But certainly what is included in the present volume reveals that while he was widely ignored, Karl Marx was also widely hailed as a titanic figure in world history.

In preparing this material for publication, I have, in most cases, omitted purely obituary notices and biographical sketches. For one thing, many were replete with errors. For another, they usually said little about the man himself, merely outlining a few highlights of his career. I have thought it worthwhile, however, to include Eleanor Marx's biographical sketch in *Progress*; first, because of its accuracy,[11] and second, because it is by Marx's daughter. Where biographical material is elsewhere included, it is because the facts, even though not always fully accurate, are intimately related to the evaluation of Marx.

The volume is divided into seven sections and two appendices, each preceded by an introduction to place the material in its historical framework. Explanatory notes have been furnished wherever it was deemed necessary to provide information on personalities and events referred to. Except where otherwise indicated, all notes are the editor's. The source of each selection is provided. Every effort has been made when material, usually of a biographical nature, has been omitted to avoid any distortion of the original meaning in the process of excerpting. In a few instances, two editorials in the same paper have been combined so as to avoid repetition.

Since the vast majority of the editorials and articles in the original were headed either "Karl Marx" or "Death of Karl Marx," I have taken the liberty of substituting titles reflecting the theme of the selection. I have also changed all titles of Marx's works referred to in the text to conform to those used in the English-language editions.

No work of this nature is the product of one man. Without the assistance of a host of institutes, libraries and individuals in several countries, this book would have never been completed. I owe a special debt of gratitude to the Institute of Marxism-Leninism in the Soviet Union, the Institute of Marxismus-Leninismus in the German Democratic Republic, the Marx House in London, the Institute Maurice Thorez in France, the Instituto Gramsci in Italy, the International Institute of Social History and Gemeentelijke Archiefdienst Van Amsterdam in Holland for graciously furnishing me copies of newspapers and magazines in their archives, or for assisting me in obtaining such material in libraries of their countries. Mr. Giovanni Grilli of Varese, Italy was most helpful in furnishing me with copies of Italian newspapers and magazines. Yvonne Kapp and Geoff Brown of London were of help in supplying copies of material in British newspapers. Professor Edward H. Shaffer of the

INTRODUCTION

Department of Economics, University of Alberta, kindly loaned me his copy of the *Voice of the People* containing the account of the Cooper Union Memorial Meeting. The Bibliothèque Nationale of Paris, the Tamiment Institute Library of New York University, the Wisconsin State Historical Society, the New York Public Library, the American Jewish Archives, Cincinnati, Ohio, Yivo Institute for Jewish Research of New York City, the Library of Congress, Harvard University Library, Columbia University Library, and the Boston Public Library were all most cooperative. I owe a special thanks to the Interlibrary Loan Department of Lincoln University for assistance in obtaining a wide variety of material in other libraries.

I have been most fortunate in obtaining the unstinting cooperation of several translators. Dr. Brewster Chamberlin of the University of Maryland and his wife Angela were of tremendous assistance in translating the large amount of material which appeared originally in the German language. Mr. Rudi Bass also assisted in translating some of the German material. Dirk Struik, Professor Emeritus, Massachusetts Institute of Technology, gave his time to the task of translating all of the material in the Dutch language, and also furnished me with important information about the nature of the newspapers and journals and contributors. Paul Russo, Assistant Professor of History, Lincoln University, translated all of the material published in the Russian press, and kindly furnished me with historical information about the journals and contributors. Andrew Suozzo of the Romance Language Department, Lincoln University, and Miss Diana Volpe translated the material published in Italian. Mircea Oprea, Department of Economics, Queens College, translated the article which appeared in the Romanian language. My wife, Roslyn Held Foner, kindly translated the material published in French and Spanish. Mrs. Marianne Russo of the Department of English, Lincoln University, was of assistance in smoothing out rough edges in the translations, and copy editing the manuscript.

PHILIP S. FONER

Lincoln University, Pennsylvania
March, 1973

1

FREDERICK ENGELS REPORTS THE DEATH OF KARL MARX

INTRODUCTION

Reports of Marx's death had appeared so frequently in the press of Europe and the United States—in large measure as expressions of wish-fulfillment on the part of those who hated the man and his ideas—that mere newspaper dispatches of his death in March, 1883 were not taken seriously by many leaders of the Socialist movement. Hence Frederick Engels moved swiftly to inform them that this time the tragic event had actually taken place. Since most accounts in the press of Marx's last illness were filled with errors, Engels also provided the world Socialist movement with a factual account of Marx's final days. Still later, to correct the accounts of Marx's illness and death already published, Engels wrote a special article for the Zürich *Sozialdemokrat* outlining for the entire Socialist movement many of the facts surrounding Marx's last days. In these letters and articles, Engels also expressed his views on Marx's historic role and significance.

In this section are the cables and letters written by Engels on March 14 and 15, 1883, immediately after Marx's death, all but the first reprinted from *The Fourteenth of March—1883: Frederick Engels on the Death of Karl Marx,* and his article for the Zürich *Sozialdemokrat.* The latter also contained tributes to Marx received too late to be read at the grave; these will be found in the next section.

Frederick Engels was born in 1820, in Barmen, Germany, the son of a religiously-inclined, tyrannical owner of textile factories in Barmen. Despite pressure upon him to pursue a business career, Engels chose writing and radical journalism. He met Marx briefly in Cologne, but in the summer of 1844, the two struck up a permanent friendship which was to profoundly influence their lives and the whole course of scientific socialism. Engels was one of the young German refugees—Marx was another—who met together in Brussels in 1845 and 1848, discussing and planning revolutionary activity. He fought in the revolutionary uprisings of Baden, and after the collapse of the Baden revolution, escaped to London. Engels worked in his father's business in Manchester for nineteen years, financially aiding the desperately poor Marx family. When he had accumulated enough capital for himself, he sold his share of the business and moved to London where he spent the last twenty-five years of his life writing his own important books and articles, editing Marx's works, and helping to direct the course of the Socialist movements in Europe and the United States. He died on August 5, 1895.

Engels collaborated with Marx on a number of books and articles—among them, of course, *The Communist Manifesto* (1848), and wrote a number of prefaces to Marx's works. A brilliant scholar and a person of immense erudition even though he never attended a university, Engels was like Marx a dedicated revolutionist. Once he had joined forces with Marx in 1844, he never swerved from his devotion to the revolution.

SPECIAL CABLE REPORT TO THE SOCIALIST PRESS

(New Yorker Volkszeitung, March 15, 1883)

LONDON, 14, MARCH 1883.

KARL MARX DIED THIS AFTERNOON.

FREDERICK ENGELS.

CABLE TO FRIEDRICH ADOLPH SORGE[2]

LONDON, MARCH 14, 1883

SORGE
135 BLOOMFIELD STREET
HOBOKEN, NEW JERSEY

MARX DIED TODAY

ENGELS, LONDON

LETTER TO WILHELM LIEBKNECHT[3]

London, March 14, 1883

Dear Liebknecht,

You will have learnt from my telegram to Frau B.[4]— the only address which I have— of the terrible loss which the European socialist-revolutionary party has suffered. Only last Friday the doctor (one of the foremost in London) told us that there was every prospect of his recovering completely if only his strength could be kept up by his taking food. Just after that he began to eat with a better appetite. Then today, some time after two o'clock, I found the house in tears and they told me he was terribly weak. Lenchen[5] called to me to come upstairs, saying that he was half asleep, and when I got upstairs—Lenchen had left the room for barely two minutes—I found him sound asleep, but asleep forever. The greatest mind of the second half of our centruy had ceased to think. About the immediate cause of death I refrain from expressing any opinion without medical advice. The whole case was so complicated that it would require reams of paper even for doctors to describe it fully. After all, it is not so important now. I have gone through enough during the last six weeks, and can only say that in my opinion first the death of his wife[6] and then, during a very critical period, Jenny's death,[7] had their share in bringing on the final crisis.

Although I saw him this evening laid out on his bed, the rigidity of death in his face, I cannot fully realise that that brilliant mind has ceased to impregnate the proletarian movement of both worlds with its mighty thoughts. We all owe what we are to him; and the movement as it is today is the creation of his theoretical and practical work. If it had not been for him, we should all still be groping in a maze of confusion.

Yours,

F. Engels

LETTER TO EDUARD BERNSTEIN[8]

London, March 14, 1883

Dear Bernstein,

You will have got my telegram by now. It all happened terribly suddenly. When our hopes were at their highest, his strength suddenly failed him and this morning he simply passed away in sleep. In two minutes this brilliant mind had ceased to think and just when the doctors had encouraged us with every hope for his recovery. What the worth of this man was, both in theory and in practice too, when great decisions had to be made, only one who has long been associated with him can realise. His mighty vision will be buried with him for years to come. It was something of which we others are not capable. The movement will go on, but it will lack that calm timely guidance of a superior mind which has saved it from so many tedious errors in the past.

More later on. It is now midnight and I have been writing letters and running about doing all sorts of things all the afternoon and evening.

Yours,

F. Engels

LETTER TO JOHANN PHILLIP BECKER[9]

London, March 15, 1883

My dear old fellow,

Be thankful that you saw Marx last autumn, for you will never see him again Yesterday afternoon at 2:45, after leaving him alone for less than two minutes, we found him peacefully asleep in his armchair. The greatest mind in our Party had ceased to think, the strongest heart that I have ever known had ceased to beat. It was in all probability a case of internal hemorrhage.

You and I are now almost the last of the old guard of 1848. Well, we'll remain in the breach. The bullets are whistling our friends are falling round us, but this is not the first time we two have seen this. And if a bullet hits one of us, let it come—I only ask that it should strike fair and square and not leave us long in agony.

Your old comrade-in-arms,

F. Engels

LETTER TO FRIEDRICH ADOLPH SORGE

London, March 15, 1883

Dear Sorge,

Your telegram arrived this evening. Many thanks. It was not possible to keep you regularly informed about Marx's state of health because it was constantly changing. Here, briefly, are the main facts.

Shortly before his wife's death, in October of '81, he had an attack of pleurisy. He recovered from this but when, in February '82, he was sent to Algiers, he came in for cold wet weather on the journey and had another attack when he arrived. The atrocious weather continued, and then when he got better, he was sent to Monte Carlo (Monaco) to avoid the heat of the approaching summer. He arrived there with another, though this time a milder, attack of pleurisy. Again abominable weather. When he was at last better, he went to Argenteuil near Paris to stay with his daughter, Madame Longuet. He went to the sulphur springs nearby at Enghien, in order to relieve the bronchitis from which he had suffered for so long. Here again the weather was awful, but the cure did some good. Then he went to Vevey for six weeks and came back in September, having apparently almost completely recovered his health. He was allowed to spend the winter on the south coast of England, and he himself was so tired of wandering about with nothing to do that another period of exile to the south of Europe would probably have harmed him in spirit as much as it would have benefited him in health. When the foggy season commenced in London, he was sent to the Isle of Wight. There it did nothing but rain and he caught another cold. Schorlemmer[10] and I were intending to pay him a visit at the new year when news came which made it necessary for Tussy[11] to join him at once. Then followed Jenny's death and he had another attack of bronchitis. After all that had gone before, and at his age, this was dangerous. A number of complications set in, the most serious being an abscess on the lung and a terribly rapid loss of strength. Despite this, however, the general course of the illness was proceeding favourably, and last Friday the chief doctor who was attending him, one of the foremost young doctors in London, specially recommended to him by Ray Lankester,[12] gave us the most brilliant hope for his recovery. But anyone who has but once examined the lung tissue under the microscope, realizes how great is the danger of a blood vessel being broken if the lung is purulent. And so every morning for the last six weeks I had a terrible feeling of dread that I might find the curtains down when I turned the corner of the street. Yesterday afternoon at 2:30—which is the best time for visiting him—I arrived to find the house in tears. It seemed that the end was near. I asked what had happened, tried to get to the bottom of the matter, to offer comfort. There had been only a slight hemorrhage, but suddenly he had begun to sink rapidly. Our good old Lenchen, who had looked after him better than a mother cares for her child, went upstairs to him and then came down. He was half asleep, she said, I might come in. When we entered the room he lay there asleep, but never to wake again. His pulse and breathing had stopped. In those two minutes he had passed away, peacefully and without pain.

All events which take place by natural necessity bring their own consolation with them, however dreadful they may be. So in this case. Medical skill might have been able to give him a few more years of vegetative existence, the life of a helpless being, dying—to the triumph of the doctors art—not suddenly, but inch by inch.[13] But our Marx could never have borne that. To have lived on with all his uncompleted works before him, tantalized by the desire to finish them and yet unable to do so, would have been a thousand times more bitter than the gentle death which overtook him. "Death is not a misfortune for him who dies, but for him who survives" he used to say, quoting Epicurus.[14] And to see that mighty genius lingering on as a physical wreck to the greater glory of medicine and to the scorn of the philistines whom in the prime of his strength he had so often put to rout—no, it is better, a thousand times better, as it is—a thousand times better that we shall in two days' time carry him to the grave where his wife lies at rest.

And after all that had gone before, about which the doctors do not know as much as I do, there was in my opinion no other alternative.

Be that as it may, mankind is shorter by a head, and the greatest head of our time at that. The proletarian movement goes forward, but gone is its central figure to which Frenchmen, Russians, Americans and Germans spontaneously turned at critical moments to receive always that clear incontestable counsel which only genius and a perfect understanding of the situation could give. Local lights and lesser minds, if not actual humbugs, will now have a free hand. The final victory is certain, but circuitous paths, temporary and local errors—things which even now are so unavoidable—will become more common than ever. Well, we must see it through. What else are we here for? And we are not near losing courage yet.

Yours,

F. Engels

LETTER TO FRIEDRICH LESSNER[15]

London, March 15, 1883

Dear Lessner,

Yesterday at three o'clock our old friend Marx went softly and quietly to sleep forever. The immediate cause of death would seem to have been internal hemorrhage.

The funeral will take place on Saturday at 12 o'clock and Tussy asks you to be there.

In great haste,

Yours,

F. Engels

THE DEATH OF KARL MARX

By Frederick Engels
Der Sozialdemokrat, Zürich, May 3, 1883

To refute some of the false rumors printed in the newspapers, I shall give a few details about the illness and death of our great theoretical leader.

Although almost cured of an old liver disease after three treatments in Karlsbad, Marx still suffered from chronic stomach pains and nervous exhaustion, which resulted for the most part in headaches and persistent insomnia. Both symptoms more or less disappeared after a visit to a seaside spa or a health resort in the summer but reappeared again with increased intensity after the New Year. Chronic throat trouble, coughing, which also added to the sleeplessness, and chronic bronchitis seemed to bother him less. But this was ultimately to be the cause of his death. Four to five weeks before the death of his wife, he suddenly came down with pleurisy combined with bronchitis and the early stages of pneumonia. The illness was very dangerous, but he seemed to recover well. He was then sent to the Isle of Wight (in the beginning of 1882) and after that to Algeria. The trip was cold, and he arrived in Algeria with another attack of pleurisy. This might not have been so serious under normal circumstances. But that winter and spring were unusually cold and rainy in Algeria. In April, they tried in vain to heat the dining room! Thus, his condition worsened instead of improving.

Marx was sent from Algeria to Monte Carlo (Monaco) but arrived with a third, though mild, case of pleurisy as a result of a cold wet crossing. The bad weather continued; he seemed to have brought it with him from Africa. Here, too, instead of regaining his strength, he had to fight with a new illness. Toward the beginning of summer he went to stay with his daughter, Mrs. Longuet in Argenteuil, and used the neighboring sulphur baths at Enghien for his chronic bronchitis. Despite the continuing wet summer the treatment succeeded, slowly, but to the satisfaction of the doctors. The doctors then sent him to Vevey on Lake Geneva, and there he recovered so rapidly that he was allowed to spend the winter, although not in London, at least on the southern coast of England. There he finally wanted to work again. When he arrived in London, in September 1882, he looked healthy and often climbed Hapstead Hill (ca. 300 feet higher than his apartment) with me without complaint. When the November fogs threatened, he was sent to Ventnor, in the southern corner of the Isle of Wight. Once again there was wet weather and fog; the inevitable result: new colds and coughs; in brief, instead of strengthening walks in the fresh air—weakening bed rest. Then Mrs. Longuet died. The next day (January 12), Marx arrived in London with a definite bronchitis. Soon he also caught laryngitis, which made swallowing almost impossible. Although he knew how to stand pain stoically, he was unable to eat adequate food and was forced to drink a liter of milk (which had a lifelong horror for him). He developed a tumor on his lungs in February. Medications were useless in this body which had grown immune to them over the past fifteen months: they only reduced his appetite and impaired his digestion. He lost weight daily. Despite this, the total illness remitted somewhat. The bronchitis almost disappeared and swallowing became easier. The doctors were very hopeful. Then I went to see him—between 2 and 3 p.m. one day—the whole house suddenly in tears: they told me he was very weak; the end seemed near. And yet he had that morning enjoyed wine, milk and soup. Faithful old Lenchen Demuth, who had raised all Marx' children and was part of the household for forty years went upstairs to him and immediately came back: "Come with me, he is half asleep." When we entered, he was asleep, but forever. One could not wish for a more gentle death than Karl Marx found in his arm chair....

And now, in conclusion, some good news:

The manuscript of the second volume of *Capital* is absolutely complete. How much it will possible to publish as it stands I cannot say; there are over 1,000 folio pages. But "The Circulation Process of Capital" and "Shaping of the Total Process" are finished in one work, organized in the years 1867-70. We have the beginning of a later version, as well as much material in critical extracts, especially about the conditions of land ownership in Russia, much of which can probably be used.

Through verbal instructions, Marx named his youngest daughter Eleanor and me as his literary executors.[17]

London 28 April 1883.

2

THE FUNERAL
OF KARL MARX

INTRODUCTION

Karl Marx was buried on March 17, 1883 alongside the grave of his wife, Jenny. (Before he was buried, many people were allowed to see him in his coffin.) A week later, the grave was reopened to receive the remains of his grandson, Harry Longuet, who died on March 21 at the age of four-and-half.

Marx's funeral in Highgate Cemetery, London, was attended by a small group of mourners: among them Engels, Eleanor Marx, Charles Longuet, Paul Lafargue, Wilhelm Liebknecht, Friedrich Lessner, Carl Schorlemmer, and Edwin Ray Lankester. The only paper to carry an account of the proceedings at the grave was the Zürich *Sozialdemokrat* which published Engels' communication with its report of the speeches and messages at the graveside.

Highgate cemetery lies above the dirt-laden fogs of the lower city. It contains expensive mausoleums of railroad kings, and simple monuments like those over the grave of George Eliot and George Jacob Holyoake, founder of British workers' cooperatives. There is also a heavy monument to Herbert Spencer. For many years, in a tiny space, there was also the grave of Marx, his wife Jenny, their grandson, and Helene Demuth (Lenchen"), the devoted family housekeeper. A small flat tombstone marked the grave, and on the slab was the inscription which eventually read:

JENNY VON WESTPHALEN
The beloved wife of
KARL MARX
Born 12 February 1814
Died 2 December 1881

AND KARL MARX
Born May 5, 1818, died March 14, 1883

And HARRY LONGUET
Their grandson
Born July 4, 1878, died March 20, 1883

and HELENE DEMUTH
Born January 1, 1823, died November 4, 1890

The question of a suitable monument to Marx was a matter of some discussion among Socialists. The Congress of the German Social Democratic Party—illegal in Germany since passage of Bismarck's antisocialist law in 1878—was scheduled to meet in Copenhagen March 29 to April 2. August Bebel wrote to Engels the day of Marx's funeral informing him that he proposed to move at that Congress a resolution that a monument to Marx should be erected. Such a monument should not be grandiose, Bebel suggested, but it should represent the gratitude of the workers of the world to their departed leader. To this Engels replied: "I don't know what should be done about a memorial to Marx. The family is against it. The simple gravestone designed for his wife and now bearing his own and his little grandson's name, would be desecrated in their eyes it if were replaced by a monument."[1] Wilhelm Liebknecht wrote later in his reminiscences of Marx:

> Marx did not want a "memorial." To have desired to put up any other memorial to the creator of *The Communist Manifesto* and of *Capital* than that which he had built himself would have been an insult to the great dead. In the heads and hearts of millions of workers, who have "united" at his call, he has not merely a memorial more lasting than bronze, but also the living soil in which what he taught and desired will become—and in part has already become—an act.[2]

The pages of *Justice* and *Commonweal* contain frequent reports of processions to Marx's grave to commemorate the Paris Commune. But the plot itself was so long neglected that in 1922 *Plebs,* a British revolutionary magazine, and *The Communist,* organ of the British Communist Party, issued a joint appeal "for funds to restore the neglected grave of Karl Marx." The appeal stated that the sum of five pounds ($25) was required immediately to restore the lettering of the inscription on the headstone and to put the grave in order, and an annual sum of 30 shillings ($6.00) for its permanent care. The appeal was accompanied by a picture of Marx's grave showing the headstone nearly buried in the soft earth and partly overgrown with weeds and unkept grass.[3]

The appeal produced a pledge from the Plebs League of Great Britain to attend to the upkeep of the grave. In the United States, the "Bolshevik" Bishop William Montgomery Brown of Galion, Ohio offered to bear the cost of restoring Marx's grave.[4] But *The Worker*, organ of the Workers' (Communist) Party of the United States felt that still more was necessary:

> We feel that something more fitting than a small headstone should mark the last resting place of this greatest philosopher of the working class.
>
> Capitalism takes care of its own. Paris boasts her Tomb of Napoleon. The Tomb of General Grant graces Riverside Drive in New York City. Recently an elaborate memorial to Abraham Lincoln was dedicated at Washington, D.C. Similarly everywhere else.
>
> Why should not the workers honor the last resting places of those who have fought and sacrificed for them. Pilgrims from many lands by the thousands annually visit the grave of Marx. These thousands should leave Marx's grave with a fitting impression upon their minds.
>
> *The Worker* believes that the workers of all countries would like to join in erecting a fitting Marx Memorial. The Communists, the true disciples of this spokesman of labor, should take the lead in this effort, should direct it. [5]

The suggestion produced no concrete result.[6] In 1956, however, the British Communist Party, seeking to erect a more prominent tombstone for Marx, found a new site for the grave midway up the cemetery slope. The Marx family grave was then moved to its present location and the ashes of Eleanor Marx were added—they had been previously held by the Marx Memorial Library on Clerkenwell Green. Today a giant bust of Marx in hammered iron stands atop a ten-foot-high granite monolith. The inscription reads: "WORKERS OF ALL LANDS UNITE."

In March, 1933, on the occasion of the 50th anniversary of Marx's death, the British workers established a different form of memorial to Marx. This was the Marx Memorial Library. In addition to making Marxist books available in England the Library was determined to keep alive the works which were at the time being burned in the streets of Germany by the Nazis.

Today the Library has over 700 paying individual members and 54 affiliated bodies. Approximately 18,000 books are in its lending and reference sections, plus pamphlets, periodicals, newspapers and other reference materials.

In the Soviet Union, the German Democratic Republic and, indeed, all of the Socialist countries there are today flourishing institutes devoted to the study and publication of the immense body of Marx's writings.

As we have noted, Engels' speech at Marx's grave has often been published. But, so far as I know, this is the first time that the full proceedings appear in print since their original publication in the Zürich *Sozialdemokrat* of March 22, 1883. This section also includes Engels' report in the *Sozialdemokrat* of May 3, 1883 in which he published the messages which had arrived too late to be read at the graveside.

THE FUNERAL OF KARL MARX

By Frederick Engels
Der Sozialdemokrat, Zürich, March 22, 1883

On Saturday, March 17, Karl Marx was laid to rest in the cemetery at Highgate in the same grave in which his wife was buried fifteen months ago.

At the grave G. Lemke laid two wreaths with red ribbons on the coffin in the name of the editors and staff of the *Sozialdemokrat* and the London Communist Workers Education Association.

F. Engels then spoke as follows in English:

On the fourteenth of March, at a quarter to three in the afternoon, the greatest living thinker ceased to think. He had been left alone for scarcely two minutes, and when we came back we found him in an armchair, peacefully gone to sleep—but forever.

An immeasurable loss has been sustained both by the militant proletariat of Europe and America, and by historical science, in the death of this man. The gap that has been left by the death of this mighty spirit will soon enough make itself felt.

Just as Darwin discovered the law of evolution in organic nature, so Marx discovered the law of evolution in human history; he discovered the simple fact, hitherto concealed by an overgrowth of ideology, that mankind must first of all eat and drink, have shelter and clothing, before it can pursue politics, science, religion, art, etc.; and that therefore the production of the immediate material means of life and consequently the degree of economic development attained by a given people or during a given epoch, form the foundation upon which the forms of government, the legal conceptions, the art and even the religious ideas of the people concerned have been evolved, and in the light of which these things must therefore be explained, instead of vice versa as had hitherto been the case.

But that is not all. Marx also discovered the special law of motion governing the present-day capitalist method of production and the bourgeois society that this method of production has created. The discovery of surplus value suddenly threw light on the problem in trying to solve which all previous investigators, both bourgeois economists and socialist critics, had been gropping in the dark.

Two such discoveries would be enough for one life-time. Happy the man to whom it is granted to make even one such discovery. But in every single field which Marx investigated—and he investigated very many fields, none of them superficially—in every field, even in that of mathematics, he made independent discoveries.

This was the man of science. But this was not even half the man. Science was for Marx a historically dynamic, revolutionary force. However great the joy with which he welcomed a new discovery in some theoretical science whose practical application perhaps it was as yet quite impossible to envisage, he experienced a quite other kind of joy when the discovery involved immediate revolutionary changes in industry and in the general course of history. For example, he followed closely the discoveries made in the field of electricity and recently those of Marcel Deprez.[8]

For Marx was before all else a revolutionary. His real mission in life was to contribute in one way or another to the overthrow of capitalist society and of the forms of government which it had brought into being, to contribute to the liberation of the present-day proletariat, which he was the first to make conscious of its own position and its needs, of the conditions under which it could win its freedom. Fighting was his element. And he fought with a passion, a tenacity and a success such as few could rival. His work on the first *Rheinische Zeitung* (1842), the Paris *Vorwärts* (1844), the Brussels *Deutsche Zeitung* (1847), the *Neue Rheinische Zeitung* (1848-9), the *New York Tribune* (1852-61), and in addition to these a host of militant pamphlets, work in revolutionary clubs in Paris, Brussels and London, and finally, crowning all, the formation of the International Workingmen's Association—this was indeed an achievement of which Marx might well have been proud, even if he had done nothing else.

And consequently Marx was the best hated and most calumniated man of his times. Governments, both absolutist and republican, deported him from their territories. The bourgeoisie, whether conservative or extreme democrat, vied with one another in heaping slanders upon him. All this he brushed aside as though it were cobweb, ignoring them, answering only when necessity compelled him. And now he has died—beloved, revered and mourned by millions of revolutionary fellow-workers—from the mines of Siberia to California, in all parts of Europe and America—and I make bold to say that though he may have many opponents he has hardly one personal enemy.

His name and his work will endure through the ages!

Marx's son-in-law Longuet [9] then read the following messages in French:

I. Message laid on the grave of Karl Marx by Russian Socialists.

In the name of all Russian Socialists I send a last farewell greeting to the most prominent master of all Socialists of our time. One of the greatest leaders has passed away, one of the most energetic fighters against the exploitation of the proletariat has died.

The Russian Socialists bow before the grave of the man who sympathized with their efforts throughout the course of their terrible struggle; a struggle they will continue until the ideals of the social revolution finally triumph. The first translation of *Capital*, that gospel of contemporary Socialism, was made into the Russian language. Students in the Russian universities were the first to be privileged to hear a sympathetic description of the theories of the powerful thinker who we have now lost. Even those who found themselves in disagreement with the founder of the International

Workingmen's Association regarding practical organizational questions had to bow before the comprehensive scholarship and higher power of the thought which was able to fathom the phenomenon of modern capitalism, the development of economic societal forms and the dependence of the whole history of man on these forms of development. And even his passionate foes in the ranks of revolutionary Socialists can do little other than follow the call which, with his lifelong friend, Frederick Engels, he shouted out to the world:

"Proletarians of all countries, unite!"

The death of Karl Mark will be mourned by all those who understand his thoughts and who recognize his influence on our time.

And I allow myself the additional words that he will be mourned more painfully by those who knew him intimately, particularly by those who loved him as a friend.

Paris, 15 March 1883

P. Lavrov[10]

II. Telegram

The Paris Brotherhood of the French Workers' Party expresses its pain at the loss of the thinker whose materialistic conception of history and whose analysis of capitalist production created scientific Socialism and the current revolutionary Communist movement. It further expresses its devotion to the man Marx and its complete agreement with his thought.

Paris, 16 March 1883

The Secretary: Lepine[11]

III. Telegram

In my own name and as the delegate of the Spanish workers Party (Madrid Brotherhood) brotherhood) I partake of the terrible pain of the friends and daughters of Karl Marx at the terrible loss of the great Socialist who was the master of us all.

Paris, 16 March 1883

José Mesa y Leompart[1]

Then Liebknecht spoke in German:

I have come from central Germany to express my love and thankfulness for this unforgettable teacher and true friend. For this true friend! His oldest friend and colleague, Frederick Engels just referred to Karl Marx as the most hated man of this century. True. He was the most hated, but he was also the most loved. Most hated by the oppressors and exploiters of the people; best loved by the oppressed and the exploited, as far as they are conscious of their situation. The oppressed and exploited people loved him because he loved them. The deceased, whose loss we suffer, was great in his love as he was in his hate. His hate stemmed from his love. He was a great heart as he was a great mind. Everyone who knew him knew that.

But I do not stand here only as a pupil and friend; I stand here also as representative of German Social Democracy, which has authorized me to give expression to the emotions it feels for its teacher, for the man who created our party insofar as one can speak of creation in this regard.

It would not be right for me to give a beautiful speech here. No one was more an enemy of the phrase than Karl Marx. His great service was precisely that he freed the proletariat, the party of the working people, from the phrase and gave it the unshakeable basis of science. A revolutionary in scientific thought and scholarship, as well as a revolutionary in scientific method, he reached the highest peak of scholarship, then descended to make science the common property of the people.

Science is the liberator of the people.

Natural science liberates us from God. Still the God in heaven lives on, even if science has killed him.

Social science, which Marx opened up for the people, kills capitalism and with it the idols and masters of the earth, which as long as they live, will not let God die.

Science is not German. It knows no limits, especially no limits of nationality. And so the creator of *Capital* must naturally become the creator of the International Workingmen's Association.

This scientific basis, for which we thank Marx, enables us to repel all the attacks of the foe and to continue the struggle we have begun with ever-increasing strength.

Marx transformed Social Democracy from a sect and from a school into a party, into a party which now fights on undefeated, and which will be victorious.

This is true not only for us Germans. Marx belonged to the

proletariat. He devoted his whole life to the proletariat of all countries. The thinking proletariat in all nations owe him thankful respect.

Marx's death strikes us as a heavy blow. But we do not mourn. He is not dead. He lives in the hearts and the minds of the proletariat. His memory will not disappear, his teachings will affect growing numbers of circles.

Instead of mourning, we will act in his great spirit; with all our strength, we will work for the earliest possible realization of what he taught and fought for. Thus can we best celebrate his memory.

Deceased, living friend! We will follow the way you have shown us to victory. That we promise you at your grave!

Also at the grave were other sons-in-law of Marx, Paul Lafargue, Friedrich Lessner, who was sentenced to five years in prison at the Cologne Communist trial in 1852, and G. Lochner,[13] also an old member of the Communist League. The natural sciences were represented by two celebrities of the first rank, the zoology Professor Ray Lankester and the chemistry Professor Schorlemmer, both members of the Royal Society in London.

Fr. Engels

A FURTHER REPORT

By Frederick Engels
Der Sozialdemokrat, Zürich, May 3, 1883

A few more announcements regarding this sad occasion have recently come to my attention which indicate what widespread sympathy it has awakened and I must acknowledge them.

On the 20th of March Miss Eleanor Marx received the following telegram in French from the editor of the *Daily News*, London:

"Moscow, March 18. Editor *Daily News*, London. Please

transmit to Mr. Engels, the author of *The Condition of the Working Class in England*[14] and the intimate friend of the late Karl Marx, our request to have a wreath placed on the grave of the never-to-be-forgotten author of *Capital*. The wreath should bear the following inscription:

"'To the defender of rights in theory and the champion of their realization in life; from the students of the Petrovskoe Agricultural Academy at Moscow.' The money will be sent to Engels immediately upon his telling us of his address and the cost of the wreath. The Students of the Petrovskoe Academy in Moscow."[15]

The cable unfortunately arrived after the burial on March 17th.

On March 31st, my friend P. Lavrov in Paris also sent me a money order for 125.50 (equal to £4.18.9) from the students of the Technological Institute in St Petersburg and from Russian women students for a wreath to be laid on Karl Marx' grave.

Last week the *Sozialdemokrat* announced that the students of Odessa also desired a wreath in their name laid on Marx' grave.

Because the money from Petersburg was more than enough for three wreaths, I took the liberty of using it for the Moscow and Odessa wreaths as well. The printing of the inscriptions, an unusual thing here, has caused some delays, but I hope to lay the wreaths next week and I will then be able to give an accounting of the money in the *Sozialdemokrat*.

From the Communist Workers' Education League in Soligen, we receive a large beautiful wreath: "For the grave of Karl Marx from the Workers of the Scissors, Knife and Sword Industry in Soligen." As we laid it on the grave on March 24th, we discovered that some desecrating hand had cut off and stolen the ends of the red silk ribbons from the wreaths of the *Sozialdemokrat* and the Communist Workers' Education League. Complaints to the authorities did not help in this instance, but may help provide more protection in the future.

A Slavic association in Switzerland which "hopes that a memorial in memory of Karl Marx will be started in his name through the creation of an international fund to aid the victims of the great emancipation struggle and also to further this struggle" sent its first contribution.[16] I retained the contribution for the time being as the fate of this proposal depends mostly on what kind of response it receives, and for that reason I am publishing it here.

London, 28 April 1883.

3

KARL MARX
A Biographical Sketch

INTRODUCTION

Of all the biographical sketches of Marx which appeared soon after his death, two were most significant. One was published in the *New Yorker Volkszeitung* of March 15, 1883, and was probably written by Friedrich A. Sorge. The other was by Marx's daughter, Eleanor, and was the first of two articles she published in the May and June issues of *Progress*, edited at the time by Edward Aveling, the British Physiologist and Socialist who had married Eleanor. (The second article was a concise exposition of the theory of surplus value and appears below.) Since both biographical sketches covered essentially the same aspects of Marx's life, I decided it best to reprint only the account written by Eleanor Marx. However, since she was reluctant to deal with Marx's personal life, the interesting final section of the sketch in the *Volkszeitung* is included there:

"Marx's family was an extremely happy one. From his marriage to Jenny von Westphalen, the sister of the reactionary Prussian minister of the trio Manteuffel-Raumer-Westphalen-came four children, a son and three daughters. The son died in childhood, and his death was a blow from which Marx never recovered; he had set great hopes on his son. The three daughters grew up to be beautiful, delicate young ladies and gave their parents much pleasure. The two eldest daughters married splendid French Socialists, Lafargue and Longuet; the latter's death a few months ago was a factor in the death of Marx, a sensitive father. All three daughters studied with their father, helped him with his correspondence, read numerous newspapers for him, underlining interesting articles, and, in general, assisted him in every way. Whoever came to know Marx's family life will never forget the impression it made upon him. Marx acted as he thought. None of his actions was inconsistent. A deadly enemy of belief in authority, he did not seek to be the authority for his children. Loving and jovial in relations with all, he evoked affection and friendship from those who had the good fortune to make his personal acquaintance.

Full of life and free and easy, he quickly cemented ties of
friendship and established informal relationships. The workers
of the entire world have lost in Marx their greatest teacher and
warmest friend."[1]

KARL MARX (A BIOGRAPHICAL SKETCH)

By Eleanor Marx
Progress, London, May, 1883, pp. 288

There is no time perhaps so little fitted for writing the
biography of a great man as that immediately after his death,
and the task is doubly difficult when it falls to one who knew and
loved him. It is impossible for me to do more at present than
give the briefest sketch of my father's life. I shall confine myself
to a simple statement of facts, and I shall not even attempt an
exposition of his great theories and discoveries; theories that are
the very foundation of Modern Socialism—discoveries that are
revolutionising the whole science of Political Economy. I hope,
however, to give in a future number of *Progress* an analysis of my
father's chief work—*Capital,* and of the truths set forth in it.

Karl Marx was born at Trier, on May 5th 1818, of Jewish
parents. His father—a man of great talent—was a lawyer,
strongly imbued with French eighteenth-century ideas of
religion, science, and art; his mother was the descendant of
Hungarian Jews, who in the seventeenth century settled in
Holland. Amongst his earliest friends and playmates were
Jenny—afterwards his wife—and Edgar von Westphalen. From
their father, the Baron von Westphalen—himself half a
Scot—Karl Marx imbibed his first love for the "Romantic"
School, and while his father read him Voltaire and Racine,
Westphalen read him Homer and Shakespere. These always
remained his favorite writers. At once much loved and feared by
his school-fellows—loved because he was always in mischief, and
feared because of his readiness in writing satirical verse and

lampooning his enemies, Karl Marx passed through the usual school routine, and then proceeded to the Universities of Bonn and Berlin, where to please his father, he for a time studied law, and to please himself he studied history and philosophy. In 1842 he was about to habilitate himself at Bonn as "Privat Dozent," but the political movement arisen in Germany since the death of Frederick William III. in 1840, threw him into another career. The chiefs of the Rhenish Liberals—Kamphausen and Hansemann—had founded the *Rheinische Zeitung* at Cologne, with the cooperation of Marx, whose brilliant and bold criticism of the provincial Landtag created such a sensation, that, though only twenty-four years old, he was offered the chief editorship of the paper. He accepted it, and therewith began his long struggle with all despotisms, and with Prussian despotism in particular. Of course the paper appeared under the supervision of a censor—but the poor censor found himself powerless. The *Zeitung* invariably published all important articles, and the censor could do nothing. Then a second, a "special" one was sent from Berlin, but even this double censorship proved of no avail, and finally in 1843 the government simply suppressed the paper altogether. In the same year, 1843, Marx had married his old friend and play-fellow, to whom he had been engaged for seven years, Jenny von Westphalen, and with his young wife proceeded to Paris. Here, together with Arnold Ruge, he published the *Deutsch Französische Jahrbücher,* in which he began the long series of his socialist writings. His first contribution was a critique on Hegel's "Rechts-philosophie;" the second, an essay on the "Jewish Question." When the *Jahrbücher* ceased to appear, Marx contributed to the journal *Vorwärtz,* of which he is usually said to have been the editor. As a matter of fact, the editorship of this paper to which Heine, Everbeck, Engels, etc., contributed, seems to have been carried on in a somewhat erratic manner, and a really responsible editor never existed. Marx' next publication was *The Holy Family* written together with Engels, a satirical critique directed against Bruno Bauer and his school of Hegelian idealists.

While devoting most of his time at this period to the study of Political Economy and of the French Revolution, Karl Marx continued to wage fierce war with the Prussian government, and as a consequence, this government demanded of M. Guizot—it is said through the agency of Alexander von Humboldt, who happened to be in Paris—Marx' expulsion from France, With this demand Guizot bravely complied, and Marx had to leave Paris. He went to Brussels, and there in 1846 published, in French, a "Discours sur le libre échange." Proudhon now published his *The Philosophy of Poverty,* and wrote to Marx that he awaited his "férule critique." He did not wait long, for in 1847 Marx published his *The Poverty of Philosophy,* and the "férule" was applied with a severity Proudhon had probably not bargained for. This same year Marx founded a German Working-Man's Club at Brussels, and, what is of more importance, joined, together with his political friends, the "Communist League." The whole organization of the League was changed by him; from a hole-and-corner conspiracy it was transformed into an organization for the propaganda of Communist principles, and was only secret because existing circumstances made secrecy a necessity. Wherever German working-men's clubs existed the League existed also, and it was the first socialist movement of an international character, Englishmen, Belgians, Hungarians, Poles, Scandinavians being members; it was the first organization of the Social Democratic Party. In 1847 a Congress of the League was held in London, at which Marx and Engels assisted as delegates; and they were subsequently appointed to write the celebrated "Manifesto of the Communist Party"—first published just before the Revolution of 1848, and then translated into well nigh all European languages. This Manifesto opens with a review of the existing conditions of society. It goes on to show how gradually the old feudal division of classes has disappeared, and how modern society is divided simply into two classes—that of the capitalist or bourgeois class, and that of the proletariat; of the expropriators and expropriated; of the bourgeois class possessing wealth and power and producing nothing. The bourgeoisie, after using the proletariat to fight its political battles against feudalism, has used the power thus acquired to enslave the proletariat. To the charge that Communism aims at "abolishing property," the Manifesto replied that Communists aim only at abolishing the bourgeois system of property, by which already for nine-tenths of the community property is abolished; to the accusation that Communists aim at "abolishing marriage and the family," the Manifesto answered by asking what kind of "family" and "marriage" were possible for the working men, for whom in all true meaning of the words neither exists. As to "abolishing fatherland and nationality," these are abolished for the proletariat, and, thanks to the development of industry, for the bourgeoisie also. The bourgeoisie has wrought great revolutions in history; it has revolutionised the whole system of production. Under its hands the steam-engine, the self-acting mule, the steam-hammer, the railways and ocean-steamers of our days were developed. But its most revolutionary production was the production of the proletariat, of a class whose very conditions of existence compel it to overthrow the whole actual society. The "Manifesto" ends with the words:

> Communists scorn to conceal their aims and views. They declare openly that their ends are only attainable through the violent overthrow of all existing conditions of society. Let the governing classes tremble at a Communist revolution. The Proletarians have nothing to lose by it but their chains. They have a world to win. Proletarians of all countries, unite!

In the meantime Marx had continued in the *Brüsseler Zeitung* his attack on the Prussian government, and again the Prussian government demanded his expulsion—but in vain, until the February revolution caused a movement among the Belgian workmen, when Marx, without any ado, was expelled by the Belgian govenment. The provisional government of France had, however, through Flocon, invited him to return to Paris, and this invitation he accepted. In Paris he remained some time, till after the Revolution of March, 1848, when he returned to Cologne, and there founded the *Neue Rheinische Zeitung*—the only paper representing the working class, and daring to defend the June-insurgents of Paris. In vain did the various reactionary and Liberal papers denounce the *Zeitung* for its licentious audacity in attacking all that is holy and defying all authority—and that, too, in a Prussian fortress! In vain did the authorities by virtue of the State of Siege suspend the paper for six weeks. It again appeared under the very eyes of the police, its reputation and circulation growing with the attacks made upon it. After the Prussian "coup d'etat" of November, the *"Zeitung"* at the head of each number, called on the people to refuse the taxes, and to meet force by force. For this, and on account of certain articles, the paper was twice prosecuted—and acquitted. Finally after the May rising (1849) in Dresden, the Rhenish Provinces, and South Germany, the *Zeitung* was forcibly suppressed. The last number—printed in red type—appeared on May 19th, 1849.

Marx now again returned to Paris, but a few weeks after the demonstration of June 13th, 1849, the French government gave him the choice of of retiring to Brittany or leaving France. He preferred the latter, and went to London—where he continued to live for over thirty years. An attempt to bring out the "New Rhenish Gazette" in the form of a review, published at Hamburg, was not successful. Immediately after Napoleon's "coup d'etat," Marx wrote his *The Eighteenth Brumaire of Louis Bonaparte,* and in 1853 the *Revelations Concerning the Cologne Trial*—in which he laid bare the infamous machinations of the Prussian government and police.

After the condemnation at Cologne by the members of the Communist League, Marx for a time retired from active political life, devoting himself to his economical studies at the British Museum, to contributing leading articles and correspondence to the New York *Tribune,* and to writing pamphlets and flysheets attacking the Palmerston "regime," widely circulated at the time by David Urquhart.

The first fruits of his long, earnest studies in Political Economy appeared in 1859, in his *A Critique of Political Economy*—a work which contains the first exposition of his Theory of Value.

During the Italian war, Marx, in the German paper *Das Volk,* published in London, denounced the Bonapartism that hid itself under the guise of liberal sympathy for oppressed nationalities, and the Prussian policy that under the cloak of neutrality, merely sought to fish in troubled waters. On this occasion it became necessary to attack Carl Vogt, who in the pay of the "midnight assassin" was agitating for German neutrality, nay sympathy. Infamously and deliberately calumniated by Carl

Vogt, Marx replied to him and other gentlemen of his ilk in *Herr Vogt,* 1860, in which he accused Vogt of being in Napoleon's pay. Just ten years later, in 1870, this accusation was proved to be true. The French government of National Defence published a list of the Bonapartist hirelings, and under the letter V appeared: "Vogt, received August,* 1859, 40,000 francs." In 1867 Marx published at Hamburg his chief work *Capital,*† to a consideration of which I shall return in the next number of *Progress.*‡

Meanwhile the condition of the working men's movement had so far advanced that Karl Marx could think of executing a long-cherished plan—the establishment in all the more advanced countries of Europe and America of an International Working Men's Association. A public meeting to express sympathy with Poland was held in April, 1864. This brought together the working men of various nationalities, and it was decided to found the International. This was done at a meeting (presided over by Professor Beesley) in St. James' Hall on September 28, 1864. A provisional general council was elected, and Marx drew up the Inaugural Address and the Provisional Rules. In this address, after an appalling picture of the misery of the working classes, even in years of so-called commercial prosperity, he tells the working men of all countries to combine, and, as nearly twenty years before in *The Communist Manifesto,* he concluded with the words: "Proletarians of all countries, unite!" The "Rules" stated the reasons for founding the International:

Considering,
    That the emancipation of the working classes must be conquered by the working classes themselves; that the struggle for the

---

*"Vogt—il lui a été remis en Août, 1859. . . 40,000 francs" is the literal text. (*Footnote in original*)

†A second edition appeared in 1872, and a third is about to be published. Translations in French and Russian were made in the seventies, and condensations or extracts of the book have appeared in most European languages. (*Footnote in original*)

‡*See below,* pp. 230.

emancipation of the working classes means not a struggle for class privileges and monopolies, but for equal rights and duties, and the abolition of all class rule;

That the economical subjection of the man of labor to the monopolizer of the means of labor, that is, the sources of life, lies at the bottom of servitude in all its forms of social misery, mental degradation and political dependence;

That all efforts aiming at that great end have hitherto failed from the want of solidarity between the manifold divisions of labor in each country, and from the absence of a fraternal bond of union between the working classes of different countries;

That the emancipation of labor is neither a local nor a national, but a social problem, embracing all countries in which modern society exists, and depending for its solution on the concurrence, practical and theoretical, of the most advanced countries;

That the present revival of the working classes in the most industrious countries of Europe, while it raises a new hope, gives solemn warning against a relapse into the old errors, and calls for the immediate combination of the still disconnected movements;

FOR THESE REASONS—
The International Working Men's Association has been founded.

To give any account of Marx' work in the International would be to write a history of the Association itself— while never being more than the corresponding secretary for Germany and Russia, he was the leading spirit of all the general councils. With scarcely any exceptions the Addresses—from the Inaugural one to the last one—on the *Civil War in France,* were written by him. In this last address Marx explained the real meaning of the commune—"that sphinx so tantalizing to the bourgeois mind." In words as vigorous as beautiful he branded the corrupt government of "national defection that betrayed France into the hands of Prussia," he denounced the government consisting of such men as the forger Jules Favre, the usurer Ferry, and the thrice infamous Thiers, that "monstrous gnome" the "political shoeblack of the Empire." After contrasting the horrors perpetrated by the Versaillists and the heroic devotion of the Parisian working men, dying for the preservation of the very

Republic of which M. Ferry is now Prime Minister, Marx concludes:

> Working men's Paris with its Commune will be forever celebrated as the glorious harbinger of a new society. Its martyrs are enshrined in the great heart of the working class. Its exterminators' history is already nailed to that eternal pillory from which all the prayers of their priests will not avail to redeem them.

The fall of the Commune placed the International in an impossible position. It became necessary to remove the General Council from London to New York, and this, at Marx' suggestion, was done by the Hague Congress in 1873. Since then the movement has taken another form; the continual intercourse between the proletarians of all countries—one of the fruits of the International Association—has shown that there no longer exists the necessity for a formal organization. But whatever the form, the work is going on, must go on so long as the present conditions of society shall exist.

Since 1873 Marx had given himself up almost entirely to his work, though this had been retarded for some years by ill-health. The MS. of the second volume of his chief work will be edited by his oldest, truest, and dearest friend, Frederick Engels. There are other MSS., which may also be published.

I have confined myself to strictly historical and biographical details of the Man. Of his striking personality, his immense erudition, his wit, humor, general kindliness and ever-ready sympathy it is not for me to speak. To sum up all—

"the elements
So mix'd in him that Nature might stand up,
And say to all the world, "This was a Man!"[2]

4

REACTION TO THE DEATH
OF KARL MARX
IN THE UNITED STATES

INTRODUCTION

Despite the fact that the vast majority of newspapers and periodicals in the United States ignored the event of his death,[1] Karl Marx was no stranger to Americans when he died. Between 1851 and 1862, he had served as one of the foreign correspondents of the New York *Tribune,* reaching 200,000 subscribers with his articles. Some carried his signature, although some were attributed to the "London correspondent," and a number were even published as editorials.[2] (The *Tribune* conveniently forgot to mention this professional relationship in its announcement on Saturday, March 17, 1883, that "Karl Marx died in London on Thursday," and it carried neither an obituary nor an editorial.[3]) During the Civil War, Marx's name became further known because of the addresses from the International Workingmen's Association to President Abraham Lincoln pledging the support of the European working class for the Union cause.[4] After the war, the contacts between American labor and the I.W.A. added to the American public's knowledge of Marx and his work, and by 1870 three sections of the International in the United States—a German, a French, and a Bohemian—made the name of Marx even more widely known. By this time, too, many of Marx's writings, including *Capital,* were available in the United States, and while the first volume of Marx's monumental work did not appear in English until 1887, English-language extracts were published in *The Socialist* and the *Labor Standard* between 1876 and 1878. When these extracts, translated by Otto Weydemeyer, son of Joseph Weydemeyer, the pioneer American Marxist, were published in 1878 in a pamphlet, the editor of the *Voice of Labor,* a Boston publication, wrote:

> It is a good thing for socialism in this country that Americans can now at least get an insight into that work which truly has been said to have made a new epoch in the socialistic propaganda. Karl Marx is admitted on all hands to have laid the foundation for the philosophy

of socialism by his scientific writing and especially by his *Capital*. No one before him has so scientifically, so profoundly, so all-sidedly, if I may so speak, criticized our present capitalistic mode of production, and such a criticism is the *sine qua non* that is absolutely essential to an understanding of what socialism proposes to do. Suppose our American editors had been able to read German, and furthermore had been able to read and understand Karl Marx, how small would they have felt themselves to be. They would never have said any more that socialism was nothing but phrases, but they would have come to a vivid consciousness of the fact that all what they had hitherto written in regard to *politico-economical* subjects had been nothing but inflated, unmeaning phrases. The debt is great which American socialists owe to Mr. Otto Weydemeyer (of Pittsburgh), for having translated these extracts; the translation seems to be very correct and a pretty fair one. The price, 20 cents, should certainly not be too high for any man who earnestly wishes to make himself familiar with the leading thoughts of the most profound living socialist, and let it again be said that without comprehending these leading thoughts it is utterly impossible to understand the *raison d'etre* of socialism, that is, understand why socialism is here now and is making all this noise in this world.[5]

It was the Paris Commune, in 1871, that brought Marx's name to the attention of many Americans who had never before heard of the prominent revolutionary leader. The Commune was the object of slander and calumny in the American press, and along with this went a campaign of vilification of the International and its foremost spokesman, Karl Marx.[6] Although Marx was residing in London, the press pictured him directing the Commune from Berlin where he was also said to be functioning as the private secretary of Bismarck. All of this, however, had the effect of arousing curiosity about Marx's real thoughts about the Commune and led American newspapers to assign correspondents to seek interviews with the leader of the International. The New York *Herald's* correspondent proceeded to distort Marx's statements on the Commune and the International, but then the *Herald* refused to publish Marx's reply to "the trash and positive falsehoods" which he charged its correspondent had attributed to him.[7] However, an interview with Marx was published in the New York *World* of July 18, 1871, apparently without mutilation, and gave American readers a clear picture of his views on the Commune and the role of the International. The interview was reprinted in *Woodhull & Claflin's Weekly* (New York).[8]

On January 5, 1879, the Chicago *Tribune* featured an interview which was really a composite of several interviews with Marx. It appeared at a time when Socialist ideas in this country were becoming more prevalent. From 1873 to 1878 the nation experienced the worst economic decline in its history up to that time, and as the U.S. Commissioner of Labor pointed out, one of the effects of the devastating economic crisis was that "it stimulated the study of panics and depressions to a greater extent than any preceding period."[9] Inevitably, the diagnosis of the capitalist system by the world's greatest Socialist thinker attracted attention. Then too, the anti-Socialist laws pushed through the German Reichstag by Bismarck in 1878 aroused interest in the ideas of the banned Social Democratic Party of Germany and those of its chief ideologist who was living in exile in England.[10] Hence the publication of the "Interviews with the Corner-Stone of Modern Socialism," as the Chicago *Tribune* headlined the article, is not at all surprising. Excerpts from the interview appeared in *The Socialist,* an English-language organ of the Socialist Labor Party, and a complete German translation appeared in the *New Yorker Volkszeitung,* with excerpts (also in German) in *Vorbote* of Chicago.[11]

In 1880, the progressive, pro-labor American journalist, John Swinton, made Marx's name and personality known to additional thousands of Americans with his account in the New York *Sun* of an interview he had with Marx, at the seaside resort of Ramsgate, during his visit to England. Swinton was immensely impressed with Marx, referring to him as "one of the most remarkable men of the day." One passage from Swinton's article, in particular, clearly illustrates the profound impact Marx had on him:

> I interrogated the revolutionist and philosopher in these fateful words. "What is?" And it seemed as though his mind were inverted for a moment while he looked upon the roaring sea. "What is?" I had inquired, to which in deep and solemn tone, he replied: "Struggle!" At first it seemed to me as though I had heard the echo of despair; but, peradventure, it was the law of life.

Marx obtained a copy of the *Sun* piece, and in a letter he thanked Swinton for his "friendly article."

It was in American Socialist and labor circles that Marx was best known at the time of his death. His (and Engels') extensive correspondence with friends and associates in the United States, with men like Joseph Weydemeyer and Friedrich A. Sorge, the outstanding socialist leaders during the pre- and post-civil War period, made Marx's ideas felt during the formative period of the labor and socialist movement in the United States. However, the most influential socialist theories among the German immigrants to the United States in the mid-sixties were those of Lassalle. German workingmen, imbued with Lassalle's idea that it was impossible for workers under capitalism to raise their wages above the bare minimum necessary to sustain life and that the only escape from poverty and bondage was for the workers to establish their own cooperative enterprises, took control of German workingmen's unions in both New York and Chicago. The Lassalleans entered trade unions in America and sought to convert them from organizations to battle for higher wages, shorter hours and other improvements in the lives of workers to associations concentrating on cooperatives and state aid to labor through the issuance of greenbacks.

The Marxists in the American sections of the First International, under the leadership of Sorge who was in constant correspondence with Marx, fought the Lassallean efforts to convert the American trade unions into purely political bodies. The "final object" of the workers' movement, Marx emphasized in letters to his American disciples, was "the conquest of political power," but such an accomplishment necessitated "a previous organization of the working class developed up to a certain point, which itself arises from its economic struggles." For this reason both the "purely economic movement" of the workers (trade-union efforts to force concessions directly from particular employers through strikes) and the "political movement" (efforts to achieve an eight-hour law) merited support, because both were "a means of developing this organization."[14] American workers learned through experience that the Marxists were correct in their approach to the problems they faced, and by the early 1870's, Marxist influence was again significant in the American labor movement, especially that of New York City.

When American labor leaders sought to rebuild their shattered trade unions after the economic depression of 1873, they turned to the Marxists in the First International for guidance and assistance. In his autobiography, Samuel Gompers, leader of the Cigar Makers' International Union and one of the founders of the American Federation of Labor as well as its long-time president, wrote that the principles of the International appeared to him "as solid and practical," and acknowledged that as a result of the influence of the Marxists there developed a clearer understanding "that the trade union was the intermediate and practical agency which could bring the wage-earners a better life."[15]

The most important central labor organization in the country at the time of Marx's death was the Central Labor Union of Greater New York and Vicinity. It was formed at a conference held on February 11, 1882, attended by delegates from 14 unions, and by the summer of 1883, it had more than 60 affiliates. The platform of the Central Labor Union was shaped by socialists who contributed "a strongly socialist spirit" to the program. Although several sections of the platform were diluted with Lassalleanism—particularly the doctrine that producer cooperatives, financed by government credit, could ultimately elimate capitalism—it did emphasize the Marxist idea that both trade union and political organization are necessary in the class struggle.

To American workers of the early 1880's life itself proved the validity of the Marxist concept of the class struggle. "The laborer and capitalists are living in war relations," declared George E. McNeill, the eminent New England labor spokesman who worked closely with the Marxists in the trade unions. The feeling prevailing among American workers that there was an ever-recurring conflict between the two classes was succintly expressed in the following excerpt from the preamble adopted by the Federation of Organized Trades and Labor Unions of the United States and Canada, later known as the A.F. of L., in November, 1881: "A struggle is going on . . . between the oppressors and the oppressed . . . a struggle between capital and labor, which must grow in intensity year by year, and work disastrous results to the toiling millions . . . if not combined for mutual protection."

It is not surprising, therefore, that copies of labor papers in existence contain, in most cases, notice of Marx's death and tributes to the man. Although Terence V. Powderly, Grand Master Workman of the rapidly rising Knights of Labor, was bitterly anti-Socialist and undoubtely prevented the Knights official organ (*Journal of United Labor*) from editorializing on Marx's death,[16] some of the local journals of the Order, such as the Denver *Labor Enquirer,* did. Moreover, members of the Knights of Labor as well as of the American Federation of Labor were among those who packed Cooper Union to the rafters in the great Memorial Meeting in honor of Karl Marx.

A VIGOROUS AND FRUITFUL THINKER

New York *Sun,* March 16, 1883[17]

On Thursday died, almost unnoticed, a man who is likely to be remembered quite as long as any of the Generals, statesmen, and diplomats whose recent disappearance from the stage of public life has been widely chronicled. The Socialist movement of our time is a phenomenon too vast and imposing to be inseparably associated with the name and achievement of any individual reformer. For its fundamental impulse and general direction we must look to the central laws and inherent imperfections of our social system. But if the title of prophet and protagonist belongs to any of its promoters, it would, by the consent of all intelligent observers, be awarded to KARL MARX. Others, like BAKUNIN, diverted for a time the attention and confidence of part of the European proletariat, or, like LASSALLE,[18] played for a brief season a more brillant part; but in him, sooner or later, workingmen throughout the world recognized their authentic guide and veritable commander. KARL MARX is dead, but the work to which he gave his life survives him in the respect commanded by the claims of labor, in the hope which he imparted, in the spirit of unity and organization which he substituted for aimless, discordant, and abortive struggle.

KARL MARX was by far the best-known, most influential, and intellectually the ablest of those *Katheder Sozialisten* or highly educated reformers who in Germany have scrutinized the assumptions and deductions of the orthodox political economists from a new point of view, and who defend their novel doctrines with a display of knowledge and ingenuity that captivate the student and compel the deference and admiration of their opponents. He was by no means a vain or self-assertive man, but he might with perfect truth have uttered the vaunt ascribed to LASSALLE, that he came to the discussion of social problems armed with all the learning of his time. His mind had been tempered and equipped in the foremost training schools of his native country, and had he not abandoned the smooth paths which lead to academical promotion, the discipline and culture of his intellect would have assured to him a place of high distinction in one of the Prussian universities. As it was, although he expended his energies for forty years on the practical object of organizing the proletariat, and in the endless correspondence and fugitive writing which such a task entailed, he was yet able to begin, and bring far toward completion, one work of comprehensive scope and abiding value—*Capital*—in which the relations of capital and labor are discussed with extraordinary penetration and breadth of view, and in which due weight is given to considerations overlooked by most economists, but fraught with momentous import to the stability of existing communities and the welfare of mankind. The appearance of this book unquestionably constituted an epoch in the history of the age-long struggle between wealth and work, between JACOB and ESAU, the heirs of the stored-up gains of proceeding generations and their disinherited brethren. It is in the book mentioned that he clearly indicates the limitations which in the interest of society itself should be imposed upon the working of the iron law of wages—the correlation of supply and demand—which, unrelaxed and uncontrolled, must always tend to lower a workman's earnings to a large subsistence, and thus chain the great majority of the human race in grinding and hopeless slavery. In the same treatise is examined the principle of individual ownership which lies at the root of our social system, and to which not only its refinement, its luxury and splendor, but much of its want and misery and crime, may be directly traced.

KARL MARX was not only a vigorous and fruitful thinker —the strongest, best equipped, and most accomplished intellect which has ever approached the labor problem from a workman's point of view—but he has been for nearly half a century the standard bearer and organizer of the great labor movement whose principles and programme he has formulated. It is true that the International Society which he founded and for some time personally directed has been virtually broken up, but the habit of cooperative effort which he instilled has transformed the laboring masses throughout Europe into a coherent, resolute, and mighty social force. They to whom his life was devoted are not are not likely to forget the watchword in which he summed up the lessons of experience and pointed out the harsh remedy. "Proletarians," he said, "have nothing to lose but their chains. They have a world to win. Let, therefore, the proletarians of all countries combine with one another!"

HE DISCOVERED THE CURE FOR MISERY

New Yorker Volkszeitung,[19] March 15, 1883

Karl Marx is dead—

These four words, sent to us yesterday from London by cable, hold in them a world event. Millions of people today will view this message that way. In the anesthetizing clatter of the machines, in the comfortless darkness of mineshafts, in the scorching heat of the blast furnaces, in all the "master countries" where there are workers who have not forgotten how to think under the deadly pressure of exploitation, and who with all their hearts and with iron will, struggle for a better future, today will be a day of sadness. Many a sinewy arm will hang dejectedly, many a tear will glide down the cheeks of men of labor—a tear about which they do not have to be ashamed, because it is no shame to weep over a loss which is suffered by not one person, not one family, not one people, but by the whole human race in its noblest thoughts and strivings.

In the development of every great ideological movement, which springs from the historical-social relationship, the phenomenon of the new idea is slumbering in the mass of the people and is embodied in some particularly sensitive strong and clear spirits. Rarely, however, has this embodiment been so completely expressed in *one* person, as modern socialism has been embodied in the life, thought and work of Karl Marx. And in the middle of his work on the battlefield of the mind, death struck him. His hand is stilled before he could complete his life's work, the scientific cornerstone of the modern labor movement, his book *Capital.* This loss will remain irreplaceable. Because even though Marx had for the most part collected the materials for the second volume of *Capital* and prepared them for working over and systematization, the powerful spirit that could master this material, that could breathe the clarifying idea into it, that could cut out the particular from the general with such a powerfully thorough sharpness, is now missing.

We must leave until a later time even a partial assessment of the *scientific* importance and meaning of Karl Marx's work. In Marx's work, socialism did not "come to the world as doctrine." Rather it held a mirror up to the world, so to speak, which showed man "why he struggles" and why he *has* to struggle under the force of actual conditions and relationships of nature and industry, and how he is forced, whether or not he wishes it, whether or not he closes his eyes to the truth, to go the way history has determined.

What Karl Marx was as a thinker, he was also as a propagandist, as a fighter for the idea for whose clarification and expression he did so much. His practical activities as the founder of the International Workingmen's Association cannot be divorced from his scientific, theoretical work. The former was the necessary result of the latter. The spirit which conceived the basic idea of *Capital* had naturally to catapult into the world the thundering words:

"Proletarians of all countries, unite!"

Because this powerful slogan so completely expressed the actual conditions, and because the internationality of capital *had to come* about vis-a-via an international association of labor, these thundering words so powerfully, and scorchingly ignited, roared from north to south and from east to west like trumpet blasts, awakening all those whom exploitation and misery had sunk into the sleep of slavery.

Therein lies a comforting thought at the death of this great man. He died in the conviction that his life's goal had been reached, that his new Evangelism had already become the mental property of the working masses of all civilized peoples and would conquer the world with great speed. And for us and all his friends there is comfort that, like no other hero in history, he is immortal. For he will live on in the memories of the masses of all peoples like no other man. We know, too, that he could have done nothing greater than he already has done.

He discovered the cure for misery. He taught how to destroy the slavery which is the basis of other slavery. Compared with Marx's accomplishments in scientific socialism, the work of all his predecessors is insignificant. Compared to his work for the fraternization of the most fragmented and most neglected of all classes in order to destroy all classes, all other bold plans in history fade into the background. No one attained the purity of his character; his words, acts, thoughts and activities were always consistent with him. As husband, father and professional man he was equally excellent, and he leaves behind an envious reputation. He was—no, he *is* a man who belonged to no nation, no country, no era. His name will live eternally in the human Pantheon—in the purest, noblest temple of fame whose gates will remain closed to the "great" exploiters of mankind.

THE GREATEST THINKER OF HIS CENTURY

Freiheit,[20] New York, March 24, April 14, 1883

On 14 March in London at the age of 65 the greatest thinker of his century, the father of modern Socialism, the trailblazer of a new science, the founder of the International Workingmen's Association, a hero of the Socialist revolution died— *Karl Marx!*

From his grave comes the call which for forty years he constantly hurled to the world: *Proletarians of all countries, unite!*

And as if possessed by a magic all-pervading power, workers everywhere have understood that their best friend was no longer with them . . . Marx's immortal service is that he taught us workers to understand our class situation. —That consciousness, that we are a particular class whose interest are opposed by the rest of society, gives birth to that class hatred which one day will be the bell tolling a new period.

KARL MARX

Irish World and Industrial Liberator,[21] New York, March 31, 1883

Karl Marx was by far the best-known, most influential, and intellectually the ablest of these highly educated reformers who in Germany have scrutinized the assumptions and deductions of the orthodox political economists from a new point of view, and who defend their doctrines with a display of knowledge and ingenuity that captivate the student and admiration of their opponents.

THE TOILERS WILL HONOR HIS MEMORY

The Carpenter, [22] New York, April, 1883

Karl Marx died in London on March 14th. As one of the promoters of the International Workingmen's Association, he was detested by all the monarchs, tyrants, monopolists and aristocrats here and in Europe. Born in Germany in 1818, he was exiled from his native land, next driven from France, and found shelter in London. A highly educated man he was one of the ablest of those who dared to take issue with the "orthodox" political economists, His work *Capital* ranks high among scientific men and has been published in all languages, excepting English. The toilers of the world all honor the memory of Karl Marx, for it was he who said: "Workingmen of all countries, unite!"

THE WORKINGMEN'S BEST FRIEND AND GREATEST TEACHER

Progress,[23] New York, March 20, May 1, 1883

Proletarians have nothing to lose but their chains. They have a world to win.

Let therefore the proletarians of all countries combine with one another.

The man who wrote those lines, who organized the International Workingmen's Association, who was feared by every crowned head in Europe and who completely demolished the heartless and cold blooded philosophy of modern capitalism is dead!

The workingmen of all the world are today mourning the loss of their best friend and their greatest teacher. On the afternoon of Wednesday, March 14, Karl Marx died at London, England, worn out with his literary labors.

No man in our present age has done for humanity so great a service as he, and none have been rewarded for their unselfish devotion so shamefully.

No narrow policy was his. He strove not for the aggrandizement of his country—he had been driven out of it. The world was his country and to do good his religion. He sought no position nor power. All that he earned was expended for the poor laborers that he loved so well. This quiet unassuming man whose death is almost entirely ignored by the public press has set on foot a movement that is shaking society to its very foundations, compelling the statesmen of every nation to trim their sails and steer their craft to safe harbors in dread of the coming revolution. Truly, the pen is mightier than the sword, for it disseminates the ideas that make the sword leap from the scabbard and causes strong men to tremble.

The International is disbanded, but its principles live and their adherents now number hundreds of thousands throughout the world. Karl Marx will never be forgotten, while a history remains in existence. Let his name be revered and his sound advice followed. His life-work is finished, and it was complete. Let us all try so to live that men may say of us as they do for Marx—"He hath done what he could for his fellow-man."

HIS NAME WILL STAND
IN THE TEMPLE OF FAME

Voice of the People, [24] New York, March 18, 1883

The Great Karl Marx is dead. The world of labor, free thought, science, the world of all those who strive toward truth through suffering, doubt and struggle is cloaked in sorrow today.

The greatest work of Marx's life was his criticism of modern political economy published under the title, *Capital*. The first volume devoted to "the process of capitalist production" appeared in London in 1867, astonished the entire literary world, causing the greatest excitement among the economists and philosophers of the old schools and throwing them into a wrangle from which they have not yet emerged, while large numbers have tacitly accepted Marx's arguments, and are in many ways weaving them into their own works. The third edition of that first volume is now in process of preparation, and the remaining two volumes, which have been repeatedly corrected in manuscript with scrupulous exactness, will soon be published by the bosom friend of the great author, Frederick Engels.

His life's work is over and it has been well done. In future ages Karl Marx's name will stand in the temple of fame side by side with those of Galileo, Newton, Humboldt and Voltaire.

ONE OF THE MOST REMARKABLE MEN OF OUR TIME

Boston *Daily Advertiser*, [25] March 17, 1883

Karl Marx, whose death occurred yesterday in London, was one of the most remarkable men of our time, although he lived in comparative obscurity, and his principal work, on Capital, is a special plea rather than an inductive or philosophical treatise. Marx was the founder, organizer, and for years the autocrat of the International. Lassalle was his disciple, and he was the principal representative of theoretical socialism. More than any other man living, Marx knew precisely what the Russian nihilists,[26] the German socialists and the French communists were doing, and if he has left any memoranda they will be worth consulting on the cause of socialism, theoretical and practical, in its widest aspects. Marx was often thought a communist and a mere revolutionist; in reality, he was a consummate socialist, and he has done work which, while it may not be liked, has to be recognized. No one can understand the present age who does not know something of what Herbert Spencer[27] called sociology.

Marx was a sociologist, as well as a socialist, a great student, and a remarkable organizer. He has impressed his mind upon his time to a degree and extent at which conservatives may be amazed, but which they cannot deny; for all this talk about nihilism, socialism, communism, and the International is but another name for the work of Karl Marx.

A MAN OF ACTIVITIES AND LEARNING

Springfield [Massachusetts] *Republican,* [28]
March 17, 1883

He was a man of activities and of learning, a graduate in the law courses of Bonn and Berlin, but all his energies were practically defeated by an early acquired enthusiasm for the impracticable socialistic idea.

THE SOCIALISTS HAVE LOST THEIR BEST MAN

The American Israelite,
[29] Cincinnati, March 23, 1883

Carl Marx is dead. The Socialists have lost their best man. Carl Marx, like Ferdinand Lassalle, was an ex-Jew, although neither of them belonged to any other religious community.

A SCHOLAR AND THINKER
Chicago *Tribune*, [30] March 17, 1883

Karl Marx, the chief of the theoretical Socialists and the founder of the "International," died Wednesday in London. A man of high intelligence, a scholar, and a thinker, he devoted his talents to warring against society and his unquestioned executive ability to the formation of organizations of a revolutionary character. His influence was manifest in every popular outbreak in Europe from 1848 to the downfall of the Paris Commune, and it is doubtful whether, outside of Switzerland, any country of Continental Europe would have afforded him a shelter.

THINKER AND FIGHTER
Chicago *Arbeiterzeitung*, [31] March 16, 1883

What Darwin was for the natural sciences, John Buckle was for the science of history, Karl Marx was for the science of national economy—a revolutionary trail-breaker of the truth. What Moltke was for the reactionary science of war, Karl Marx, the thinker, was for the proletariat—a field-marshall of the revolution. He was the most knowledgeable historian of his times, and unbeatable logician and organizer. The much-feared International was his work. Karl Marx showed the world that all relationships, including the economic, are controlled by the law of necessity; in such a way he explained the past, characterized capitalism of the present with irrefutable sharpness, and predicted its inevitable collapse. He prophesied and proved the collapse of capitalism, and gave the coming revolution form and content. He organized its fighters and gave them a common program which even today stands as an unequalled socialist document—the *Communist Manifesto*.

"Proletarians of all countries unite," was the key to his program, and through this program the old society will fall. Under the flag on which the glowing letters of the solidarity of all oppressed stand, the great revolution will begin. With this slogan, the new society will emerge and stand.

HIS MEMORY WILL LIVE
LONG AFTER KINGS ARE FORGOTTEN

Labor Enquirer, [33] Denver, March 24, 1883

A dispatch from Paris, under date of March 16, noting the death of Karl Marx, who died in London, near Regent's park, on the fifteenth. Karl Marx, or "the man of earthquakes," as he was called was the founder of the International Workingmen's Association and was one of the most remarkable men of the nineteenth century. For the past forty-two years he has played an inscrutable but puissant part in revolutionary politics. At his death he was sixty-three years of age and was up to his last moments in the perfect and active use of his superior faculties. In the recital of his travels in Europe in 1880, referring to a visit paid by the writer to "the man of earthquakes," John Swinton says:[34]

"He is a man without desire for show or fame, caring nothing for the fanfaranade or the pretense of power, without haste and without rest, a man of strong, broad, elevated mind, full of far-reaching projects, logical methods and practical aims, he has stood and yet stands behind more of the earthquakes which have convulsed nations and destroyed thrones, and do now menace and appal crowned heads and established frauds, than any man in Europe, not excepting Joseph Mazzini himself.[35] The student of Berlin, the critic of Hegelianism, the editor of papers, and the old-time correspondent of the New York *Tribune*, he showed his qualities and his spirit; the founder and master-spirit of the once dreaded International, and the author of *Capital*, he has been expelled from half the countries of Europe, proscribed in nearly all of them, and for thirty years past has found refuge in London."

Out of respect to the wishes of the deceased, who always avoided unnecessary demonstration, the funeral was very private, and only a few faithful friends and members of the family followed to their last resting place the remains of one whose life-struggle had been for the oppressed of all nations, and whose memory will live sacredly long after kings, monarchs and emperors are forgotten or remembered only to be cursed.

HIS LIFE WAS NOT A SUCCESS

(Daily Alta California, March 18, 1883)

Karl Marx, the revolutionary agitator whose name a few years ago was so frequently mentioned in connection with the International Society, is dead, after a life of sixty years, all the waking days of which were spent in agitating against the most powerful Governments in Europe and the strongest institutions of society. His life was not a success, and at the time of his death he had witnessed the failure of every extensive project on which his hopes had been set and for which he labored with such ability. He was compelled to fly from Germany after the unsuccessful revolutionary attempts of 1848; the International Association, which promised to be such an epoch marking organization, had fallen into ruins within a few years after its birth, and the socialist ideas which he tried to propagate failed to make a lasting impression. His death at this time will serve principally to bring to mind once more that splendid failure, the International, and call attention to the falsity of the premises on which it is builded. It is seldom that events break up and scatter a popular delusion so effectually and so dramatically as was done in this case. It is the Socialist theory that the primary division of mankind is into classes and not nations; that the interests of the laboring classes of different countries are more nearly identical than those of the laborer and capitalist of the same country, and that the laborers all over the world needed only to be brought to understand their true interests to work in perfect harmony. It was not until 1865 that the International was fully organized, and it is a proof of the power of Marx's influence that, although he came into it only after it was in partial operation, he was, without question or objection, accepted as its head.

For a time the society spread with a rapidity that provoked the alarm of European statesmen and inspired a certain dread even on this side of the Atlantic. But an event was close at hand which was to signally demonstrate that blood is thicker than water and that a great international confederation of the labor classes was the unsubstantial fabric of visionaries, which would not withstand the first rude shock of the actual world. That event was the Franco-German war. When that began, the International Association melted away and sank out of sight. Frenchmen and Germans rushed to arms with no thought of a bond of sympathy in the common rights of labor, and the doctrines of Marx were cast to the winds in a single day. It demonstrated that nationality was a vital principle that swayed the world with a thousand times more power than the social philosophy of Marx, LaSalle, Blanc, and all the other European writers of the same or kindred beliefs. The International never recovered from the shock. The wreck was irretrievable, and Marx was glad to embrace the first opportunity to escape from the ruins. Since that time he has been but little before the public, and it is probable that no one was better aware of his own utter failure than himself.

HIS SPIRIT YET LIVES

Burnette G. Haskell in *Truth*,[36] San Francisco, April 7, 1883

The death of Karl Marx saddens me. And yet he is not dead. That grand figure filling the puny theatre of this world with a model of newer and more heroic manhood, that mighty presence has not left us alone and leaderless to wage the desperate fight of the future. No! His mind and thought and soul are with us yet. The holy spirit of this free man yet lives for us upon the pages of his philosophy and shall serve as a guiding angel to point the way to that onstriding Future when we shall deck his statute with the flags of victory and crown his lofty memory with wreaths of flowers.

5

THE COOPER UNION
MEMORIAL MEETING

INTRODUCTION

On March 21, 1883 the New York *Sun* carried the following news report:

TRIBUTES TO KARL MARX

A Great International Memorial Meeting of Workingmen Thousands Turned Away from the Doors of Cooper Union—Addresses in English, German, Russian, Bohemian, and French.

If the great hall of Cooper Union had been twice as large as it is, it could not have held the vast throng of workingmen who gathered last evening to do honor to the memory of Dr. Karl Marx. Long before the hour set for the meeting, every seat was taken, and hundreds stood at the door. They went away only when they saw there was no hope of getting within earshot of the speakers. The audience was composed of people of all trades, from all lands —Americans, Germans, Russians, Italians, Bohemians, and French. There were many ladies present. On the platform were many men prominent in such meetings. . .

The article then gave a summary of the proceedings, extracts from several of the speeches, and the text of the resolutions adopted—a full column in all.

The Cooper Union Meeting of March 20, 1883 was the outstanding memorial event held anywhere in the world in the weeks immediately following the death of Marx. The absence of any such meeting in Germany is understandable; between October, 1878 and October, 1890 when it was repealed, Bismarck's Exceptional (anti-socialist) Law outlawed socialist organizations and publications, and provided for the persecution of members. But in England and France where there was no such proscription, not one meeting was held to honor the memory of the father of socialism. The absence of a meeting in France may have been due to the split which took place in the French Workers' Party (*Parti Ouvrier*) at the Congress of St. Etienne, September 25, 1882, and resulted in exclusion of the

Marxists from the Party on the ground that they could not "obey both the decisions of the Congress, and the will of a person who is himself located in London outside of all Party control." Engels denounced the action and accused those responsible of being "guilty of direct treachery."[1] As for England, both Marx and Engels had repeatedly criticized the desire of the British trade union leaders to achieve "bourgeois respectability," and the failure of these men to organize a meeting in honor of Marx's memory appears to have borne out the criticism.

Furthermore, as British scholars have noted, this period was marked by a decline of radical ideology among the artisans of London, and the emergence of a new white collar working class which was essentially conservative. These factors, together with the rise of a labor aristocracy, help explain the lack of attention to Marx's death in British working class circles.

In the United States, on the other hand, the year of Marx's death was one of sharpening class conflict, increasing influence of Marxist ideas in working class and trade union circles, and one in which few trade union leaders were aiming at "bourgeois respectability," a tendency which was to appear in strength during the opening decade of the twentieth century. Thus to the working class of the United States and its labor and socialist movement—the Cooper Union meeting was initiated by the Central Labor Union of Greater New York and Vicinity, most of whose leaders were socialists—belongs the credit of having accorded the recently-departed Karl Marx the greatest tribute.

The Cooper Union meeting was not the only one held in the United States in the weeks following Marx's death where a tribute was paid. A memorial meeting took place in the hall of the Brooklyn Labor Lyceum on March 18, and was attended by German-Americans of all trades.[2] (For several days, beginning on March 16, the American flag atop of the Lyceum building flew at half-mast in Marx's honor.[3]) On March 18, too, at a meeting in Cleveland to commemorate the heroes of the Paris Commune, Paul Grottkau, leading socialist in the city, concluded his speech on the Commune with a tribute to Marx. "What Kepler was for astronomy, what Darwin was for the natural sciences," he declared, "Karl Marx was for the newest science, national economy and history." At the end of his tribute,

Grottkau asked the audience to rise "in honor of the powerful spokesman for the people who had just died," and remain standing for several minutes. He then urged the audience "to live and act on the basis of the principles outlined in Marx's teachings. Never stand on the side of the people's oppressors. Rather, like Karl Marx, always stand for the interest of the exploited, and, like him, work for the final emancipation of the oppressed."[4]

At a session of the Executive Committee of the Socialist Labor Party of Chicago, a motion was adopted calling for a meeting to be held in honor of Marx on March 25, and that the occasion be used for a discussion of the advisability of nominating a list of candidates for the forthcoming municipal election. The Chicago *Tribune's* account of the meeting read in part:

> The Socialistic Labor Party met yesterday afternoon at No. 54 West Lake street to celebrate the deeds of Karl Marx and to consider the advisability of placing in nomination a city ticket. In honor of the occasion, the hall was decked with bunting and on the walls were mottoes—such as: "No Titles to Land," "Liberty, Fraternity, and Equality." A wide band of black bunting, in the center of which was a portrait of the renowned socialist whose praise was the object of the gathering, extended the width of the room. . . .
>
> Paul Ehman gave an epitome of Carl Marx's life, and closed with a warm tribute to his efforts to advance Socialism.
>
> Julius Vahitech, ex-member of the German Reichstag, then spoke at length in German. He gave a sketch of Marx's works, and in conclusion appealed to the audience to agitate in the spirit of Carl Marx, and to remember his watchword: "Workingmen of all countries, unite."

The Chicago *Tribune* however, took delight in reporting that the meeting degenerated into a brawl between the socialists and the anarchists, led by "Dynamite" Dusey, who "gave vent to an inflammatory speech, during which he characterized the Stars and Stripes as a 'dirty rag,' and pronounced the Emperor of Russia 'the foremost reformer of the age.'" The remarks were condemned by the socialists, and after "a general wrangle," between the anarchists and socialists, the latter gained control of the meeting, and went on to adopt a resolution denouncing the system of voting as being so organized as to make it impossible for a minority party to express itself politically, and that, therefore, no political action should be taken in the forthcoming spring elections by the party as a whole. In the effort to bring the meeting to a close before the anarchists started a new battle, the men on the platform adjourned the gathering before resolutions on the death of Marx could be proposed and adopted.[6]

The Chicago *Arbeiter Zeitung* of March 26, 1883 under the heading, "In Tribute to Karl Marx," carried the news that the "Official" section of the old Chicago "National Socialist Labor Party" held a meeting at which Paul Ehmann read "the biography of the illustrious Karl Marx paying tribute to the invaluable service which he rendered labor." Another speaker, Julius Vahleteich, described as "formerly a member of the Imperial German Parliament, now a member of the staff of the Chicago servile newspaper," spoke on the "labor question in general," but "also paid tribute to Karl Marx, the man of great merits."

What made the Cooper Union meeting in New York so remarkable, was not only its size—in its account *Progress*, organ of the Cigarmakers' Progressive Union of America, called it "The Greatest Demonstration Ever Held in the American Labor Movement in Honor of Any Man"[7]—but the fact that it represented an alliance of different elements who were often at odds with each other but who were ready to abandon their differences in paying tribute to Karl Marx. The meeting brought together for the first time members of socialist and anarchist groups, members of the Knights of Labor and the American Federation of Labor, single-taxers and socialists, and workers of different nationalities and languages. Furthermore, it represented the first time that foreign-born workers, especially the German-Americans, joined with native-American workers in a significant undertaking. Indeed, the Cooper Union meeting marked the beginning of an effort to end the isolation of the German-American Socialists from the native-American working class, a step which Engels repeatedly urged.[8]

Then again, the Cooper Union meeting was also significant in that its proceedings, though in an abbreviated form, were reported in a number of leading commercial journals and in labor and socialist journals throughout the country.[9] In this way, even those in this country who had learned nothing of Marx's death and of his great contributions to the labor and socialist movements through their own local newspapers, were able to obtain such information. (It is likely that when the editor of the *Daily Alta California*, who had written in that paper on March 18, 1883 that Marx's "life was not a success," read accounts of the Cooper Union meeting in California labor papers, he began to have second thoughts.) In short, the Cooper Union meeting was an event of major significance not only in the historical record of reaction to Marx's death but also in the development of the American labor and socialist movements.

The fund raised among trade unions and by the Socialist Labor Party to organize the Cooper Union meeting had a surplus when the gathering was over, and so this was deposited into a special fund for the publication of an edition of *The Communist Manifesto* in the English language which would be circulated among trade unions and other interested groups. (Unions which helped organize the meeting were to receive 300 free copies of the *Manifesto*.) The fund was augmented through the sale of a portrait of Marx specifically drawn for the Cooper Union meeting. The English-language edition of the *Manifesto* was later published and widely distributed. However, Engels was distressed by the quality of the translation.[10]

The Cooper Union meeting had another interesting aftermath which involved Engels. This related to the speech by Johann Most, the leader of the anarchist movement in the United States, which concluded the meeting. Johann Most spoke of having been the popularizer of Marx's works in Germany, and related that when he had met Marx in London before coming to the United States, he had literally received his blessings. His assertion left the impression with the audience that Marx's writings were part of the foundations of anarchism, and soon Most's friend were boasting of him as "the most competent and hard-working distributor of the ideas which Marx had given to the German proletariat."[11]

On April 2, 1883, Phillip Van Patten, socialist Secretary of the

Central Labor Union of Greater New York and Vicinity and one of the two secretaries at the Cooper Union meeting, wrote to Engels:

> When all parties were united in connection with the recent memorial celebration in honor of Karl Marx, many loud declarations were made on the part of Johann Most and his friends that Most had stood in close relation to Marx and had popularized his work, *Capital,* in Germany and that Marx had been in agreement with the propaganda which Most had conducted. We have a very high opinion of the capacities and activity of Karl Marx, but we cannot believe that he was in sympathy with the anarchistic and disorganizing methods of Most, and I should like to hear your opinion as to the attitude of Karl Marx on the question of anarchism versus socialism. Most's ill-advised, stupid chatter has already done us too much harm here, and it is very unpleasant for us to hear that such a great authority as Marx approved of such tactics.

Engels responded to Van Patten's communication on April 18, 1883, and noted that anarchism and Marxism had nothing in common. ("The anarchists stand the thing on its head. They declare that the proletarian revolution must *begin* by abolishing the political organization of the state. But the only organization that the proletariat finds ready at hand after its victory is precisely the state.") "Does it require my express assurance that Marx opposed this anarchist nonsense from the first day it was put forward in its present form by Bakunin?" The whole history of the International Workingmen's Association proved this, and Sorge who was present at the Hague Congress in September, 1872 where the anarchists were expelled from the International, could furnish further details.

> And now for Johann Most.
> If anyone asserts that Most, since he became an anarchist, has had any relations with Marx whatever or has received any assistance from Marx, he has been deceived or he is deliberately lying. After the publication of the first number of the London *Freiheit,* Most did not visit Marx or me more than once, or at most twice. Just as little did we visit him—we did not even meet by chance anywhere or at any time. In the end we did not even subscribe to his paper any more, because there was "really nothing" in it. We had the same

contempt for his anarchism and his anarchist tactics as for the people from whom he had learned them both.

To be sure, Marx did help Most with revisions of the second edition of his translation of extracts from *Capital,* published as a "popular summary," but he had allowed his corrections "to be inserted only on the expressed condition that his name should never be brought into any connection even with this corrected edition of Johann Most's compilation."

Engels gave Van Patten permission to publish his letter.[12]

In this section is the full report of the Cooper Union meeting based on accounts in three newspapers: *Voice of the People, New Yorker Volkszeitung,* and *Freiheit.* None of the three papers carried a complete account, but each did contain some aspect of the proceedings omitted in the others. By combining the reports in all three, it was possible to present the fullest account.

The report of the meeting is preceded by the resolution adopted at the Central Labor Union of Greater New York and Vicinity which brought the meeting into existence, and is followed by the editorial in the *New Yorker Volkszeitung* on the day following the meeting, the report by José Martí, the Cuban "Apostle," who attended the meeting and wrote of it appreciatively in his dispatch of *La Nación* of Buenos Aires which published it on March 29, 1883, and a poetic summary of some of the proceedings published in Germany in 1893 and reprinted here and in an English translation which, however, does not retain the original rhymes.

LET US ALL UNITE IN HONORING HIS MEMORY

Proceedings of the Central Labor Union of Greater New York and Vicinity
Voice of the People, New York, March 25, 1883

The following communication was next read:

Fellow-Workmen: The world of workers has lost one of its greatest teachers and one of its warmest friends. You have all heard of the death of Karl Marx, the great expounder of political economy, whose teachings have laid the cornerstone of that ideal structure which we are all called upon to assist in erecting—the structure of the labor republic of the future, in which the laborer is to reap the full fruit of his toil. Karl Marx was the one who over thirty years ago called upon all workingmen of all countries to unite and organize for the purpose of establishing justice upon the earth. The remedies he proposed for existing evils you find embodied in all labor reform platform; every true advocate of labor reform repeats them in his speeches and writings. Marx proposed the nationalization of the land. the assumption of production, and the distribution of the means of life by the laboring masses themselves. You, as his disciples, are pledged by your own free will to assist in carrying out those propositions which alone are calculated to free us from capitalistic oppression. His death recalls to our minds the duty we owe all our brothers who today are mourning the great loss we are suffering through his demise. Let us all unite in honoring his memory. We have called a mass meeting for tomorrow evening at the Cooper Institute. We expect you and the members of your unions to participate in that meeting. Let us show that labor knows how to honor its friends and workers. Fraternally yours,

> *George G. Block,*
> *Secretary of the Committee*
> *on Arrangements*

A committee of five were appointed to represent the union at the meeting tonight and to draw up resolutions to be then read. The Chairman spoke feelingly of Marx's efforts in 1866 to liberate Irish prisoners, and said that it would not be long before monuments to his memory would be erected all over the world. The members rose from their seats and stood three minutes silently in honor to his memory, and a contribution of $9.12 was taken up to assist in defraying the expenses of the Cooper Union meeting. The following resolution was also adopted unanimously:

> Whereas, The working classes of the world have lost in the death of Karl Marx, the great apostle of the international unity of labor.
>
> Whereas, The Central Labor Union has proclaimed, in the platform of principles, the sympathy and help which every nationality of workers owes to every other; and,
>
> Whereas, This union is formed by all classes of labor, from all quarters of the world, be it,
>
> Resolved, That we unanimously proclaim our deep and lasting sorrow for this untimely loss, and, while desiring to avoid committing any union to special details of any system of action, we unite in our tribute of reverence for the memory of Karl Marx, and our profound sense of regret at his death.

LET EVERY TRUE FRIEND
OF LABOR ORGANIZATIONS ATTEND

Voice of the People, New York, March 18, 1883

On last Thursday morning the news of Karl Marx's death shocked and saddened all workingmen of New York who were acquainted with the life and the labors of that greatest philosopher and social economist of modern times.

On next Monday evening, March 19, there will be a popular mass meeting at Cooper Institute, called by the leading labor advocates and the officers of all the progressive trades unions and labor organizations of New York City, for the purpose of honoring the memory of Karl Marx and expressing the universal regret felt at his decease.

Able speakers will address the meeting, notably John Swinton and other prominent champions of the labor cause. All factions and all elements will be represented on the platform and in the audience, as the meeting will be entirely cosmopolitan and non-partisan in character—a proletarian workingmen's mass meeting, pure and simple. Let every true friend of labor organizations attend.

MOURNING FOR THE TEACHER[13]
(Report of the Proceedings of the Cooper Union Meeting)

The Voice of the People, March 25, 1883; *New Yorker Volkszeitung*, March 20, 1883; *Freiheit*, 1883, III, p.24.

THOUSANDS PAYING TRIBUTE TO THE MEMORY OF KARL MARX
COOPER INSTITUTE PACKED TO ITS UTMOST
CAPACITY—THOUSANDS UNABLE TO
GAIN ADMITTANCE

On last Monday evening, March 19, the large hall of Cooper Institute was crowded to suffocation before 8 o'clock, by six thousand workingmen and women, who filled all the seats, packed the aisles, lined the walls, and densely thronged the lobbies and entrances, so that after 8 o'clock five thousand people, tired of struggling and perspiring in their attempts to gain entrance, were obliged to turn away. The capitalistic papers admit that a hall twice the size of Cooper Institute would have been filled to overflowing by the masses that came to testify their regard for the memory of the great labor champion, Karl Marx. People from all lands and of all nationalities were there. French, Bohemian, German, Italian, Russian, Scandinavian and Spanish—all foreign languages were well represented, while great numbers of Irishmen and Americans demonstrated their presence by appreciative applause of John Swinton's excellent and scholarly memorial in honor of the deceased philosopher.

Back of the speaker's desk was a large crayon portrait of Karl Marx framed in evergreens, with black and white bands, and with a wreath of immortelles above it. Over the picture were the words in large, black letters,

"Vive l'Internationale!"

On each side were red flags, most of them bearing mottoes, among which were:

"Our object, reorganization of society independent of priest, king, capitalist, or loafer."

"Abolish War by Organizing Labor."

On the sides of the hall were large cloth signs with the words:

"Workingmen of all countries, Unite! "

The reading desk was draped in black, and on its front was the letter "M" in white. Beethoven's Funeral March was rendered by the organist, after which the meeting was called to order by P. J. McGuire, Secretary of the Brotherhood of Carpenters of North America,[14] who said: "We have met here for no purposes of hero worship. It is not so much to honor Karl Marx as the principles he advocated." He then announced the following list of officers of the meeting:

Chairman, Edward King; Vice-Presidents, Wm. Horan and John Ritter; Secretaries, Phillip Van Patten for the English and Justus H. Schwab for the German languages.[15]

Mr. King, upon taking the chair, said the meeting was not in any sense political or partisan. It was a cosmopolitan gathering for united regret at the death of a cosmopolitan man. All shades of opinion among the labor organizations of New York were represented, and all kinds of progressive labor men had for a few hours dropped their factious differences and antagonisms in order to honor the memory of the great teacher of them all.

The Socialistic Liedertafel, a singing society with over sixty members, then sang a funeral dirge.

The Chairman then introduced as the first speaker Victor Drury,[16] who said:

We have met to regret the death of one of those men who, although not in the acceptation of some a workingman, has at least aided the workingmen of the world to fight the greatest battle that was ever fought in the world, and that is the battle of the weak and the poor against the rich. Karl Marx has been despised and scorned, as have all those who have pushed themselves forward as thinkers and fighters in the International. The International has been laughed at and termed dead, but your presence tonight is proof that it still lives! And as long as a single drop of blood flows in the veins of thinking workers, the International brotherhood of workers will continue. The work begun by the International will be led in spite of everything, to a glorious ending. The International was founded on a basis as firm as a rock. It had an indestructible program which was: (1) the abolition of standing armies; (2) the abolition of frontiers; (3) the fusion and union of the people. Kings, aristocrats, and loafers of all descriptions understand that when workingmen unite they will have to do their share in the world's work. If they do not do this we will say with St. Paul: 'if you do not work you shall not eat.' Another idea we have in Karl Marx's own words: 'Workingmen of all countries, unite.' He announced that labor creates all wealth, and that labor is entitled to its share of the wealth which it has created. Marx was of greater value for the International than any other man has been, for he proved that only labor creates all values and that the emancipation of the working class can only be brought to reality by the workers themselves. No one, no king, no prince, no capitalist will help you. There are only two classes: the workers and the idlers, and therefore all governments have united against the workers, for the governments are in the hands of the idlers.

The International had a hard battle, for at the beginning the workers did not want to hear anything about its ideas. But it has made progress and has conquered the hearts of the workers. The fight which it has led against authority, aristocracy and professors, has led to victorious results. In that struggle so many have fallen and met no recognition that to-night I look upon this assemblage here as a tear drop which falls upon the graves of the unknown leaders of the labor movement.

John Swinton[17] was then introduced and was greeted with loud applause. After an earnest and close scrutiny of his audience he said:

It is to make requiem for Karl Marx, who has just left the world, that we are here to-night. Karl Marx I met for the first and last time, and his companionship enjoyed, when he welcomed me to his marine villa during the visit I made to England in August of 1880. He was at Ramsgate, the great seashore resort of the Londoners, and there I found him in his cottage with his family of two generations. This saintly-faced, sweet-voiced, graceful woman of suavity who welcomes me at the door is evidently the mistress of the domicile, the wife of Karl Marx. And is this massive-headed, generous-featured, courtly, kindly man of 60, with the busy masses of long revelling gray hair, that remarkable man of the times, Karl Marx!—student of Berlin, critic of Hegelianism, editor of papers, democratic revolutionist, author of *Capital*, founder of the once-dreaded International, proscript and refugee, who for forty years has played an inscrutable but formidable part in the revolutionary politics of the world, and who has stood behind more of the earthquakes which have convulsed nations and shattered thrones, and do yet menace and appall crowned heads and established frauds, than any other man in Europe, not excepting Joseph Mazzini.

During the summer half day I spent with Karl Marx at Ramsgate I was often surprised by his words. His dialogue reminded me of that of Socrates—so free, so sweeping, so creative, so incisive, so genuine—with its sardonic touches, its gleams of humor, and its sportive merriment. He spoke of the political forces and popular movements of the various countries of Europe—the vast current of the spirit of Russia, the motions of the German mind, the action of France, the immobility of England—speaking hopefully of Russia, philosophically of Germany, cheerfully of France, and somberly of England, referring contemptuously to the "atomistic reforms" over which the Liberals of the British Parliament spend their time. Surveying the European world, country after country, indicating the features and the developments and the personages of the surface and under the surface, he showed that things were working toward ends which will assuredly be realized. It was evident that this man, of whom so little was seen or heard, was deep in the times, and that, from the Neva to the Seine, from the Pyrenees to the Urals, his hand was at work preparing the way for the new advent. Nor was his work wasted any more than it had been in the past, during which so many desirable changes had been brought about, so many heroic struggles had been seen, and the French republic had been set on the heights. As he spoke, the question I had put, 'Why are you doing nothing now?' was seen to be an inquiry of the unlearned, and one to which he could not make direct answer.

Karl Marx spoke freely of his contemporaries, the stormy Russian Bakunin, the brilliant German Lassalle,[18] the Frenchman Rochefort among others[19], and I could see how deeply his genius had taken hold of men who, under other circumstances, might have directed the course of history. I found, too, that Mr. Marx was an observer of

American action, and his remarks upon some of the formative and substantiative forces of American life were full of suggestiveness.[20]

The afternoon passed very quickly for me. He prepared a walk to the beach. There we found the family, the wife and his two daughters with their children and husbands. It was a happy little gathering. Marx understood no less subtly than Victor Hugo how to be a grandfather, but he was more fortunate than Hugo, for his married children survived, in order to enliven his old days. As we strolled on the beach, I could not help but notice how friendly the old man was with the boys and girls who met us. 'I love children,' he said, 'I love them all,' at the same time crouching down, in order to kiss a girl, whose delightfully dimpled cheek he had previously stroked.

With all courtliness, Karl Marx accompanied his American guest to the railway station, where for a half hour of waiting he gave full play to his sportive humor, thus answering my attempts to provoke him to graver philosophy. As I was on the point of being whirled away to London, I saw him from my car window waving his hand in farewell. And thus beyond my sight forever in this world passed Karl Marx.

Here, then, through this visit, I had found in Karl Marx such a man as I had imagined him to be—a man without desire for show or fame, caring nothing for the fanfaronade of life or the pretence of power, without haste and without rest, a man of strong, broad, elevated mind, full of far-reaching projects, logical methods and practical aims.

Friends, this old world of ours is very poor in men who unite intellectual genius with the supreme moral qualities—the spirit of self-sacrifice for the love of truth. Of men of this kind there have at no time been many within sight. Nature has always been shabby in supplying them though she furnishes vermin without stint. Even when they appear mankind does not welcome them, but is apt to treat them with contumely, or to outlaw or imprison them, or to hang them. Perhaps we have as many of them in these, our hard days, as there ever were at any other time. Germany has given the world Karl Marx; in our own country we find Wendell Phillips,[21] not to speak of John Brown;[22] Italy can show us Mazzini, not to speak of Garibaldi;[23] France, Victor Hugo,[24] not to speak of Rochefort; Russia, Chernychevsky;[25] Spain, Pi y Margall;[26] Ireland, Michael Davitt;[27] and other countries yet others. Ay, there are ten righteous men to be found in this Sodom of a world; and therefore there is hope that the storm of fire and brimstone may yet be withheld from mankind. All these various men of many lands and languages seek certain great things in common. They aim at the establishment of man's welfare and well-being in life through right ideas and practices, and the abolition of those wrongful things and ways which plays havoc with mankind. They hold that this work is within men's power; that it is practicable; that the way of doing it can be found, and is not too hard. If more than this ye would know, to him who knocks the door shall be opened.

Now take notice, my hard-headed hearers, that these men are not mere dreamers, much less impracticables. Mazzini may have dreamt for forty years of a united Italy, but he lived to see it. Wendell Phillips may have dreamt for forty years of Negro emancipation, but he lives to rejoice over it. Victor Hugo may have dreamt for forty years of a French republic, but he lives to enjoy it. Chernichevsky and Pi and Davitt are dreaming of countries unshackled, and who can tell what they may yet live to see? Karl Marx dreamt of something greater than national liberation, even of the enfranchisement of mankind, and he saw through his lifetime the generation in the natural and moral world of the forces by which it is yet to be brought about.

Here, now, in a few words, I would sum up:

First—Karl Marx was a man of lofty mind, true and free, equipped with all the knowledge of the times.

Secondly—It was by his moral nature, his generous and radiant qualities, his faith in right and love of man, that his mind was controlled.

Thirdly—Karl Marx did extraordinary work in the world, and when the history of the last forty years is revealed, and the movements of which he was a promoter, and which are now in progress throughout Europe, are brought to their consummation, the depth and scope of his work will be known.

Fourthly—Karl Marx proclaimed fruitful ideas to mankind—the comprehensive ideas of unity and self-help incarnated in the International Association, that have become the watchwords of the world's workers; the creative ideas upon political economy, social forces, industrial cooperation and public law that are found in his *Capital*, and the other great underlying ideas of the Revolution whose star will soon appear over Europe.

Fifthly—Karl Marx gave up his whole life for the disinherited, neglecting the personal ends he might have subserved and the prizes he might have won, rendering himself liable to the hostility of power, by which he was made an outlaw.

Finally, in giving all to mankind, Karl Marx gave that which was more than aught else when he gave himself.

In losing him from among us how great is the loss. Comrades everywhere join with us in lamentation. In many of the workshops of our country eyes are moistened by the news of his death. In the workshops of all the many-tongued nations of Europe there is grief that a light bearer has fallen. Hundreds of young students in many lands are touched with regret for the loss of a master. His moral offspring, now prisoners for truth in Germany, Austria, Russia, Spain, Italy, are bewailing his loss. Tears are shed for it in the wastes of Siberia.

But, though dead, he yet liveth—liveth in the heart of mankind, in the spirit that broods over the earth, and in the everlasting principles proclaimed by him, under which we wait for the world's renovation.

Stay with us, mighty shade! And yet farewell, dear friend, farewell! "

The following resolutions were read by Phillip Van Patten in English and Justus Schwab in German, and adopted by a unanimous vote, every person in the room rising to his feet:

RESOLUTIONS

The World of Labor is plunged in sorrow. Its most powerful thinker, its noblest hero, Karl Marx, is no more. His life and the entire power of his great intellect have for thirty years been devoted to the cause of the laboring people. In the field of social-economic science he was the first to prove, by statistical facts and by reasoning based upon universally recognized principles of political economy, that capitalistic production must necessarily lead to the monopolizing and concentrating of all industry into the hands of a few, and thus, by robbing the working class of the fruits of their toil, to reduce them to absolute slavery and degradation. In the field of the *practical* struggle against the despotic rule of capitalism, Marx was also the first to disseminate among the masses in all countries the idea of the solidarity of interests of all workingmen, and by founding the International Workingmen's Association gave to this idea its first and most complete embodiment. He it was who, by formulating the constitution and declaration of principles of the International Workingmen's Association, laid the foundation for the modern progressive labor movement that is overpowering both hemispheres. He it was who first conceived and proclaimed the practical aim and object of this movement—the solution of the social problem of our time— *public ownership of the land and the means of labor.*

What the man of thought and action, Karl Marx, accomplished will remain imperishable in history. Equally great as the man of ideas and the man of action, true and firm, his name will remain immortal while a single human heart beats for justice and liberty. Upon these considerations, and in view of the fact that at this moment millions of people are overwhelmed by the same sentiments, we, men and women of all nationalities, citizens and toilers, in mass meeting assembled, declare:

First—In common with the workers and the disinherited, with the true friends of liberty of all countries, we deplore the death of our great thinker and champion, Karl Marx, as a grievous and irreparable loss to the cause of Labor and Freedom.

Second—We pledge ourselves to keep his name and his works ever in remembrance, and to do our utmost for the dissemination of the ideas given by him to the world.

Third—We promise, in honor of the memory of our great departed, to dedicate our lives to the cause of which he was the pioneer, the struggle in which he left so noble a record, and never at any moment to forget his grand appeal: *Workingmen of the World, Unite!*

Dr. Adolphe Douai[28] next addressed the meeting in German. He said:

To estimate the importance of Karl Marx before Germans and in the German language is actually 'carrying coals to Newcastle.' The Germans who have not yet studied his writings, especially *Capital,* are to be pitied, if they have not had any opportunity to do so, and if they have not done it for other reasons, they are to be condemned. Especially is this true of the man of learning, for whom the study of this strictly scientific work has no difficulty, as it did for hundreds, yes thousands of workers, who did not, however, desist, until they understood it. There is nothing in the entire history of learning which is more disgraceful than the manner in which the German scholars, even specialists in Marxist subjects, treat Marx's work, how they have condemned it to death by silence. Even if they do not agree with the results of such an important research, it was and still is their professional obligation to refute it, and if they are not able to refute it, they should admit this fact. Such is proper conduct for the scholarly sense of honor and scholarly conscience. But except for a few, they have done none of these things.

The governments and the exploiting classes have honored this irrefutable work by forbidding the propagation of its truths as soon as they saw that it was understood by thousands of intelligent workers. They have passed special laws against the followers of Marx; they have taken away their freedom of speech, press and assembly, and have proven thereby that this work contains irrefutable truth and that its propagation must be hindered by force if they are to continue to exist. Yes, in all of Europe, with the exception of England and Switzerland, power is set against the word, the word which speaks truth, and for the followers of Marx there is no freedom of speech. Has a scientific work ever been given a more decisive proof of worth than this? But at the same time the working class has learned that force can only be defeated by force. It has once again been confirmed, in the words of Marx, 'that power is still the midwife of all great innovations.'

It is proper for us as Germans to honor this pride of our nationality, this eternal contribution of our Marx. No scholar of our nationality has achieved anything greater in his field of study than Marx, not even Copernicus, who revolutionized astronomy. He has revolutionized that science which touches most deeply the general welfare of all peoples, which has a greater effect on all people than does religion, yes, even more than the natural sciences of history. He has given to his people the greatest honor that can be bestowed by a scholar and the greatest blessing to all people. This gospel of the liberation 'of the people is at the same time the greatest scientific work written in the German language because of its wealth of old and new facts, its keeness of logic, by which the grouping and development of these things are carried through, and finally through the sagacity of its conclusions, explanations, and comments. Marx has revolutionized the science of political economy by demonstrating the true source of wealth, and by pointing out the injustices of capitalistic methods of usury and profit-taking, the monstrous outrage of private property in land, and the necessity for a radical reconstruction of society. Therefore his works are feared and treated with silence by the powers that be and those who are their servile tools and dependents.

Dr. Douai's address was frequently interrupted by tremendous applause, and closed amid a general roar of approval.

Secretary Van Patten then read the following letter from Henry George:[29]

I am unable to accept the invitation of our committee to address the meeting at Cooper Institute, but I desire to express my deep respect for a man whose life was devoted to efforts for the improvement of social conditions.

I never had the good fortune to meet Karl Marx, nor have I been able to read his works, which are untranslated into English. I am consequently incompetent to speak with precision of his views. As I understand them, there are several important points on which I differ from them. But no difference of opinion can lessen the esteem which I feel for the man who so steadfastly, so patiently, and so self-sacrificingly labored for the freedom of the oppressed and the elevation of the down-trodden.

In the life and in the teachings of Karl Marx there were the recognition of two profound truths, for which his memory deserves be held in special honor.

He was the founder of the International—the first attempt to unite in a 'holy alliance of the people' the workingmen of all countries; he taught the solidarity of labor, the brotherhood of man, and wherever his influence has reached it has tended to destroy those prejudices of nation and race which have been in all ages the most efficient means by which tyranny has been established and maintained. For this I honor Karl Marx.

And I honor Karl Marx because he saw and taught that the road to social regeneration lies not through destruction and anarchy, but through the promulgation of ideas and the education of the people. He realized that the enslavement of the masses is everywhere due to their ignorance, and realizing this, he set himself to work to master and to point out the social economic laws without the recognition of which all effort for social improvement is but a blind and fruitless struggle.

Karl Marx has gone, but the work he has done remains; whatever may have been in it of that error inseparable from all human endeavor will in turn be eliminated, but the good will perpetuate itself. And his memory will be cherished as one who saw and struggled for that reign of justice in which armies shall be disbanded and poverty shall be unknown and governments shall become co-operation, that golden age of peace and plenty, the possibility of which is beginning even now to be recognized among the masses all over the civilized world.

I join with you in paying to such a man the tribute of brotherly regard.

Sincerely yours,
Henry George.

The following telegraphic despatches and communications were then read:

Boston, Mass., March 18.

Comrades: The Section of Boston combines with you in mourning the loss of the great teacher and friend of the Proletariat, Karl Marx. Although his body has perished, his glorious teachings will forever be a beacon-light to every friend of Humanity and Justice. Fraternally,

The Boston Section S. L. P.
E. Neugebauer, Secretary.
New Haven, March 18.

The Socialistic workingmen of New Haven in mass meeting assembled to-day expressed their hearfelt sorrow at the great loss to the labor movement through the death of the master mind, Karl Marx. Permit us to join you in echoing his battle cry: Proletarians of all lands, unite! Fraternally,

M. Ruther, Secretary.
Meriden, Conn., March 19, 1883.

To the Secretary of the Karl Marx Memorial Mass Meeting at Cooper Institute:
At the Convention of the Connecticut Turner Societies, held at Bridgeport yesterday, March 18, 1883, it was

Resolved, That it is with sincere regret that we received the sad news of the death of Karl Marx, the great champion of the rights of man, the man who fought tyranny and the oppression of the laboring classes by capitalists and monopolists. In his death we mourn the loss of a good and true man, but whose principles embodied in his works and treasured up in the hearts of his fellow men will never die.

By order of the delegates,
Louis Kroeber, Secretary.
Trenton, N.J., March 19, 1883.

To the President of the Karl Marx Memorial Meeting in Cooper Institute:
Allow me to join with you in offering a tribute of love and veneration to the memory of my friend and tutor, Karl Marx. Marx is dead, but his work will live forever.

J. P. McDonnell. [30]

By resolution of the meeting the following cable despatch was then ordered sent to Frederick Engels, the bosom friend and companion of the deceased:

To Frederick Engels, 122 Regent's Park Road, London, England:
The proletarians of New York, assembled in Cooper Institute, honor the memory of their immortal Karl Marx.
Proletarians of all countries, unite!
The Secretary.

S. E. Shevitsch,[31] editor of the New York *Volkszeitung*, speaking in English, said:

An interview published in one of the morning papers contains the expression, 'If you want to see to what extent Socialism has spread in America, just come to Cooper Institute this evening.' I hope that the editor of the *World* is now here and can see with his own eyes whether there are any Socialists in New York City.[32] This is the greatest international memorial festival which I ever saw in my life, and it is to honor a man like Karl Marx, who belongs, not to one nation or one hemisphere, but truly to all men who live upon this earth. This meeting is a proof that the laboring population of New York City feel what a man Karl Marx was. Though perhaps thousands of them have not read his works, thousands of them embody his ideas and are ready to live, struggle and die for them. I was born in Russia, and am to speak in that tongue to those of my fellow countrymen who do not speak English. I will say to American students that the Russian people, students, youth, have been among the first to acknowledge the noble ideas of Karl Marx. His ideas are in all Russian universities, in all Russian villages, in all those dark dungeons in which the Russian Government buries those who strive to struggle for freedom in Russia. The ideas of Karl Marx will never die as long as there in one Russian revolutionist in the world.

Mr. Shevitsch then spoke in Russian, in order, he said, to carry out the International idea of the meeting. He asked all Russians present to respond by saying "Yes" to show that they were there. Some fifty men shouted "Dah." Mr. Shevitsch said the principles of Marx were the same as those of Tchernikoff.[33] Once more changing his language, Mr. Shevitsch ended with an address in German:

The greatness of Marx consists in the fact that he told the world for what, and because of what, it would fight. He has proven that the development of the bourgeoisie, as it now is, was a historical necessity. The colossal, the world-conquering power, which speaks from his works, consists in the fact that he proved that the capitalistic means of production had to develop out of the existing relationships. The greatness of Marx is to be seen in the fact, as the highly esteemed speaker before me said, that in this country, where one does not even understand this man's language, such a splendid gathering has taken place in his honor, a meeting such as no political loafer could ever bring together.

The International was the embodiment of Marx's works. The man who wrote *Capital* had to become the founder of the International. He could not do otherwise. The International is dead in form only, but in reality it will and can not die. It still lives and will also live, especially when the people are liberated and joined together in brotherhood.

Let us tonight pledge ourselves to live only for the ideas that Karl Marx promulgated; let us struggle for their realization, and, if necessary, die for them." (Great applause.)

Joseph Bunata[34] spoke briefly in the Bohemian language, and was evidently understood by hundreds of those present, to judge by the applause.

Teophile Millot[35] delivered an address in French. He said:

Marx is an universal character. He represents the universal brotherhood of man, the abolishment of national prejudice and extinguishment of national hatred. The enlightened workingmen of all countries have perceived that their interests are identical and mutual, and that unity is strength. Therefore, they are organizing in accord with Marx's appeal, and will not rest until the capitalistic system is overthrown and replaced by co-operation. Marx is dead, but the International is imperishable and the future belongs to labor!

P. J. McGuire said:

This meeting is a satisfaction to the men who have worked so long and so faithfully in showing that we workingmen of all nations have no quarrels to fight among ourselves, but are united against our oppressors, the capitalists. A few months ago trades unions of

England, from Manchester and Liverpool, sent delegates to Paris to join with their fellow-workingmen in saying that no more trouble was wanted between these countries, but that all workingmen of both countries should unite. That meeting of 6,000 men was held close by the Bastille.

The attempt of Napoleon to kill the International had ended in killing Napoleon himself. He hoped that this work, which had been begun by the trades unions of Europe, would lead to a grand and glorious issue of universal union among the workingmen.

Johann Most[36] was the last speaker. In his speech he said:

Ten years ago at this time I was in jail in Saxony. But I count that period as one of the most beautiful of my life. For back then I had the opportunity for the first time to study the works of Karl Marx and to popularize them—later to bring excerpts of them into circles of the masses which had not yet become acquainted with the writings of their greatest theoretician.

Whoever, like myself, has had the chance to immerse himself into the scholarly accomplishments of this man whom we honor today, knows that such a man must live *forever*.

Under the mound of dirt around which the workers of the entire world sadly are gathered in spirit, lies that which was mortal in Marx—his body. His spirit, which he expressed in his works, is eternal.

When those such as Gorchakov,[37] Gladstone,[38] Bismarck,[39] Lehmann,[40] Theirs and the other crowned and uncrowned monsters of this world are long forgotten, Karl Marx will be remembered.

When the memorials and statues to the old and new Caesars have turned to dust, that memorial which Marx gave humankind, his greatest work, *Capital*, will still shine with its original freshness.

He belonged to those mental giants who discover new truths, formulate new ideas and open for the world new avenues of progress. Only very few of this type arise in a century.

If in spite of this the men of average scholarship have not duly appreciated the importance of Marx, it is due to a fact which Marx himself expressed best when he wrote: The bourgeoisie has made the lawyer, the doctor, the priest, the poet, the man of science into its *paid wage-earner*.

Paid wage-earners. of the bourgeoisie, beggars before the doors of the rich and powerful, corrupted creatures of the machinery of the state which is nothing more than the organized political power in the hands of a thieving horde to further the enslavement of the proletariat—such learned ones *can* not recognize what they are not *allowed* to understand.

Their employers are the representatives of capital whose history Marx correctly branded when he wrote: 'As money in Augier comes into the world with natural blood spots on one cheek, capital is born dripping blood and dirt out of every pore from head to toe.'

The excuse of the learned ones that Marx's works cannot be understood because they are too erudite, is unacceptable because Marx concentrated into short sentences the same things he dealt with so thoroughly in long sections.

He said, for example: 'The Communists can express their theory in *one* word: Removal of private property!' And further: 'The bourgeoisie is producing its own grave diggers. Its overthrow and the victory of the proletariat are equally unavoidable.'

It is also wrong to believe that Marx was only a critic of the present situation who thought only about tearing down and not building. Clearly and sharply he showed what will and must come: 'In place of the old middle class society with its classes and class conflicts will stand an *association* in which the *free development of the individual is the condition for the free development of all.*'

Thus, as he worked for the proletariat alone he expected an active participation from it in return. Of all the classes which stand today against the bourgeoisie, he said, *only* the proletariat is *really* a revolutionary class.

He wrote unceasingly about revolution. What he wrote about the Communists in general referred to himself particularly: 'The Communists support everywhere *every* revolutionary movement against the present social and political conditions. The Communists declare openly that their goals can only be attained through the violent overthrow of all of the current social order. Let the ruling classes shake before the Communist revolution. The proletariat have nothing to lose but their chains. They have a world to win.'

When I saw Marx for the last time three years ago, he was already ill and he said to me: 'I will not see the triumph of our cause, but you are young enough, you can still live to see the people win the victory.' This man fought for forty years; some revolutions sped by him; some victories, some defeats he saw; but he never doubted.

For us younger ones such perserverance must be a model. It is our task to go to the people, to preach to them, to drag one worker after the other into our ranks. In this way we will reach our goals. The social question is just as important here as in Europe, and who knows how soon the battle will break out here. Who knows how soon martial law will be declared here? So organize yourselves not only for defense, but for attack against the capitalist beasts.

You can honor Marx best by not resting in the great work of liberation, in the preparations for the great social revolution.

The speaker was loudly applauded by the Anarchists present.

The greatest memorial mass meeting ever held in the labor movement of America then came to an end by the singing of Carl Sahm's grand chorus, "Work and Pray" (*Bet und Arbeit*), rendered by the Socialistic Liedertafel. The tremendous gathering dispersed singing "La Marseillaise." Never will that demonstration be forgotten by the workingmen of New York. The effects will soon be noticeable throughout the entire labor movement.

KARL MARX LIVES

New Yorker Volkszeitung, March 20, 1883

Under the powerful, unforgettable impression of yesterday's demonstration to honor our eternal thinker and fighter, we find no words to express what we and certainly each of the unnumbered thousands who filled the gigantic hall of the Cooper Institute (pressed shoulder to shoulder for three hours) have felt.

If we can find a word for this feeling, it is the one that we have placed at the beginning of our remarks.

Karl Marx lives! That was indeed the thought, the overpowering feeling that pervaded yesterday's meeting. The eternal spirit of the thinker, the powerful will of the fighter floated over the masses of the proletariat of all countries, all tongues, which have turned up to honor their teacher, their friend.

Had Karl Marx himself been present at the meeting yesterday not merely his eternal spirit, his immortal ideas which are conquering the world, he would have received the conviction that his life, suffering and work have not been in vain, that his call to battle, which is directed at the proletarians of all countries, has also penetrated millions of workers on this side of the ocean, and has sowed a seed which bears a thousandfold harvest.

New York's proletariat will not forget yesterday's observance. The impressions received yesterday will not be wiped out in the business of daily life. The spirit of this immortal man has seized the people forever!

HE DESERVES TO BE HONORED

By José Martí

(José Martí, *Obras Completas*, La Habana, 1946, vol. IX, p. 388)

Look at this large hall. Karl Marx is dead. He deserves to be honored for declaring himself on the side of the weak. But the virtuous man is not the one who points out the damage and burns with generous anxiety to put it right; he is the one who teaches a gentle amendment of the injury.

The task of setting men in opposition against men is frightening. The compulsory brutalization of men for the profit of others stirs anger. But an outlet must be found for this anger, so that the brutality might cease before it overflows and terrifies. Look at this hall: dominating the room, surrounded by green leaves, is the picture of that ardent reformer, uniter of men of different peoples, and tireless, powerful organizer. The International was his creation: men of all nations come to honor him. The crowd, made up of valiant workers, the sight of whom affects and comforts, shows more muscles than jewels, and more honest faces than silk underwear. Labor beautifies: it is rejuvenating to see a farm-worker, a blacksmith, or a seaman. By manipulating the forces of nature, they become as beautiful as nature is.

New York goes on as a kind of whirlpool: however much it

surges and heaves in the rest of the world, in New York it drops down. Here they smile at one who flees; out there, they make him flee. As a result of this kindness, a strength has come to this people. Karl Marx studied the methods of setting the world on new foundations, and wakened those who were asleep, and showed them how to cast down the broken props. But being in a hurry, with his understanding somewhat clouded, he did not see that children who do not have a natural, slow and painful gestation are not born viable, whether they come from the bosom of the people in history, or from the womb of woman in the home.[41] Here are the good friends of Karl Marx, who was not only a titanic stimulator of the wrath of European workers, but also showed great insight into the causes of human misery and the destiny of men, a man driven by a burning desire to do good. He saw in every one what he carried in himself: rebellion, highest ideals, struggle.

KARL MARX MEMORIAL

"in Cooper Institute, New York, March 19, 1883*"
By Leopold Jacoby

In workers' clothes many thousands
Sit and occasionally stand,
And their murmuring tumultuously fill
The grand hall.

There all the languages in all the tongues
Of the nations of the world
Ring out a farewell salute
To the dead warrior.

*This is a translation from *Buch der Freiheit: Gesammelt und herausgegeben von Karl Henckell*, Berlin, 1893, pp. 244-245

The Englishman spoke, "Beloved in huts,
Feared in the Palace,
He lived, acted, and fought
Without haste nor rest.

"He whose name shook the
Factory's windows
Where machine's racket
Is hailed today in our cities and in the country!"

The Russian: "Where despots
Reign through terror and darkness
And where millions tear at their chains,
There Marx is commemorated."

The Frenchman: "As a liberator of the world
He fought against hate among people and war
And this memorial gathering
Guarantees us the victory."

The German said: "Today in front of everyone
We want to pay with love,
Tribute to the thinker
As well as the fighter.

"As once Copernicus created new
The knowledge of the heavens,
So from his mouth rang out
The prophetic words.

"The knowledge of the suffering of the masses
And of the torment of labor.
The idols already lie dying,
Capital!

"He fought for our struggle on the earth
And gave it a sharp sword,
So that a new world would be,
Therefore honor him!

"No one else has ever given us
The equal of the gift of those thundering words:
'Workers of all countries,
Unite!'"

6

REACTION TO THE DEATH
OF KARL MARX
IN EUROPE

INTRODUCTION

This section includes the reaction to the death of Marx as recorded in the press of ten European countries. Some of these articles were written by men forced into exile and so were published outside the authors' native countries. The material ranges from a single expression, as in the case of Spain and Romania, to a fairly extensive body of opinion, as in Holland, Italy, and Russia.

Expelled because of his political activity from Prussia, Belgium and France, Marx went to England in 1849 and lived in London until his death thirty-four years later. There he wrote many of his most important works, the innumerable articles as foreign correspondent for the New York *Tribune*, and completed much of his research for *Capital*. (The British Museum on Great Russell Street was only a ten-minute walk from his third-story apartment at No. 28 Dean Street which he occupied from 1849 to 1856, and not too far from the house in Maitland Park into which he moved in 1864 after a six year residence at Grafton Terrace in Kentish Town.) But if one scans the contents of most British newspapers and periodicals in the weeks following Marx's death, one might easily conclude that he had been a resident of another planet. Apart from the pieces included in this section, the only other mention of Marx's death in the British press seems to have appeared in a twenty-eight line obituary in the *Annual Register* of London, which acknowledged that since he had settled in London, Marx was "recognized as one of the chief Socialist leaders," and that *Capital*, written in the same city, was "the textbook of Socialism."[1] *The Guardian*, *Reynolds Newspaper*, a Liberal-Labour paper, and *The Jewish Chronicle* among many others published in London, failed to make note of Marx's death in their pages. While the *Illustrated London News* had room it its "Obituary of the Week" column of March 17, 1883 for reports of the death of several relatively obscure individuals, it found none for Karl Marx.

Outside of London, only the *Manchester Guardian* carried

anything of Marx's death. The article was the fifth leader, and was probably written by a member of the Democratic Foundation founded in June, 1881. There could have been few men other than Henry M. Hyndman and Ernest Balfort Bax, organizers of the Federation, who could have written such an accurate and sympathetic account.[2]

The ill-informed notice in the London *Daily News* had an interesting sequel. On March 19th a letter appeared in the *Daily News* from Eleanor Marx:

To the Editor of the Daily News

SIR,—In the obituary notice of my father in this morning's *Daily News*, I find certain inaccuracies, one of which I cannot allow to pass uncontradicted. It is said there of the International: "Marx drew up its first programme, and it may be asserted that so long as the English element, represented by him and by English working men like Mr. Odger and Mr. Lucraft, held sway, its aims were mainly such as no Liberal politician would very seriously dissent from . . . At successive Congresses . . . the ascendancy passed to agitators of the 'Red' type, and before the war of 1870 altered the state of Europe, the International had split into two sections, one of which merged in the Commune and the other, of which Marx continued to be the head, found its headquarters in America." It is not for me to inquire in how far an English Liberal politician would "very seriously dissent from" views represented by Mr. Odger and Mr. Lucraft; but it is the fact that Mr. Odger and Mr. Lucraft threw up their positions as members of the General Council the very day that this position made them co-responsible for the manifesto of the International on the "Civil War in France", a glorification of the Commune, and entirely drawn up by my father. I am, Sir, yours obediently,

Eleanor Marx
41, Maitland Park-road, N.S.
March 17.

The limited number of comments in the German press was to be expected in the atmosphere prevailing during the operation of Bismarck's anti-socialist law. (The tributes of the exiled German Social Democrats appear in the section dealing with

Switzerland.) *Neue Zeit* the theoretical organ of German Social Democracy (edited by Karl Kautsky from 1883 to 1917) was the only Socialist publication permitted to appear, but a cautious approach characterized the contributions; so cautious, indeed, that when the journal was threatened with governmental suspension in 1884, Engels assured Kautsky that it would be "no misfortune for the Party."[3]

Apart from *Neue Zeit*, two German papers commented on Marx's death, and much of their space—apart from biographical details—was devoted to an exposition of how unoriginal Marx's ideas were. However, both did concede his considerable influence and his devotion to the working class.

No man was more insulted, none more calumniated than Marx; the hysterical article published in the reactionary *Neue Freie Presse* of Vienna is evidence that the campaign of slander did not cease with his death. However, citizens of Austro-Hungary were at least able to read an appreciative tribute by Leo Frankel, one of the leaders of the Paris Commune, in the *Arbeiter-Wochen-Chronik*, published in Budapest

Among the French papers of 1883 at the Bibliotheque Nationale issues for March are missing for three papers. Fourteen carried no mention of Marx's death, and of the nine which did, five merely published a brief obituary.[5] Only five newspapers in France included editorial comments on Marx,[6] and of these four were appreciative of his work and achievement. One of these was *La Justice*, edited by George Clemenceau, and with which Charles Longuet, Marx's son-in-law was associated. The nasty piece by Paul Brousse in *Le Proletaire*, organ of the Workers Party, understandably aroused widespread indignation in socialist circles. However, it might have been expected that Brousse who had been an enthusiastic anarchist in 1873 and thorough-going revisionist ten years later, would have betrayed his shallowness in his comment on Marx's death.

In general, the discussion in the French press, including the socialist press, was a reflection of the limited influence of Marxism in France at the time. "During the lifetime of Marx and Engels," one scholar has recently observed, "their considerable theoretical achievements did not make much of an impact and were certainly not followed up or discussed in intellectual circles. Paul Lafargue . . .possessed a fine gift of sarcasm and wit and was successful as an organizer and teacher in the ranks of the *Parti Ouvrier*. But as a theorist his work is not remarkable. Indeed, it was with regard to some of his French epigones of this period that Marx uttered his famous, 'I am not a Marxist.' "[7]

The only negative note struck in the entire Dutch press was in the confused and ill-informed article by R. Maclester Loup in *De Gide* (which may be found in the next section). Otherwise those in Holland who commented on Marx were uniformly respectful, including commentators in the papers of the commercial bourgeoisie.[8] The articles by Ferdinand Domela Nieuwenhuis, the Dutch freethinker who turned Socialist and later Anarchist, are among the most thoughtful which appeared anywhere.[9]

In 1872 Engels observed that "the situation in Italy is such that the Bakunists are for the present the masters of the situation within the International."[10] The influence of Bakunin was still strong in Italy when Marx died, but Marxism was asserting itself forcefully. Actually, some of the most confirmed Bakunists were moving from anarchism to socialism. Thus Andrea Costa, Bakunin's friend and disciple, became a Marxist after a long stay in Paris (part of which was spent in prison) , and in 1881 founded the "Partito Socialista Rivoluzionario di Romagna." The following year he was elected a member of the Italian Parliament—the first socialist deputy in Italy. Costa's paper, *Il Sole Dell'Avvenire* of Ravenna, carried a biographical sketch of Marx and a brief but respectful editorial comment. A longer article appeared in the Socialist paper, *La Plebe* of Milan. In addition, *La Lega Democratica* of Rome, a radical though not socialist paper, carried a biographical sketch and an editorial evaluation of Marx.[11] In 1962 *Avanti* of Rome published an article on the reaction of the press of Turin to Marx's death. This article is included in the present section. The lengthy discussion of Marx by Professor Achille Loria of Turin will be found in the next section.

This section closes with what is certainly the most interesting of all the reactions in the European press to Marx's death—that in Tsarist Russia. For one thing, in no other European country was there such wide coverage of the event, and that, too, in spite of the fact that most liberal newspapers which would probably have commented had already been suspended, including *Golos (The Voice)* of St. Petersburg, the leading liberal newspaper which was suspended in mid-February, 1883. To be sure, many papers of different political hue in St. Petersburg, Moscow and in the provinces, such as *Moscow News, Moscow Flyer, Saratov Diary, Warsaw Diary, Volga Messenger (Kazan), Kievan, The Week* (Moscow), *Moscow Gazette, Contemporary News* (Moscow), confined themselves to reporting that the "famous Socialist" or "famous author of *Capital*" had just died, although a few added the note that he was "one of the top-ranking scholars of our time." But at least Marx's death was not, as in most European countries, ignored by the vast majority of the newspapers and journals. Even the biographical sketches were presented with some attempt at accuracy. Furthermore, the general tone both of the brief reports and longer editorial comments was one of respect for the man and his work. Indeed, only three or four of the Russian papers which commented on Marx—and these were the most reactionary in the country—denigrated his contribution, charged that there was nothing original in his work, or labelled Marxism as being based on "vulgar materialism."[12] Apart from these few articles, the discussion was both serious and laudatory. Some of the commentary was written by the leading social scientists in Russia; the article in the Moscow *Law Messenger* was by A. I. Chuprov, Professor of Economics at Moscow University and the leading pre-Revolutionary economist of Russia, who delivered the same tribute to Marx in a speech on March 28, 1883 to the Statistical Section of the Moscow Law Society. There is also the fact that the only Jewish paper anywhere in the world to discuss Marx's ideas in the weeks and months after his death was the *Voskhod Weekly Chronicle* of St. Petersburg. (The *American Israelite* of Cincinnati, it will be recalled, merely devoted a few sentences in its comment.) The article in the St. Petersburg journal is also interesting because of the many attempts to depict Marx as an anti-Jewish bigot.[13]

The final article in this section has an interesting history. Funds to place wreaths on Marx's grave were raised by students in Moscow and St. Petersburg and the "People's Will Circle" (a terrorist organization). They organized an evening meeting in honor of Marx at Elsavetgrad in the south of Russia where funds for a wreath were contributed. The Petersburg Central University Circle of the People's Will was already publishing an illegal journal (printed on hectograph) called *Studenchestvo (The Student Body)* when news of Marx's death reached Russia.[14] The Circle had published *The Communist Manifesto* and issued two editions of *The Civil War in France* so that it was not surprising that its journal joined the movement for placing wreaths on Marx's grave. In connection with this campaign and in tribute to the man it sought to honor, it published the article "For a Wreath for Marx" which closes this section. Though reflecting the lack of theoretical clarity to be expected from the movement it represented, the piece in *Studenchestvo* is a moving tribute to Marx by the revolutionary students of Russia.

When one adds to the material in this section the telegrams sent to Marx's funeral from Russian students and societies and the article "Marx on the Russian Socialists," in the following section, it becomes clear that nowhere else in Europe was as much attention paid to the death of the father of Socialism as in Russia. This will probably come as a surprise to many readers, but one must remember that Marx's works circulated rather widely in Russia. The censorship's lenience stemmed from the belief that Marx's economic theories were too abstract to incite radical behavior, and that discussion of them might even serve as an antidote to the bomb-throwing proclivities of Russian radicalism. Furthermore, Marx's exposure of the evils of capitalism met with an appreciative response from those in Russia who believed it was possible for their country to avoid such evils by skipping the stage of capitalist development as they understood it. Thus the wide popularity of *Capital* in Russia—its translation was begun by G. A. Lopatin soon after it appeared in German, completed by Nikolai Franzevich Danielson, and published in 1872—and the appearance of serious discussions of Marx's economic theories in scholarly journals by the "legal Marxists" paved the way for the response to his death.

However, all this should not leave the impression that to be associated with Marx and Engels was easy in the Russia of 1883. To discuss Marx's economic theories was one thing: to become involved in Marxist political activity and to be known as one of Marx's followers, quite another. This is illustrated by an interesting aftermath of Marx's funeral. On March 24, 1883, Engels wrote to P. L. Lavrov that he did not know how to respond to the telegram the students of the Petrovskoe Agricultural Academy at Moscow had sent to the London *Daily News*, since it was not signed by any specific name. "But I would like to tell these splendid children that I have received their telegram and carried out the task entrusted to me." Lavrov wrote back on March 26 suggesting Engels write to one of the well-known professors of the Academy:

Yesterday, I made inquiries about the professors and I think a good choice would be Professor Ivaniukov. He has done work in political economy and on the question of peasant emancipation. If you write that you know him as the author of these works, your letter will not compromise him, especially since it will be evident from the contents of the letter that he had nothing at all to do with the business. Another approach is to write to Moscow University, to Kovalevskii. . . . In these times, however, it is more dangerous to send a professor a letter in which his friendly relations with you are evident than to write to a man whom you do not know at all.[15]

ENGLAND

HIS INFLUENCE WILL NOT DIE WITH HIM

Pall Mall Gazette, London, March 16, 1883

It is extraordinary that the death of Karl Marx should have been allowed to pass by us almost unnoticed. The great German Socialist has, indeed, for years been little before the eyes of the public. Since the collapse of the International, of which he was at once the moving spirit and the directing mind, he has exercised no visible influence upon contemporary politics. But every one who knows anything about the subsequent workings of the Socialist propaganda is well aware that Marx's influence long survived his recognized leadership, and could indeed only terminate with his death. We speak, of course, of his personal influence, derived, as it was, not only from his intellectual superiority, but from a firm and noble character, marred by a certain imperiousness of disposition. His influence as a thinker and writer will not die with him; indeed, it is destined to increase. Marx is little read, but no man who ever read him with patience and intelligence has failed to be struck by the strength of reasoning and the vastness of erudition which are buried beneath his involved and difficult style. *Capital,* unfinished as it is, will beget a host of smaller books, and exercise a growing influence on men of all classes who think earnestly on social questions.

OBITUARY

DEATH OF DR. KARL MARX

The Times, London, March 17, 1883

Our Paris correspondent informs us of the death of Dr. Karl Marx, which occurred last Wednesday in London. He was born at Cologne in the year 1818. At the age of 20 he had to leave his native country and take refuge in France, on account of the radical opinions expressed in a paper of which he was editor. In France he gave himself up to the study of philosophy and politics, and made himself so obnoxious to the Prussian Government by his writings that he was expelled from France, and lived for a time in Belgium. In 1847 he assisted at the Workingmen's Congress in London, and was one of the authors of the "Manifesto of the Communist Party." After the

Revolution of 1848 he returned to Paris, and afterwards to his
native city of Cologne, from which he was again expelled for his
revolutionary writings, and after escaping from imprisonment
in France, he settled in London. From this time he was one of
the leaders of the Socialist party in Europe, and in 1866 he
became the acknowledged chief. He wrote pamphlets on various
subjects, but his chief work was *Le Capital,* an attack on the
whole capitalist system. For some time he had been suffering
from weak health.

A REALLY DISTINGUISHED NAME

Manchester Guardian, March 19, 1883

The name of the late KARL MARX was a power in Democratic
France; he receives ungrudging praise from papers that differ
from one another on most occasions, and the *Intransigeant* and
the *Bataille* lament in unison over his grave. Yet there is
something for French writers to forget in this instance, for KARL
MARX was undoubtedly a German. There are Germans and
Germans, however, and this one was born in the Rhenish
provinces, and was an enemy of Prussia; while Prussia returned
his hostility with interest. All these are so many points in his
favour; and for the rest his positive services to the democratic
cause were almost inestimable, according to the papers just
named. He founded the International; the first idea came from
him, and, above all, that precious thing in democratic politics,
the "formula." This formula was not the bloody thing it
afterwards became; the International was primarily an economic
conception; the workmen were to combine together to secure
their rights, and to prevent capitalists from playing them off
nation against nation, in the industrial war. It was inevitably

political as well as economic, but whether in MARX's view it was inevitably revolutionary as well is not quite clear. For the thinkers of the party he did still greater service in writing his book on *Capital* which is frankly recognized on the Continent as the Bible of the modern Socialistic movement, an arsenal of weapons for discussion in favour of the most sweeping social changes. It was a peculiar service to the Revolution to give it that basis of argument of which it had long felt the want in our critical age. KARL MARX came, and platform orators could henceforth speak by the card. He was the philosophic father of the movement, and he was prepared for the function by his studies as well as by the natural bent of his mind. He had written on German philosophy before he began to write on modern politics: his revolutionary ideas took root in the profoundest thinking of our time. For the modern Socialist he was a bulwark as well as a beacon; but for him they might have been carried away by the specious Caesarism of LASSALLE, his friend and pupil, who executed all sorts of fantastic personal variations on the theme of the pure doctrine. An argument of KARL MARX set this right. PROUDHON's vagaries, too, were corrected in the same way; his rather paradoxical *Philosophy of Misery* drew down an answer from the sage—*The Misery of Philosophy*—which was one of his happiest efforts. For all these reasons the French Democrats have found little difficulty in forgetting country, if not party, in their tribute to this really distinguished name.

DEATH OF KARL MARX

Daily News, London, March 17, 1883

The death is announced of Dr. Karl Marx, the German Socialist. He had lived to see the portion of his theories which once terrified Emperors and Chancellors die out, while the substantial truth which lay therein was ripened under other care than his own. He was born at Trier (Treves), May 2, 1818, his father being a Prussian official of some importance in the district. The family it is stated was of Jewish extraction. His early university distinction opened the way to lucrative public employment, but this he from the first declined, and commenced his career as editor of the *Rheinische Zeitung*—the result being that he shortly found it expedient to fly to Paris with his newly wedded wife—sister of Herr Von Westphalen, afterwards a member of the Manteuffel Cabinet. In Paris he co-operated with Arnold Ruge and Heine in the publication of the *Deutsche Französische Jahrbücher* and *Vorwärts*, the chief outcome of which was the necessity for his removal to Brussels. Here he spent the years from 1846-7 in study, and produced his first distinctly socialistic book, *The Poverty of Philosophy*, a reply to Proudhon. In 1847 he attended the Workingmen's Congress in London, and in the English capital his chief work may be said henceforth to have been carried out. On the dissolution of the Prussian Chambers in 1848, he started a new *Rheinische Zeitung*, which lasted but for a few months, and advocated the refusal of taxes until all popular demands were conceded. A brief sojourn in Paris, during the revolution of June, was followed by a compulsory flight to England, whence he continued to edit the *Rheinische Zeitung*, printed at Hamburg. In 1859 appeared a work which may be called the precursor of his chief production. It was entitled *A Critique of Political Economy*. But the most notable achievement of Marx was the part he took in founding the *International*, which may be said to have had its birth in September, 1864, at a meeting presided over by Professor Beesly.[16] Marx drew up its first programme, and it may be asserted that so long as the English element, represented by him and by English working men like Mr. Odger and Mr. Lucraft, held sway, its aims were mainly such as no Liberal politician would very seriously dissent from. The subjects discussed at the Geneva Congress (1866) were such as: strikes, and the means of preventing them; standing armies; shortening of the hours of labour; religious ideas, their influence on social, political, and intellectual movements. At successive congresses, at Lausanne, Brussels, Basle, and the Hague, the ascendancy passed to agitators of the "Red" type, and before the war of 1870 altered the state of Europe, the *International* had split into two sections one of which merged in the commune, and the other, of which Marx continued to be the head, found its headquarters in America. It is absurd to suppose, as both advocates and opponents have professed to do, that the *International* had any material influence on the events which brought about the war of 1870. An address written by Karl Marx about that time might indeed bear this interpretation, but impartial history will relate that on the whole, its opposition to war on economical as well as moral grounds has been among its most prominent features. It remains to say a word on Marx's great work *Capital,* published first in 1869, and revised in 1872. The main doctrine—that capital is simply the robbery of the workman by the capitalist, and that if the true value of labour were paid capital could not exist—is illustrated especially by facts from English Blue-books.[17] It is noteworthy that though the work has been translated into French, and summarized for the Italian workingman, no summary even exists in English. The form in which the principles are enumerated—in mathematical formulas, may have something to do with this neglect; but undoubtedly another reason is that English working men would not care to be identified with these principles in their bald form.

A SEVERE BLOW

The Republican, London, March, 1883, p. 483

The death of Karl Marx is a severe blow to the Socialistic party in Europe. He was for many years the guiding spirit of the movement, and there is now no man able to fill so well the position he long occupied. A full biography of Marx appeared in this journal in November last, and to that account of the man and his work we are not now prepared to add anything; but we have reason to believe that a forthcoming number of the Swiss *Sozialdemokrat* will contain a complete account of his career; and we hope to be able in a future issue to give our readers a satisfactory view of the life-work of this remarkable man.

BY HIS DEATH THE PROGRESS
OF HUMANITY IS RETARDED

Progress, London, April, 1883, p. 254

KARL MARX, foremost of the Socialist party, has passed away. The best comment on his many-sided nature is furnished by the names of those present by his grave-side. His daughter Eleanor, his two sons-in-law, his friend of forty years, Herr Engels, Herr Liebknecht, leader of Socialism in Germany, Professor Schorlemmer, of Owen's College, Professor Ray Lankester, of Oxford and University College, London, Dr. Edward B. Aveling,[18] and Mr. Ernest Radford. Messages from the working-men of France, of Russia, of Spain, were read by M. Longuet, and Herrn Engels and Liebknecht spoke over the dead man. By his death the progress of humanity is retarded.

SWITZERLAND

HE GAVE SOCIALISM
A SCIENTIFIC FOUNDATION

Der Sozialdemokrat, Arbeiterstimme, Zürich, March 17, 1883[19]

An extremely painful news report reached us just as this number went to press. *Karl Marx,* the man who first gave Socialism a scientific foundation, who was in the truest sense of the word a thinker and a fighter, who devoted his whole life to the proletariat, the man whose name is mentioned with high respect in all countries where there are Socialists, and particularly among German Social-Democrats who proudly honor Marx as their intellectual head, is dead. A telegram from his co-worker, Frederick Engels, informs us that he died on Wednesday (yesterday) March 14, at 3 o'clock in the afternoon. He died after long suffering which hindered him in bringing his life work, *Capital,* to completion.

We are not in a position today to describe what Social Democracy and what science lost with the death of Marx. Such extraordinarily rich knowledge, coupled with a still rarer critical faculties, and such passionate devotion of himself to the struggle of the proletariat, have never before been united in one man. In this man, who has been described as cold and without feeling, pulsed true passion. He was as demanding in his approach to science and politics as he was of himself. He was ruthless with politicians and scientists. He hated all sham emotionalism, seeing in it the support of all "Pfaffen," who are the enemies of decisive action.

Marx was not quite seventy years old. Marx was in the midst of his work when death took him away shortly after it had robbed him of his wife and oldest daughter. Two daughters stand next to Frederick Engels mourning at his grave. With them, mourn hundreds of thousands of workers the world over.

Marx died in exile which he had voluntarily extended in order to complete his studies in total independence. Even though he saw Germany in chains and enslaved, he still did not view it pessimistically. He set his hopes on the German workers, and continually expressed his joy about the clever, manly solidarity with which they made the anti-Socialist laws ineffective. He, who worked for the social revolution for more than two generations and thus had the right to become impatient, understood and knew the difficulties of the struggle in Germany. With the conviction that the German proletariat was capable of achieving a high, historical mission, he died. (The Social Democrats of Switzerland also treasure the deceased. They also feel pain at his death. He will remain in their memory forever. We will honor his memory as we follow his call: "Proletarians of all lands, unite.")

IN HIS WORK HE ERECTED
A PERMANENT MEMORIAL

Der Sozialdemokrat, Zürich, March 29, 1883

Almost the entire European press has devoted detailed obituaries to our recently deceased great pioneer, including our enemies who were the butt of the deceased's sharp criticism. It was not to be expected that his critics would present a just and impartial view of this extraordinary man. However, it is significant that no paper dared ignore his scientific significance. Nonetheless, they attempted to bring up small, mean things such as the myths which have long since been disproven. The *Neue Freie Presse*, the main organ of the Vienna corruptionists, even regaled its readers with the distorted falsehood of Karl Vogt that Marx sneered at his own followers and had respect for the aristocracy. One look at the *Communist Manifesto*, *Capital*, and his other works shows the absurdity of such charges.

The Socialist workers' press, foreign and domestic, with one exception,[20] gave clear proof of how much the class-conscious proletariat felt the loss they suffered through his death, how much they are aware of his significance, how much the progressive elements feel they owe him. Since there is so little space in this party organ, we intend to collect these voices of the proletariat in a special memorial issue, illustrated with a picture of this eternal fighter for the social revolution. We know well that this man in his work, in his creativity, erected a memorial as permanent as stone and ore. But we believe, along with the masses for whom he was a pioneer, that we will do a service for the people in publishing this memorial issue.

GERMANY

AN UNSELFISH AND HEROIC LIBERATOR OF THE WORKING CLASS

Kölnische Zeitung, Cologne, March 16, 1883

We have received the telegraphic report that Karl Marx died yesterday, March 15, 1883, in Argenteuil, a suburb of Paris. Our young school of national economics stands collectively in Marx's debt. Marx had more continuing influence on the domestic politics of all civilized states than any other of his contemporaries. National economics particularly in Germany, can cite no other person who has had a more decisive and revolutionary effect on the masses as well as on the academic world than Karl Marx. Of course this is not to say that Lassalles's system of inherited rights is not a work which will retain its importance for all time, and will remain indispensable for both friend and enemy of Social Democracy on this question.

It is not possible in this short space to do justice to Marx's scientific importance and political influence. All domestic politics in Germany stand at the moment under the influence of modified Marxist viewpoints. We limit ourselves to short excerpts with regard to his life and works.

As to the extraordinary significance of Marx's thinking there can be no doubt. An objective judgment about him can hardly be offered today. Blind hate on one side and exaggerated admiration on the other have made objectivity impossible. But that he was an unselfish and heroic liberator of the working class, a staunch opponent of capitalism, and in a certain sense, a liberator of the enslaved masses, is certainly true. He was, too, one of the sharpest thinkers and most accomplished dialecticians, despite Proudhon, which the national economic scene ever had. One errs, however, if one believes that Marx did it all on his own. Better than most men of his age, he knew the English writers and used their opinions often very cleverly disguised. What would some of his current admirers say if one could prove that his theory of labor, indeed, the normal working time as value measurement, came from Adam Smith: they probably would not believe it, and yet it is so.[21] In any case, one may say about the deceased that his *Capital*, published in 1867, and the earlier critical work, *Critique of Political Economy* (1859), will long remain controversial, but nevertheless indispensable for anyone who becomes seriously involved in social and economic questions.

SOCIALISTS HAVE LOST THEIR REAL FATHER

Vossiche Zeitung, Berlin, March 18, 1883

The death of Karl Marx awakens memories of F.Lassalle and the relationship between these two leaders of the Socialist movement. Their personal relationship was very close in 1848 in Cologne where they both joined along with Engels and other comrades around the red flag of the *Neue Rheinische Zeitung*.[22] Thereafter they went their separate ways; nothing is known of a later meeting or regular correspondence. Nevertheless the intellectual connection was very close, whereby Marx was almost always the giver and Lassalle, the receiver. As early as their time in Cologne, Lassalle received from the older Marx, whose convictions were even then solidified, the inspiration for his later social and political studies and agitation, and from then on the younger man was under the influence of Marx's ideas. The following passage in the foreward to Marx's main work, *Capital*, shows clearly the relationship of dependence in Lassalle stood to the teachings and works of Marx: "*Enpassant*. Even though Lassalle took, almost word for word, from my writings, the whole general theoretical sense of his economic works, i.e., on the historic character of capital, on the connection between the relationship of production and the means of production, etc., including the terminology I created, this process was conditioned by propaganda considerations. I am naturally not speaking of his detailed thoughts of his use of the ideas with which I have nothing to do."

The last sentence shows a sharp malice: Marx wants to say that Lassalle lacks a logical thought process and a consistent development of the fundamentals. And in reality this is true. As much as Lassalle had more breadth of viewpoint and of education, more spirit and elegance of description, and strength as agitator, he stood behind the master in terms of logical sharpness and ruthlessness of thought. In this sense Marx stands alone among socialist writers. If one accepts his first premises, there is no stopping through the chain of strong and final consequences which follow one another tightly. Lassalle's successors also follow the trail of Karl Marx; indeed since Wilhelm Liebknecht took the intellectual leadership upon himself, these thinkers have taken up Marx's theories with the strict discipline and consistency which Marx thought lacking in Lassalle. Lassalle still attempted to form some relationship with the existing state order and cloaked his socialism in nationalism, but after his death, Liebknecht diverted the movement back into Marx's path of international communism. Marx's manifesto to the "proletariat of all countries", his "inaugural address", his statutes for the International became the shibboleths of the movement; his *Critique of Political Economy* and his *Capital* became the arsenal from which they took their sharpest weapons. What Liebknecht, Bebel and the whole collection of minor apostles minted was coin from the quarries of the great ore supply of Karl Marx. The anti-Socialist law silenced German Social Democracy; if they could talk they would openly confess at Marx's grave that in his death they have lost their real father. His spirit still rules in the circles of our politically schooled workers; indeed, our arm-chair and state socialists, our leading social reformers also stand consciously or unconsciously under his influence. Whoever wants to destroy social democracy, not only in its external aspects but also in its fundamentals, must continually return to Karl Marx.

HE WAS A MAN!

Neue Zeit,[23] *Stuttgart, I, 1883. (pp. 197-98, 236-41)*

Karl Marx. Just prior to editorial closing, news reached us of the death of Karl Marx, dead in the midst of his work from a broken heart over the death of his wife and the recent loss of his daughter. Like Charles Darwin and Richard Wagner,[24] Karl Marx died after he had received the undivided respect of friend and foe. As with the name Darwin and the name of Wagner, so too the name Marx represents a program, a political, social and scientific meaning. Marx was more than just a national economist who created some new academic opinions; he created for the social sciences what Darwin did for the natural sciences, even if the methods and paths of development are basically different. It was the principle of development which both used to break scientific ground. Marx brought history into national economic and national economics into history; he founded the historical viewpoint in national economics and the materialistic viewpoint in history and united the two divisions of knowledge in an organic whole. With these few words one can, of course, only sketch, in an unsatisfactory manner, the importance and meaning of the thoughts of the deceased. If Marx' name was in the mouths of everyone in public life in the past years, he belongs to those thinkers whose works are more talked about than read and more read than understood.

No pomp, no noisy demonstrations—and yet one realized throughout the civilized world that an extraordinary man had died. The obituaries in the European and American press showed this: written by political enemies they recognize almost without exception the vital importance of the deceased and pay him the tribute, often reluctantly, of awestruck respect which they had for the most part stubbornly refused him during his life. . . .

Marx's criticism of Hegel's philosophy of law, and his essay on the Jewish question[25] allowed us to recognize the powerful master of the dialectic who had returned to earth from the heaven of philosophy, and who, on earth, was determined to struggle with earthly problems.

By 1847 his view had been sharpened and expanded. He looked behind the scenes of history and saw the driving forces under the surface. Thus, the phrases of that "crazy year" which dominated the world could not ensnare him. A revolutionary out of passion and logic, he did not fool himself for a moment about what friend and foe thought was revolution, but brought under his sharpest criticism the revolutions and revolutionaries of the day no less than the reactions and reactionaries. Some of the idols of the revolution, whose tinsel he removed by showing their snotty philistinism to a laughing public, later revenged themselves through publishing lies and hateful notices in German and foreign newspapers which portrayed Marx as a boundless seeker for dominance, an ice-cold, calculating demagogue who, with no heart and ice-water for blood in his veins, only had one goal: to build himself up at the expense of everyone else.

In London, in the capital of the most economically developed country in the world, in the center and heart of the capitalist system, he found the right place for himself. Nowhere else could he have observed the secrets of the capitalist production process with the same success or researched with the same thoroughness.

He did not, as other exiles, fall into the trap of attempting to direct the events of his homeland from such a distance. His critical understanding saved him from succumbing to the illusion that the movement which failed through its own mistakes, inabilities and immaturity could be galvanized back to life through artificial agitation and conspiracy.

The coup d'etat of Louis Bonaparte in December 1851 inspired him to write *The 18th Brumarie of Louis Bonaparte*, a work written for the occasion—as Goethe wrote poems for particular occasions - which, free from solemnity, describes the origins of the coup in the flaming language of wrath, mercilessly draws and quarters the putschist and his accomplices, and is not only an historical judgment but one of the most brilliant historical studies in our literature.

Marx's break with Bakunin deserves a few words. Bakunin was the noisiest representative of those professional conspirators who wanted to make "revolution", but who in reality only played into the hands of the reaction. Rooted in the thoroughly ideological point of view that the Revolution (regardless of what was understood by it) could be created by the force of the thought and will of "revolutionary" men, Bakunin's viewpoint was bound to find a decisive enemy in Marx who was attempting to study the laws of organizational development of all historical occurences. We would not even mention this as such were it not the characteristic opinion in wide circles which knew Marx only as the head of the Communist League and the International Workingmen's Association, and which advanced the view that Marx was a conspirator and spent his entire life trying to make putsches and revolution. Marx was exactly the opposite of a conspirator. The customary portrait drawn by these circles, resembles Bakunin not Marx, who, himself, removed Bakunin and his followers from the International Workingmen's Association, precisely because of this Rinaldo Rinaldini viewpoint.

Let it be remarked in passing that already before 1848 Marx had criticized and shown to be ridiculous one of these revolution-makers—namely the fulminating silver-obsessed (dynamite had not yet been discovered) but basically tame, Karl Heinzen.

His work, *Capital*, continued to develop. The more he investigated—with his gigantic energy—the further into investigation he was driven. With that hunger for truth and honesty of self-criticism which sets the princes of scholarship apart from the mean minded, he set for himself the highest standards, examined with painstaking care each new fact, was ready at all times to sacrifice the laboriously attained concept, even if it was the fruit of years of research and thought, to a better insight.

Science can thus still expect something meaningful in the second part of *Capital*. Nothing can be added to the scientific importance of Marx. Through the investigation of the historical and economic laws of development, Marx has placed himself at the side of the greatest thinkers and scholars. No one can or will take that from him.

Marx's teaching is an historical fact which may make many

uncomfortable, but cannot be ignored or defamed. It has the same meaning for science as Darwin's teaching: as Darwin did with natural science, so Marx dominates the economic science of society. And as various representatives of natural science today either fight Darwin's thought or are rooted in it, so the representatives of political economy divide themselves into those who fight Marx and those who adopt his teaching. A look at the list of names in the latter category shows that they have the greatest scientific weight. Even the enemies of Marx's system must pay him the homage of using weapons to fight him which they borrowed from his thought. But enemies and friends unite in the recognition of the scientific importance of the investigator Marx, and considering the whole Marx: the investigator and the politician-enemy and friend unite in the judgment: he was a Man!

AUSTRIA-HUNGARY

ONE OF THE MOST IMPORTANT CONTEMPORARIES

Neues Wiener Tagblatt, Vienna, March 17, 1883

In Argenteuil near Paris, a German driven from his fatherland died yesterday without having seen with his own eyes the beloved ideal he searched for. No shining medals will be carried on velvet pillows behind the coffin of this man; no title or uniform characterized him. He was no minister, no general and he had no rank in the intellectual hierarchy; his person was not the object of a mystical folk cult and no legends wove themselves around his name as they did around the names Garibaldi and Lassalle. Nonetheless, Karl Marx must be recognized as one of the most important contemporary figures. He was the master of a discipline which was often and incorrectly known as being dry, terribly sober and unimaginative; Karl Marx mastered the field of economics and from this position wanted to overthrow and reorganize the state and society. In this way economics becomes socialism.

. . . Karl Marx stands high above the mass of socialists Because of his deep and sharp understanding, he even elicited respect from his enemies while finding in his own socialist world hardly more praise and understanding.

Karl Marx said to himself that political freedom even if expressed in the most beautiful laws was not enough to keep the people from oppression. . . .

It must be pointed out that Karl Marx was well equipped to carry out his task. He knew the financial history of the states as perhaps no other man in Europe; he was at home in all areas of economics and he knew also the secrets of banking and the stock market. The blind faith and madness of socialism is not to be found in this man. . . .

Marx stood against the principles of nationalism. In 1866 when these principles brought about a war, Marx founded the International. He clearly understood the issues of the period and his studies of nationalism have the value of serving as a counterweight to fanaticism, superstition, prejudice and dark errors, the mad conception of a ruthless egotism which is now taking hold in the areas of politics, social thought and economics.

HE RAISED THE BATTLECRY
OF HATRED AND DESTRUCTION

Neue Freie Presse, Vienna, March 17, 1883

We remove our hat before the corpse of such a great foe. We honor the powerful mental energy even in its most frightening form which, with thundering hammer blows, demanded the destruction of middle class society. He drew through the mud that which is most prized by the human heart—the homeless one who never knew devotion to the fatherland, the love of country. He poured the poison of hatred and envy into the minds of the poor. They could never follow the cunning dialictic which he developed in the eight hundred pages of his major work, but they stood with shy awe before the volume which reported a dark saga to them. This cold thinker who used the most scholarly apparatus, who was apparently lost in abstract deduction removed from the earth, knew how to find words which struck into the heart of the poor like an unsheathed dagger, and which are continually stuttered by them like a prayer.

Today the deadly foe of the middle class left this life and went back to the only sphere in which a gloomy equality is possible. He himself had never looked need in the face[26] and in this, as in his origins, he is similar to Lassalle from whom he is otherwise fundamentally different. Lassalle was a national, Marx a cosmopolitan. Both wanted to organize the proletariat, one on the foundation of the fatherland, the other on that of the world. Marx cried out: "What have the workers to do with all these wars? Their interests are everywhere identical." He had no trace of the temperament and originality of Lassalle. He sat in his room or in the British Museum to build his mathematical formulas; he lived only in the ice-cold region of computation, and even the terrible antithesis of his proclamation stemmed from the head not the heart.

Marx tore the worker from the hearth. He wanted to force him as an alien into our society without any feeling for our successes, without partaking in our suffering. Can one understand now the honor given this thinker and agitator by our aristocrats? Is that not written petroleum? Marx is the father of Social Democracy, with which no peace or reconciliation is possible, which repressed sympathy with its cruelty, which demands not only revolution but what is even worse—treason. He is responsible for the fact that so many innocent moths, confused, throw themselves into the flames, and for the fact that the awakening of political consciousness leads not to liberation but to downfall.

Of course tragedy caught up with even this fighter for social revolution. What remains of all the theories he invented, of all the dreams he tried to advance scientifically? What is the basis of value? The necessary time required to manufacture something. The mass is completely equal and the rabbit is as valuable as the doe because one needs the same amount of time to shoot both. The famous formulas are just as destroyed as the infamous attempts to realize them. Marx preached that the proletariat of all lands should unite, and out of his heart sprang the idea of an international organization which would embody the solidarity of the workers, would be an influence wherever the struggle against capital existed, a struggle which would cover all nations and people. Marx was the soul of this organization which was to put such power in his hands as no mortal ever had, and was to have brought millions under his influence. This giant child died almost as it was born. Marx was forced to withdraw from the International,[27] tarred with the brush of being called a reactionary, a representative of authoritative principles, a man who was childish enough to demand that all individuals recognize the truth, justice and virtue of the organization's program. How ancient that all sounds today! The collectivists have been overtaken by the anarchists. Bakunin is the God to lay sacrifices before. Dagger, dynamite, theft are the weapons of the struggle. Fanatical young girls sacrifice their purity for the higher cause and become courtesans. The life of a person weighs as much as a feather. The methods of overthrowing society are different, but the words still come from Marx.

The death of Karl Marx will not bring about reconciliation, and even in the face of the coffin which carried the remains of this important man, the antipathy which his individuality elicited will not be repressed. His mental power made him one of the most important forerunners of the reaction which sweeps freedom away like the Borgias. His concepts have become normal in the mouths of statesmen who, when he invented them, would rather have thrown him into chains. Marx was a demon who fought against middle class order without inner conviction. As one of his most devoted admirers pointed out: Marx laughs at the fools who pray with his proletariat catechism as he does at the communists and the bourgeoisie; the only ones he respects are the aristocrats, the pure ones, those with the consciousness of it. Marx was one of those destructive forces who lets loose war, destroys every idealism, forges weapons for despotism, and warns the citizenry that a terrible crisis threatens which must shake the foundations of the state. Woe to the unscrupulous who play a frivolous game with such armament. A day may come when no misery will equal theirs! Karl Marx raised the battle cry of hatred, destruction, the overthrow of freedom and property. His scholarship was an imaginative lie, his doctrine despair. The damage he created will pass like his corpse. Already the middle class holds out the olive branch, and soon the workers will recognize that freedom is the first guarantee of prosperity.

ONE OF THE NOBLEST MEN
TO WALK THE EARTH

Arbeiter Wochen-Chronik, Budapest,
March 23, 1883

One of the most important men of our century, one of the brightest stars ever to shine in the scholarly heaven, one of the noblest men to walk the earth: Karl Marx, the founder, the creator of scientific modern socialism is no more. He ended his struggle—a rich life which he dedicated fully and totally to the emancipation of the working people—on March 15 in exile in London. He was a relentless and sharp foe of those toadies of the ruling society who are partly too shallow to recognize the economic drives of our world and partly to cowardly to draw the consequences. These mean minds could do nothing else to avenge themselves than at first to ignore the researches of the deceased, and when this no longer was possible, to twist his teachings around so that they could at least appear to fight it. Who would declare themselves bankrupt? To acknowledge Marx' teaching means nothing less than a declaration of bankruptcy for the political economy taught for the state at all universities, and, at the same time a recognition of the untenableness and unnaturalness of our society based on the exploitation of the masses. It is a meaningful sign of our times when the representatives of the bourgeois world, the papers of all party directions, present obituaries devoted to the man who through the sharpness of his intellectual armament was the most terrible foe of the capitalist society. Even though with visible discomfort, they can not escape lifting their hats before his greatness, his overwhelming logic and his strict scientific deduction.... His pupils will speak after the social revolution has come, and well note that Marx was for this revolution what the Encyclopediasts, Voltaire, Diderot, and others were for the bourgeois, the so-called great French revolution.

The social revolution will be brought closer the more widely the scientific teaching of Marx is spread throughout the masses. The economic relationships at least in the industrial states are already at the point where they demand a change from capitalist methods of production to socialist methods. In addition, the contradiction between the increasing concentration of wealth in the hands of fewer and fewer capitalists and the daily expanding, but threatened proletariat will force change.

The meaning and importance of Marx as an agitator is most clearly demonstrated in the founding of the International Workingman's Association, which was proclaimed on September 28, 1864 in St. Martin's Hall.

Aside from his social-economic theories, Marx distinguishes himself from others who have worked in his field through his historical point of view. Marx showed that from ancient and mediaeval times the entire history of society down to the present has been one of class struggle, involving on one side the maintenance of political and social power of the ruling classes, and on the other the conquest of power by the socially and politically oppressed. Marx showed that the historical development of human society is tightly related to a society's production relations of which are followed by change in the principles and ideas of the society which adjusts itself accordingly so that the ruling ideas of any time appear to be always only the ideas of the ruling classes.

Marx lies now on the bier. He died in the middle of his rich creativeness and wherever a thinking worker, a selfless teacher, a true friend of the people lives, here this most meaningful and most noble of all friends of mankind will be mourned. He is dead, but his spirit, which fills the whole world of thinking workers, remains alive, and will remain so even after we who think of ourselves as his pupils mourning him, have sunk into the eternal night.

Leo Frankel[28]

FRANCE

KARL MARX

La Justice, Paris, March 17, 1883

Karl Marx has just died in London, following a chest ailment contracted slighly more than a year ago at the bedside of his dying wife. Several months later, the doctors had sent him to Algeria, then to Nice. Last summer, he came to spend two months in Argenteuil at the home of Ch. Longuet, his son-in-law, which enabled him to take the treatment of the waters of Enghien. By October, he believed he was well enough to return to England, where he hastened to put the finishing touches to his great work, *Capital*, which was to be divided into three parts, of which only the first volume had appeared in 1869. He was staying at Ventor, Isle of Wight, when he learned of the unexpected death of his elder daughter, Mme. Longuet. In his weakened condition, he could not withstand this final blow, and he declined rapily in the last two months.

The life and work of Karl Marx deserve more than hastily written notes. However, here are some biographical details which have the merit of being factual.

Marx was born in 1814 in Trèves, where his father practiced the profession of law. He himself began by studying law, first at Bonn University, later at the University of Berlin. But he had too inquiring and scientific a mind to be cooped up in the dry and sterile study of jurisprudence. His inclination towards the historical side of the law, Roman as well as German, impelled him toward the actual study of history.

Meanwhile he devoted himself passionately to philosophy and even, although already a skeptic in this respect, to metaphysics. In Berlin he met Bruno Bauer, Feuerbach, and others—the whole "Hegelian Left," in whose ranks certain biographers have even included Marx.

It was about this time that, taking the advice of a university comrade, Frederick Engels, who remained his most devoted friend until his death, Marx devoted himself to the study and critique of political economy. Immediately after he earned his doctor of philosophy degree, he returned to the University of Bonn, where he began to teach a course as a "privat-dozent."

He had been lecturing there a short while when Frederick William III died (1840). The heads of the liberal bourgeois democracy, believing the moment had arrived to give constitutional reforms an energetic forward thrust, offered the not quite 21-year-old Karl Marx the editorship-in-chief of the *Rheinische Zeitung*. His original and audacious polemics soon alarmed those in power who started by censuring the paper; later, dissatisfied with the results, they ended by suppressing it.

So Marx went to Paris in 1843 with the young woman he had just married, Berthe-Caroline von Westphalen. There he published, in collaboration with Arnold Ruge, a Hegelian of the Left, and a democrat (who later, like so many others, was to prostrate himself before Bismarckian chauvinism) the *Deutsch Französische Jahrbücher*. This periodical, to which Heinrich Heine also contributed, was neither teutonic nor exclusively of any other nationality.

Marx then began a relationship with the leaders of French democracy. But the Prussian government refused to allow him to remain in Paris; he was expelled at the request of the Ambassador, Alexander von Humboldt (1846).

He sought refuge in Brussels, where, the following year, he published the most noteworthy work of his youth, a passionate, biting, but sound critique of the *Economic Contradictions* of Proudhon. The great Franc-Comtois polemicist, moreover, had nothing to complain of: he himself had sought the debate, and he ended a friendly letter to Marx with these words: "I await your critical judgment."

Immediately after the February Revolution, Marx received an invitation to return to France, by dispatch from a member of the new government, Flocon. But he did not stay very long. The revolution broke out in Germany and he returned at once to Cologne, where, with Frederick Engels, and the lyric revolutionary poets Herweg and Freiligrath, he brought out the *Neue Rheinische Zeitung*. This was the brilliant period of his "vie de combat." His newspaper immediately became a force because of its skill and depth as well as its verve and colorful style. At the time of the coup d'état in Berlin, Marx published in his paper an appeal to the people to organize a refusal of the tax, and if the government took no notice, to answer force with force.

The state of siege suspended the paper and forced the editors to leave Cologne. But as soon as the siege was lifted Marx began the struggle again. He was tried time and time again. He acted as his own attorney and the jury acquitted him.

In the spring of 1849, the Prussian government expelled him. He returned to Paris, where the reactionaries were already beginning to win. They wanted to shut him up in the Moribihan. So he went off to establish himself in London, where he lived until his death.

We will pass lightly over the last 30 years of Marx's life, since we will have a chance to come back to this when we study his theories and his works.

Until 1864 he was involved almost exclusively in the study and research which were to comprise the three volumes of the work which places him in the front rank of the critical economists and socialists of our century, that is, *Capital.*

In September, 1864, the German, French, English, and Italian workers who started the International Workingmen's Association, called on Karl Marx. He was, from the very beginning, secretary for Germany. But his influence was felt chiefly in the first impetus of the organization, and in his remarkable publications of the General Council, almost all of which he wrote himself. Marx knew, and handled perfectly, especially in writing, the most important European languages. But above all, he understood thoroughly the political and economic situation of the different countries. Any one of these rare qualifications would have sufficed to make him the leading spirit of the General Council, since the Council had neither director nor president. His true role there will not be clearly understood until the history of the International is written, and it has not yet even been drafted.

Karl Marx, as we have said, leaves the work unfinished of which the first part, "The Production of Wealth" has produced a veritable revolution, even in the teaching *ex cathedra* of political economy, everywhere that teaching has not yet become mummified. However, we think that the second volume, "The Process of Circulation of Capital," is already advanced to the point where it can be published by the closest friend and the most worthy interpreter of Karl Marx, F. Engels.

The third volume was supposed to be a critical analysis of all economic literature. We are very much afraid that Marx, who regarded this last volume as a light, easy, almost pleasurable work, left only a few sketchy fragments of it.

Among the writings of Marx which we have not cited, we point out an admirable study of the *coup d'état* of December 2nd: *The Eighteenth Brumaire of Louis Bonaparte.* Undoubtedly a French publisher will be found to translate and publish it.

DEFENDER OF THE COMMUNE

Le Citoyen et La Bataille, Paris, March 17, 1883

One of the greatest thinkers of our time has just died—Karl Marx, who was certainly the most perfect revolutionary genius of this century. . . .

It was *Capital* which revealed to the world of learning an irrefutable revolutionary economist. In vain all the critics have tried to find fault with the most complete, most veracious, most precise methodical social analysis we have to this moment. The work of Karl Marx, translated into all languages, is the indispensable key today to all socialist studies. It is this work which has founded German socialism, and its revolutionariness has triumphed over the attacks of Lasalle, the sorry disciple of Karl Marx. If German socialism did not somersault into Lassallean Caesarism, it is because of Karl Marx.

The enormous revolutionariness studies demanded by this colossal work did not prevent Karl Marx from taking an active part in our recent struggles. The first idea of the Intermational came from him, and he gave it its first format.

We will not relate in detail the role Karl Marx played in this organization, and how he was ill-served, even betrayed, by ambitious people, who wanted to take over the International. But we are impelled to relate how he defended the Commune and welcomed its defenders.

The brochure which Karl Marx published in June 1871, *"La Guerre civile en France"*, is the most perfect piece ever to come from the pen of this master. Its publication assuredly aided the sympathetic welcome extended by the enlightened classes of England to those defeated in this Revolution. These people found in Marx a fraternal hospitality. In order to help the exiles of the Commune, he condemned himself to penury and wore out his friends; there was not a refugee who did not get from him some solace or help.

All the world's socialists will bow down before this prodigious tomb. The revolutionary socialists of France will be much affected, and from the banquets of March 18th, they will send a word of farewell to the man who was the most powerful glorifier of the advent of the proletariat.

HIS WORK HAS PRODUCED
A VERITABLE REVOLUTION

La Republique Radicale, Paris, March 18, 1883

. . . His principal work, of considerable import, is *Capital*. It has produced a veritable revolution in economic systems. The influence of the works of Karl Marx, which has been very great, will be even more important when after the political question has been resolved, we will shortly have to confront the social question.

A MISFORTUNE FOR HUMANITY

L'Electeur Républicain, Paris, March 18, 1883

Mourning for Karl Marx will be worn not only by his family but by all those who know that the death of a thinker is a misfortune for humanity.

Karl Marx, Socialist, of the Saint-Simon family and the Fourier family, in pursuing the discovery of the laws governing the formation of capital and the transformation of the methods of production, was the true creator of the collective school. By founding the International Workingmen's Association, he put into practice the doctrine of solidarity and gave life to an idea. . . .

When a man has, from his youth, struggled and suffered for his ideas; when he has been persecuted, imprisoned, outlawed because of them; he ends up having only one fatherland: humanity and the family. Such was the case with Karl Marx, before whose grave friends and adversaries alike will bow, united in feelings of respect and regret.

KARL MARX

Le Prolétaire, March 24, 1883

Death has just robbed contemporary socialism of a great thinker, a distinguished economist. Marx is no more. Fortunately his theoretical work is apparently finished; "The Process of the Circulation of Capital," the second volume of his work, *Capital*, is advanced enough to be published; and the third volume is only a rough draft. . . .

Marx proved himself to be a powerful thinker in economic matters as well as an unparalleled analyst and critic. He was the first to speak of a materialist conception of history, and if socialism has finally and irrevocably taken a scientific course, he is the one to whom we are indebted. But must one, for this reason, declare, as Engels does, that the Marxist doctrine has become the *Credo* of world socialism? Or, as M. Lavroff does, that *Capital* is the socialist *Gospel?* Must one "make *complete communion* with the doctrine" like the passionate devotees of "agglutination?" That would be too much. But was he a great man? He was not God. Like Owen, like Saint-Simon, like Fourier, like Proudhon, he has been surpassed today. Contemporary scientific work has considerably enlarged the bases of materialist history, and as far as communist evolution of property is concerned, the theory of *Public Service* which takes its origin from the international Congresses of Brussels and Berne, held in 1874 and 1876 outside of the influence of Marx, leaves Marxist communism far behind it, in Utopia. I should discuss Marx further as an agitator. But on this subject I would have to evaluate his role in the International and his influence in the different workers' parties. Here I must workers' I cannot write a single word which might offend the sorrow of his relatives and friends, and enemy that I am of cowardly capitulations of conscience, I cannot bring myself to gloss over the truth.

Paul Brousse

HOLLAND

A REMARKABLE MAN

Neuwe Rotterdamsche Courant,[29] March 18, 1883

This remarkable man whose death has been mentioned by us, and about whose life we have already written some particulars, deserves a little more commemoration, because of his profound scientific studies and the great influence he has had on the labor movement of the century.

Let us begin, however, by correcting the account of his death. He did not die last Thursday in Argenteuil, but in London. This mistake, according to the Paris *Justice,* is because some time ago, he came to Argenteuil, where one of his daughters, Mrs. Charles Longuet, was dangerously ill. However, after her death, Marx returned to London, already himself clearly suffering from the illness that was fatal to him and brought him to his grave. There he died in his home, almost 65 years old (he was born on the 5th of May 1818 in Trier).

It is known that Marx worked expecially in philosophic and economic fields, and in a direction into which he was driven neither by birth, nor education, nor kinship. By birth, Marx was a Jew, the son of an employee in the service of the Prussian

State. By marriage, he became the brother-in-law of the Count von Westphalen, who was a member of the reactionary von Manteuffel cabinet which suppressed with violence the last convulsions of the Revolution of 1848-49. Such a background does not suggest the direction of the life of Marx, who became the father of the International which was the sworn enemy of Prussia, and the militant fighter against the power of capital which he believed was personified in Judaism.

At Bonn and Berlin he studied law, but already at that time, philosophy and economics were his favorite studies. In 1841, when he was 23 years old, he gained the Doctor's title, and established himself as lecturer (Privatdozent) in Bonn. He attracted the attention of the owners of the *Rheinische Zeitung* in Cologne with a few articles he wrote, after which he acted as chief editor of this paper, exactly at the time that the liberals in Prussia fostered the illusion that the death of King Frederick William III, and the ascension to the throne of the "liberal" Crown Prince, would bring the Constitution promised in 1815. It is well known how cruelly this illusion was destroyed, and how Frederick William IV who, at Koenigsburg at his coronation, cried woe to those who might dare to lay his hands on him, the annointed of God. It is well known that this king even surpassed his father in his reactionary leanings. The *Rheinische Zeitung* and its editor, Karl Marx, were among the victims of this absolutist period.

From Paris, where he with Arnold Ruge, published the *Deutsch-Französische Jahrbücher* (of which only one issue saw the light of day), he was exiled through the diplomatic influence of the Prussian government, which also persecuted him in Brussels, resulting in his exile from there. He established himself in London where no diplomatic action could further hamper his freedom to act and think. Only there did his socialist deliberations attain the communist form which he defended until his death. This communism he confessed, for the first time, in his *Poverty of Philosophy*, which was published as an answer to Proudhon's *Philosophy of Poverty*. Briefly and accurately, one can express the fundamental idea of this Communism in the following way:

"The proletariat which originated and grew up through and

with the present mode of production, will, as soon as it has reached full development, bring an end to all the existing antagonism to Communism, because Communism shall be the final form to which the preceding history of human society and its faulty forms of organization must lead. This full development of the proletariat presupposes on its side, knowledge of its true condition, and understanding of its vocation. And the proletariat has to be brought to that knowledge and understanding." In these words we find both the foundation of the philosophic and economic creed of Karl Marx, and an explanation of his role as an agitator.

It would, of course, lead us too far afield if we were to discuss particulars concerning the many fruits of his active spirit, which will probably be recovered in his legacy, partly in manuscript, and partly in print in different languages. But we will mention the role he played from 1847 to 1872 as the head of the international labor movement. The Congress in London, in 1847, attended by Communists from all parts of the world, represented birth of the International, whose first manifesto and statutes, both written by Marx, spread terror throughout Europe. The Congress at The Hague, marked the death of the International although ostensibly it continued to exist in New York at the headquarters of the federalist wing, no longer under Marx's direction. This death was already prepared in 1871 by the federalists by the way in which they, from the 18th of March to 27th of May in Paris, had brought into practice their principles under the so-called reign of the Commune.

Marx took an active part, with his pen, in the revolutionary movement in Germany in 1848-49. He lived in Cologne, and started there the *Neue Rheinische Zeitung*, to which the famous poet Freiligrath contributed. However, after the suppression of the rebellion in Baden, by which the last armed resistance was broken, Marx again had to return to London.

These few items about his life as an agitator should suffice. We also have to be brief with respect to his writings, especially since a dry summary would be useless to the reader. We prefer to give here a short summary of the first volume of his principal work, *Capital*, which if we are not mistaken, still is the only volume that has appeared of that work which he decided to write in 1859 under the title, *Critique of Political Economy*. This first volume alone is a volume of 800 pages in small print, and is very difficult to digest.

We finish our sketch with the short summary of this book, which we take from the biographical sketch of Karl Marx presented in 1879 by the lawyer Mr. A. Kerdyk in *Men of Importance*.[30] It cannot claim any completeness, yet can give some idea of the life and aspirations of the remarkable man. We read on p. 56 of this sketch:

"It is certainly a daring thing to try to compress in a few sentences the drift of a reasoning which is so complicated. Yet I believe that this can be done, in the main as follows.

"The value of all objects which men exchange with each other—that is the *exchange* value, to be distinguished from the *use* value, determined by the usefulness of these objects for human life—depends on the quantity of labor necessary to produce them. This, of course, should not be taken in the sense that an object produced by a poor devil with many hours of labor, would have greater value than what would have been produced by an able worker in a short period, but it has to be understood that by reduction of all kinds of labor to ordinary hand labor, the normally required (socially necessary, as Marx expressed it) labor time is the measure of value. Capital does not produce new value, because the produced object does not contain more capital than has been used for production; labor alone creates value. Yet the worker does not enjoy the fruits of his toil. Indeed, while the capital-owning employer intrudes himself between the worker and his product, the performance of labor is itself a commodity which the employer buys for a price equal to the production costs of labor; and these costs are exactly as much as the worker needs to live and to continue to work. While the worker works, for example, twelve hours a day, he receives as wage only a value which can be produced in six hours of labor, because this is sufficient for the maintenance of his life. In this way we get, because of the wage relation, between the laborer and the capitalist employer, a difference between the value which the first produces and that which the capitalist pockets as unearned profits, in order to increase it more and more. The capitalist has then some means at his disposal to increase his profits: the more workers he employs, the more 'surplus product' he appropriates from the hours of labor over and above those in which each worker produces the value of his wage; the longer the hours of labor, the larger also the advantage the worker brings to the employer; the more productive the employer can make labor with the aid of machines, the smaller becomes the number of hours that can be held as the equivalent of the value of labor. We have to add something to this. Under the rule of capital and free competition, periods of industrial prosperity alternate with periods of depression almost with the certainty of a law of nature. When times of depression come, then the employers dismiss the unnecessary workers, who have to be kept alive by relief at a cost to society, until such time as the employers can rehire them. This is the reserve army of industry which enters the labor market again when times get better, and then prevents the workers who have been kept at work from gathering the fruits that otherwise would have come to them as a result of the increased demand for labor. All this is not the result of personal arbitrariness, but the inevitable result of the capitalist mode of production. It is the secret of 'plus making'—an injust and unhappy situation that necessarily has to end with the worker himself, or better still, society, taking possession of the means of production—i.e., capital."

HOW RICH A LIFE![31]

Recht Voor Allen[32] (Justice For All), Amsterdam, March 24, 1883

Karl Marx died last week. Feared and hated as few men ever have been, he was at the same time, highly honored and appreciated. He has now been torn from the ranks of Socialism after an active life full of dedication.

How rich a life!

Whatever we may say about him, whatever the hatred of the powerful who persecuted this great man and now will persecute his memory, nobody can or may contest him the honor of having been one of the greatest figures of the nineteenth century. Of him it can be said with full truth what can only rarely be said of a man: he was a man cast of one piece and his life carries the proof of it.

As a man of science, he is a man of the first magnitude. Professor Beesley says that in his knowledge of the history and statistics of the industrial movement in all parts of Europe, Marx has *no equal*. Albert Lange stated that without doubt, Marx was the most learned and keenest economist of our time. Rudolph Meyer claims that Marx's work, *Capital*, is the greatest scientific witness of modern German economics.

Yet many people, usually university professors and such, believed that they made themselves great and noble by gnawing at the reputation of this man, whose shoelaces they are not worthy to untie. He, the giant, was surrounded by dwarfs who wanted first to kill him by silence and after this could no longer be done, called him all kinds of names and warned against his "enormities."

He, the serene man of science, was called a demagogue who incited by hollow phrases the stupid masses and made them dissatisfied! He, the philosophical mind, was represented as the Knight of the Sorrowful Figure tilting against windmills!

But what did he care for the prattle of pygmies?

He went his own way, and by his endeavors, founded for himself a monument not of metal or stone but in the hearts of thousands of workers on both continents. If all princes and ministers die at the same time, even then the honest sorrow in the hearts of the working people will not be so great as for this one man who never had a single government position and yet was feared as one of the great powers that governments had to contend with.

What Lassalle said of himself—he could say it even if some find him an arrogant witness—holds also perfectly for Marx who, as we believe, was Lassalle's superior: "He carries the full armor of the whole culture of his century."

Marx was going on seventy, but despite his age and his

weakened health still worked a good deal, so we expected that the second part of his famous work, *Capital,* would soon appear. Yes, we foster the quiet hope that it has been completed to such an extent that his great and worthy friend, Engels, can see it through to publication. . . .

Endowed with great gifts and full of dedication for the proletariat, Marx always worked for the liberation of the workers. If we want to honor him not with our lips but with our deed then we engrave into each other's memory his words: "YOU HAVE NOTHING TO LOSE BUT YOUR CHAINS OF SLAVERY. PROLETARIANS OF ALL COUNTRIES, UNITE". . . .

ROMANIA AND SPAIN

NOT ONLY A THINKER BUT ALSO A FIGHTER

Dacia Viitoare [Future Dacia], Paris, April 1, 1883

At the time that No 4 of *Dacia* came out we learned with great sorrow about the death of illustrious economic scientist Karl Marx. He dies at the height of intelligence, with still unfinished works. Karl Marx was born in 1814 in Cologne. After finishing the law studies he enters as chief editor at the *Rheinische Zeitung*. Persecuted for his political ideas he comes to Paris from where he is expelled in 1846 by Guizot following the request of the German government and takes refuge in Belgium. Returning to France he took part in the revolution of 1848, was interned at Morbihan from where he escaped and took refuge in London where he also died on the day of March 15. Last year he lost his wife and companion in misfortunes, two months ago his daughter, the wife of Mr. Ch. Longuet the editor of the journal *La Justice*. These domestic misfortunes also shortened his days. He leaves two daughters: one unmarried and the other one the wife of the socialist Paul Lafargue.

His most important works are: *Contributions to the Critique of Hegel's Philosophy of Right; Introduction; The Poverty of Philosophy* written in French and through which he attacks Proudhon's book *The Philosophy of Poverty;* a pamphlet on Napoleon III's coup d'etat; a pamphlet on the Commune, *The Civil War in France* which contributed very much to the sympathetic reception found by the communards who took refuge in England. He leaves completed one volume: "The Process of Circulation of Capital" which will be published by his comrade in struggle Engels and will be a continuation of *Capital*. From a third volume: "The Process of Capitalist Production as a Whole," he unfortunately does not leave more than fragments.

The work that gained him immortality however is: *Capital*, a true social anatomy which adversaries have tried in vain to repudiate. By finding the historical and economic laws which govern the social world, he founded incontestably the scientific socialism, which up to him was only a generous utopia.[33]

Before him many great hearts were upset by social injustices and proposed as remedy various admirable plans for reform, but almost all homeric, which if they had as a goal everybody's happiness, did not have reality as a base. Almost all projects for renovation were *a priori fantasist* concepts whose sole value was often only the ardor of their supporters. Before him there were *socialist schools*, but not one general socialist idea sufficiently accepted, to unite the proletarians of diverse nations.

Marx did not propose any speculative system, he analyzed the facts and explained scientifically the march of humanity and especially the present period—capitalist. History is the struggle of classes be it the dominant ones among themselves: *bourgeoisie, feudalism, old patriarchate,* be it between those ruling and the ruled: slaves, serfs, proletarians. Material interests cause the struggle among classes; some try to relegate the work to others. The material conditions, that is the mode of production have determined and will determine: the form of property, the mores, social, juridical, institutions, etc.

The period through which we are passing is the capitalist period characterized through the production of *exchange values* that have replaced the production of *use values* of other times.

The exchange value of an object is the average human labor needed to produce it, having in mind that the work applied to an object that cannot be useful is not counted. This is the cornerstone of Marx's system, which not being breakable, gives the whole system the solidity of granite. The worker does not receive the exchange value, but only a salary. The difference between the paid salary and the object's value, that is part of the worker's labor goes into the purse of the exploiters that possess the instruments of work and form their capital.

The working class must work for its maintainance and for the maintainance and enrichment of those who have acquired the instruments of work. Production however becomes more and more *a social act, collective*; the capital concentrates continuously. The exploited class will finish the evolution socializing the instruments of work also; supressing the antagonism that exists between *production-social* and *appropriation-capitalist*. When the worker will possess the instrument of work only then will he be able to have the integral product of his work and the classes will disappear.

This is as short as possible the theory of Marx back to what as disciples we will constantly return.

Marx was not only a thinker but also a fighter. He was the initiator of the foundation of the International Association of Workers whose sublime devise was: *the emancipation of the workers will be done through them-themselves*, and which disappeared in 1872 through internal fights on the one side and the persecution of the International association by the governments.

If posterity will remember with gratitude one man, this will be Karl Marx who contributed so much to elaborating the emancipating idea of humanity. The recognition of this truth is the most deserved homage that we bring to the memory of the great thinker.

A. Andries

ONE OF THE MOST EMINENT MEN OF THE NINETEENTH CENTURY

La Illustración Española y Americana, Paris, No.XI, 1883, p. 179

The famous German socialist, Karl Marx, has just died in London—on the 14th of March— of a chest ailment, contracted little more than a year ago at the bedside of his dying wife. Several months after he had acquired the germs of his illness, the doctors sent him to Algiers and later to Nice. Last summer he came to spend two months in Argenteuil, near Paris, in the house of his son-in-law, Charles Longuet, editor of *La Justice*. Believing that he had recovered sufficiently, he went back to England in October of the same year, since he wished to put the finishing touches to his great work *Capital,* which was to be divided in three parts, and of which only the first volume has been published (1869). He was on the English Isle of Wight, when he learned of the unexpected death of his oldest daughter, Mme. Longuet; she had died in mid-January of that year. His broken health could not endure this final blow, and from then on he declined rapidly. . . .

After the dissolution of the old *International* in 1872, in the Congress of the Hague, Karl Marx retired almost completely from militant politics, devoting himself eagerly to finishing his work, *Capital,* which was to be the Gospel of the socialism of our time. His constant idea, his most burning desire, was to give the working class, so disturbed in every country, a scientific theory, a body of doctrine which would serve as a basis and a defense against useless and aimless agitation.

For this concept, and as a thinker, as the discoverer of the laws of economic evolution, particularly those governing the origins of capital and the necessary metamorphosis of the means of production, Marx will go down in history as one of the most eminent men of the nineteenth century.

As we have said above, Karl Marx did not finish the work, the first part of which, devoted to "A Critical Analysis of Capitalist

Production," produced a veritable revolution in the economic ideas of our time, and even in university instruction in political economy, especially in Germany. We have reason to believe that the second volume of *Capital,* or "Process of Circulation of Capital," is sufficiently advanced so that it can be published under the direction of the most intimate friend and the most worthy interpreter of Marx; Frederick Engels. The third volume, "The Process of Capitalist Production as a Whole," was to be a critical analysis of all economic literature. We are afraid that Marx, who considered this last volume a light, easy work, almost a recreation, left only a few fragments and notes for it.

In conclusion, a curious fact: Like Manin, [34] like Disraeli, [35] Karl Marx came from an old family of Spanish Jews, who probably emigrated to Holland at the end of the fifteenth century, and settled later in Germany. His lively temperament, his frank, affectionate character, and even the type and features of his physiognomy clearly revealed his Mediterranean (or Southern) origin. His childhood friends called him *El Moro* (The Moor.)

This man whose enemies have insisted on presenting as a cold, calculating character with a stony heart, possessed on the contrary, the most tender and loving heart in the world, and the proof of this is that the loss of his wife and of his adored daughter was enough to cause his death.

The profound philosopher, having lived so many years a life devoted to thought, dies wounded in the heart, a victim of his love as a husband and a father.

Seldom has so complete a cerebral organism been joined to such an exquisite delicacy of feeling.

J.M.L. [36]

ITALY

A PROFOUND THINKER

La Lega Democratica,[37] Rome, March 17, 18, 1883

Paris. March 15. The German socialist, Karl Marx died in Argenteuil near Paris.

Another Information from Paris.

Karl Marx died in a country cottage near Paris, where he lived for some time.

He was the patriarch of the authoritarian Socialism of the latter part of the century. His struggles with Bakunin are known to all who are interested in the study of social science and economics.

Capital was Marx's most serious work. Marx was one of those studious types that Germany produces. His theory was based on the application of experimentalism to all the laws of future society. The past did not exist for him. He was a profound thinker, an impassioned philosopher who was not stopped by any consequence of his theories.

SOCIALISM HAS LOST A GREAT MAN

Il Sole Dell'Avvenire[38] The Sun of the Future, Ravenna, April 1, 1883

Karl Marx is dead! Socialism has just lost a great man, but if the man is gone, his works remain for mankind to learn from.

DISCOVERER OF THE LAWS
OF ECONOMIC EVOLUTION

La Plebe, Milan, April, 1883

He died in London on the 15th of March at three in the afternoon. In the midst of Socialist agitation which in varying degree is spreading throughout all European countries, the news of the death of Karl Marx, who contributed so greatly to the expansion of Socialist theory, will at least produce a certain impression in everyone, although in a different way. . . .

In 1867 he published the first part of *Capital* entitled *The production of wealth* (Ed. Henry Oriol, 11, rue Bertin-Poiree, Paris. Fr. 5) which produced a veritable revolution, even in the *ex cathedra* teaching of political economics, wherever this teaching is not yet mummified. In *Capital* Marx pointed out the two trends, which, after the appearance of the works of Smith and Ricardo, occured among the scholars of economics. One group, among which Proudhon and Marx must be counted in the first line, have wealth deriving from the principal posed by Smith—from *work;* the others, like Say and the economists, put another element beside work, which according to them, is really the creator of wealth: *utility.*

For Marx, a man's labor is at once the source and the measure of all values; and consequently he combats the accumulation of capital as theft from the working classes. He considers the mechanization of industry as a means of exploitation completely to the advantage of capital and he maintains that pauperism and the relative surplus of population are in indirect proportion to the production and development of wealth. "As much as capital increases—he says—so much the worse off becomes the working class. The law of population surplus makes the working class into a new Prometheus. Accumulation of wealth means, on the one hand, accumulation of poverty, of suffering, of slavery, of ignorance, on the other hand, an increase of brutality and moral degradation."

The illustrious economist of Liege, De Laveleye, wrote thus about the first part of this work:

> When you read Marx's book and you feel yourself confined within the gears of his steel logic, you are overwhelmed by a nightmare, because given the premises, which are taken from more authoritative works, you don't know how to flee from the consequences; and because at the same time his erudition, vast as well as sure, permits him to cite in support of his thesis, most important extracts from a number of authors, and numerous as well as pungent facts taken from parliamentary inquiries and from the industrial and agricultural history of England.

The unfortunate Carlo Cafiero published a brief but good Italian outline of this part of Marx's *Capital*.

Unfortunately this most important work remains incomplete; but *Justice* whose editor is Charles Longuet, son-in-law of Marx, has made it known that the second volume, "The Process of Circulation of Capital," is already sufficiently advance to be able to be published by Marx's closest friend and worthiest interpreter, Frederick Engels.

The third volume, "The Process of Capitalist Production as a Whole," a critical analysis of all economic literature. "We fear very much," says *Justice*, "that Marx who considered this last volume light, easy, almost a work of pleasure may have only left rough drafts."

The *Address* with which the International justified the Paris Commune, defending it, is also Marx's work.

Beyond having taken a most active part in the direction of the International—and the history of this great association when it is written will give its judgement on this part—Marx also busied himself with the more recent founding of some current workers' parties. But above all as a thinker, as a discoverer of the laws of economic evolution, and especially of those which preside over the genesis of capital and the mandatory transformations of the means of production, Marx will remain one of the most eminent men of the XIXth century.

From the family of Saint-Simon,[39] Fourier,[40] and Owen,[41] he has contributed as they have and as much as they have to the discovery of new ways which lead to the emancipation of humanity. To him, after Proudhon, we owe the historical and scientific character which modern socialism has taken, in place of the utopian and sentimental socialism of the first half of the nineteenth century.

Contemporary socialism loses in him its scientific leader, its profoundest thinker.

A.P

Marx's death inspires the following reflections among our friends of Rimini's *Alfabeto* (Alphabet):

Modern sociology is not, in our opinion, with Marx; the unyielding omnipotence of the State yearned for by the German Socialist, would necessarily lead to oppression, to the violation of individual liberty, but not necessarily anarchy or communism. These theoretical ideals of a perfect humanity, to which every social revolution must come one step closer, are not able to be foreseen on the immediate horizon without ignoring historical laws.

Modern Socialism, according to us, must be eclectic and experimentalist: it must know how to harmonize the mission of the State—developing within the orbit of a wide decentralization—with individual liberty, with the mission of workers' associations, possessors of capital and labor.

But it is not less true, whether you agree or not with his ideas, that Karl Marx was one of the most splendid intellects and one of the most noble hearts that have honored the people's cause. Even his most dogged opponents agree.

Therefore we likewise designate him for the gratitude of the workers.

A SURVEY OF THE TURINESE PRESS
ON THE DEATH OF MARX

Avanti, May 7, 1962

Many of its judgments prove more accurate than the opinions that Italian scholarship has continued to express for years.

In March of 1883 the bourgeois newspapers of Turin referred to and commented upon the news of Marx's death which occurred on the 14th of the month in London. After the publication of *Capital*, after the Paris Commune and the great activity of the International of the years 1870-1872, the figure of Marx had emerged from the obscurity in which it had been kept for many years by the "official culture" of the European countries and facts about him circulated in the international press. The dailies and the periodicals of Turin also joined in the discussion of the event.

On March 16, 1883, two days after the death of the thinker, the *Gazzetta di Torino* communicated that "Present-day *Justice* makes it a certainty that Karl Marx died in London." The following day the *Gazzeta Piemontese*, ancestor of the present-day *Stampa*, confirmed the news, but at erroneously held "Karl Marx died suddenly yesterday at Argenteuil in the neighborhood of Paris." In the same issue it published an article entitled "Karl Marx" with some biographical allusions. The article had been probably drawn up in Turin by a contributor to the newspaper who had put together a few lines based on the outline of brief and simple-minded biographies of the German author existing in Italian. It was inaccurate but gave information on the most important events of Marx's life and cited the titles of his work in French.

A few days later, the 20th of the month, the well-known *Gazzetta del Populo* concerned itself with the death of "the German Socialist," qualifying the matter as the "event of the day." The person and the work of Marx were praised and, with allusions taken from French newspapers, it acknowledged in him "the historical and scientific character (?) which contemporary Socialist has taken today, in place of Socialism founded on the utopia or the sentimentalism of the first half of our century." The article ended with an unusual notation: "The death of the German Socialist will certainly influence European politics; but Prince Bismarck outlives his greatest enemy."

A RARE APPRECIATION FOR THOSE DAYS

By Gian Bario Bravo

On March 22, in the *Gazzetta di Torino*, Petruccelli della Gattina, one of the few people in Italy who had in his hands a book of Marx which was not the *Compendio* of *Capital* by Carlo Cafiero, in a bombastic article entitled "Pene a Lavoro!" (Bread and Work!) wrote in the way of an epitaph: "Peace to the great thinker, to my friend, Karl Marx, who died in London a few days ago." It would be interesting to research this declaration of "friendship," considering the fact that Petruccelli lived in London for a few years. On the same day the *Gazzetta Piedmontese* put to the presses a correspondence from the English capital on the funeral of the 17th of March and reported extracts from the funeral orations of Liebknecht, Lavroff and Engels. The words of the latter were reproduced in a form that differed from that published in the *Sozialdemokrat* of Zürich (and printed in translation in Italy only in the April issue of the *Plebe* of Milan), but which was substantially a summary of the speech that was given: the fact stands to demonstrate the contacts of the author of the article with the German Socialist society of London, and perhaps also an acquaintance with Engels

On the 25th of the month, finally, the *Nuova Rivista* in its death notices carried a more rigorous portrait of Marx than those preceding it, lavish with eulogies, defining him as the "most famous German social revolutionary" and a "daring thinker, profound philosopher, synthetic and organized genius." Following the line of the daily press calling the *Communist*

Manifesto the "Gospel of the disinherited," it stated that Marx "was not a blunderer, nor was he greedy with his own means: his doctrines were convictions to which he sacrificed himself."

But already on March 22 the *Gazzeta Piemontese* had published an introduction to a long article, continued the following day and occupying the entire central portion of the newspaper, entitled "Karl Marx and Scientific and Rational Socialism," bearing the signature of Dall'Enze, from Geneva. Dall'Enze was a rather well informed follower of Mazzini who had not very well understood the actual motive of Marxian Socialism, which opposed both republican democracy and Bakuninism. He gave a portrait of Marx written clearly, with enthusiasm and certainly not hostile. From it came the figure which was to be present among all those who in the decade '70-'80 had participated in the struggles of the European workers' movement, even if they were antagonistic in the confrontations of the Marxist International. His description did not correspond to reality, but was sincere: "Karl Marx was a man of average height, robust, broad shouldered, sturdy, with a wide thorax, bull-necked with curly hair and nostrils, thick sensuous lips scarcely hidden by a grey moustache; everything about him showed force of will, passion without hatred; [he was] one of the handsomest types of the Jewish Slav. His long beard, his thoughtful gait, his secure and slow movement like that of a man who bears the weight of a great utopia and the moral responsibility of a great revolution on his shoulders. His superiority was derived from a vast, well-balanced mind, guided by great study and held in check by reason and experience in human affairs." Besides uncertain bits of news on the assertions of Marx, on his participation in ideological-revolutionary movements occurring before the 1880's, on his activity during the years of the First International, Dall'Enza cited as an expert, passages and chapter titles of the most important works of the German philosopher. He related some "original" biographical events, made value judgments which, considered historically above and beyond the struggles and the polemics of the time, could be taken up even today in a discussion, if only to refute them. Thus a newspaper of liberal outlook but intimately conservative such as the *Gazzetta Piemontese* expressed on the *Communist Manifesto* an evaluation which in the Italy of that time was rare to find in the well-known worker and Socialist newspapers. Touching upon the publication of the pamphlet (and attributing it only to Marx, without mentioning Engels), Dall'Enza related in the Turin newspaper that, after 1848, the *Manifesto* had become "the standard militant Socialism, the catechism of the disinherited, the bible upon which the German workers and the greater part of the English workers vote, take oaths, and fight."

These judgments appeared in some Turin newspapers in March of 1883; from then on the publicists and Marxian biographical studies have completed enormous passages which are more advanced, but even today the question mark which Dall'Enza put at the beginning of his article is still valid—the question mark asking who Marx was and what his teaching had represented: "Who is this who fills the world with his fame, who makes the hearts of millions of men beat, who makes kings tremble on their thrones, who makes the bourgeois millionaire shudder with fear?" The answer was: "The new David who slays the giant of feudal and bourgeois Caesarism is a Jew, and his name is Karl Marx." The author ended effectively with total praise for the work and the person of the German philosopher: he was gone, but his principles lived on "among every people" and they spread "in the world in the name of justice, of peace and of social equality, which were the breath of his life." In these words was the value of the article, which showed itself superior by far to the elaborations and opinions which Italian academic scholarship had continued to express for many years.

RUSSIA

ADDRESS OF RUSSIAN SOCIALISTS
Der Sozialdemokrat, Zürich, March 15, 1883

Valued Comrades:

We have been instructed by a number of Russian Socialists in Geneva and Zürich to convey to the German Social Democrats through delegates to the Party Convention, their most profound sympathies. At the same time, they express the deep desire that the Congress in its proceedings reach fruitful results for the common cause of the proletariat.

We and our friends could not let this opportunity go by without expressing our deep pain at the death of Karl Marx, the great teacher and master of the proletariat of all countries. The high respect and honor which our Comrade, P. L. Lavroff, gave at the grave of the noble departed, we also express in the fullest sense. We too are completely convinced that the early death of the intellectual leader of the intellectual proletariat is just as total a loss for the Russian Socialist Revolutionary movement as it is for the labor movement in progressive countries. Therefore we express the hope that the German Social Democratic Party Congress will initiate an international fund-raising effort for one of the great precursors of modern Socialism, so that the honor in which he is held by Socialists of all countries can be expressed through a memorial stone. We hope such funds will also provide for a people's edition of his collected works.

We close with the assurance that we follow the struggle of the German Social Democracy with intense interest, and we will greet with joy, progress in its internal development.

Hail the Social Democracy in all countries! Greetings and Solidarity.

Plekhanov[42]
Vera Zasulich[43]
P. Axelrod[44]

A REMARKABLE ECONOMIC WRITER

Vsemirnaia Illiustratsiia [Illustrated World],[45]
St. Petersburg, No. 742, 2 April 1883, pp. 283–286.

Karl Marx, one of the most remarkable economic writers of recent times, passed away on 16 (4) March. He is usually regarded as a combination of two personality types: the armchair scholar and the political activist. It is the latter activity that has hitherto made a fair evaluation of his scientific works difficult. Most have seen in him only the founder of an international association and an agitator driven out of most countries. Few, therefore, have been inclined to undertake a detailed criticism of his politico-economic system, imagining that they would find only propaganda for anarchism and communism. This prejudice, moreover, has in part been justified by the nature of Marx's activity in the political arena, although in the economic sphere this prejudice is contradicted by reality.

Karl Marx, the son of a mining official, was born in Trier in 1818. Receiving his education at the universities of Bonn and Berlin, he became an ardent Hegelian and joined the party of the liberal bourgeoisie. His collaboration on the *Rheinische Zeitung*, which was published in Cologne and which he began to edit in 1842, was marked by a series of articles against the plundering of the forests and the irregular activities of the Rhenish *Landtag*. As a result, the publication was closed, and Marx moved to Paris. His first work there was "Critique of Hegel's *Philosophy of Right*", published in *Deutsch-Französische Jahrbücher* which he began to edit with Ruge with the aim of bringing together the critical opinions of France and Germany. He then wrote several pamphlets against the Prussian government, for which at Prussia's demand he was exiled from Paris. Moving to Belgium, he published "A Discussion of Free Trade" there in 1846, and a few months later *The Poverty of Philosophy* directed against Proudhon's *Philosophy of Poverty*. Marx and Engels then brought out the *Manifesto of the Communist Party* and Marx began to agitate among the workers; he was therefore asked to leave Brussels. Taking up residence in Cologne, Marx began to publish *Neue Kölnische (sic) Zeitung* in which he appealed to the citizenry to withhold taxes. As a result, after the city was put under martial law, he was forced to flee to Paris. But he did not remain there very long either since the government uncovered his connection with those responsible for the insurrection of 19 June 1849 and threatened to send him to Brittany.

After having moved to England, Marx devoted himself to his research in political economy for which the "British Museum" offered invaluable resources. At the same time, the young scholar wrote for the American newspaper, the *New York Tribune,* in order to earn a living, and only occasionally did he otherwise appear in print. In this period of his activity, at least, one can point to only two pamphlets that caused a sensation: *The Eighteenth Brumaire of Louis Bonaparte* and *Revelations About the Trial of The Cologne Communists.* In 1859, however, he published the remarkable work entitled *Zur Kritik der politischen Oekonomie,* which later appeared in condensed form as the first chapter of *Capital.*

Marx's literary activities did not, however, interfere with his dedication to political agitation. The "International Association", which became famous under the name the "International", was organized in 1864 thanks to Marx's efforts. He was elected a member of the provisional central council of this Association and he drew up the draft of its regulations. Since Marx's activity in this area does not come within the purview of our article, we shall confine ourselves to noting that he always opposed anarchism and the theories of Bakunin and that as a consequence a schism occurred in the Association.

In 1867, the most remarkable of all the works of this German economist appeared —*Capital,* translated into Russian in 1872. As the basis of his theory, he posits the idea that every economic system constitutes merely a transient phenomenon and that economists are mistaken when they assume that the division of labor, credit, and money are fixed categories. That mutability of the forms and phenomena of social life which distinguishes the development of nations depends on changes in the conditions of material production, these being the conditions that determine both juridical relations and state structures. The author shows how the feudal economy was transformed into a handicraft economy and the handicraft economy into the factory economy, and the distinguishing feature of the latter is posited as the production of commodities serving to satisfy the demands not of those who produce them but of extraneous persons. The inherent value of a commodity is determined by the worker's time that goes into it and this is expressed in the commodity's price. The worker sells the use of his labor for a given time and he receives for the duration of that time the value of the essentials necessary for his and his family's subsistence. Out of the discrepancy between the worker's wage and the value of the product he makes arises surplus value and this is kept by the capitalist-entrepreneur. The unchanging portion of capital in the production process is called constant capital, and the changing portion is called variable capital. By means of the division of labor, the increase of the worker's hours, and the use of machines, the capitalist can increase the amount of surplus value he receives. Capital is accumulated not by savings and frugality, but by production in large quantities of a commodity in demand, and production is limited only by a lack of labor.

Having formulated this sophistical point of view, Marx finds that capitalist agriculture leads to the expropriation of the peasantry and the exhaustion of the soil. In the sphere of industrial capital, he assumed the destruction of private property. The best way to eliminate these harmful consequences, in his opinion, is the cooperation of free laborers, and the communal ownership of land and the means of production.

Such is the essence of this theory, formulated with the dialectical skill of an expert Hegelian and reflecting the tremendous erudition of the author. Marx's sophistries, nevertheless, could not escape the notice of serious economic writers and they have been pointed out to him. But even these critics found in Marx's works many sound ideas and a mass of statistical and historical data that he used to support his conclusions. Perhaps the second volume of *Capital,* which has already been prepared for the press, will contain some response to the criticisms raised against him, but judgment on this will have to await this volume's appearance in print.

After everything is said and done, it is impossible to deny the tremendous significance of Marx for economics. He has moved it forward and his original views have compelled people to discuss issues that touch on social questions of the first importance. One may disagree with Marx and censure his political activity, but one cannot deny his conviction, or the brilliance of his exposition.

In his last years, moreover, Marx virtually ceased being active in politics and devoted all his efforts to research, studying the economic situation of Russia and the United States. The illness that brought him to the grave, unfortunately, hindered his working with his former energy.

ONE OF THE GREATEST REPRESENTATIVES OF MODERN ECONOMICS

Iuridicheskii Vestnik [Law Messenger][46] Moscow, April, 1883, Vol XV, No. 4, pp. 715–720

Karl Marx, one of the greatest and most eminent representatives of modern economics died in London on 20 February (4 March). His name and works enjoy immense fame in the learned world and they evoke the most contradictory evaluations. One finds, on the one hand, enthusiastic reviews asserting that his studies constitute an epoch in the realm of political economy. On the other hand, one encounters efforts to denigrate Marx's works in every possible way, to deprive them of even a shade of scientific significance, to accuse him of bor-rowing ideas, etc. But just the ferocity of the attacks and the enthusiasm of the reviews demonstrate that we are dealing here with an outstanding individual, a towering personality, a scholar the likes of whom one rarely encounters. . . .

Marx's studies have some very unusual features, not only in their conclusions, but also in their methodology. In the latter respect, they are distinguished by the use of the Hegelian dialectic. Marx regards all economic phenomena as transient, and in this he differs from the representatives of classical political economy who considered essential economic relations as permanent and stable and who applied principles pertinent to the contemporary European economic system to the way of life of savage tribes. The task of economics, according to K. Marx's doctrine, consists in the study of the continuity of phenomena and the discovery of the laws that govern the economic relations of every given stage of development. He introduced the idea of the mutability of the phenomena of social life as early as his *The Poverty of Philosophy*. This proposition emerged for him under the influence of Hegel's philosophy. But, according to Marx, it is not ideas that govern the world, but rather economic relations, and in these he recognizes the influence on morality, customs, the family, religion, and ideas. If Marx's idea of the continuity of phenomena was developed under the influence of Hegel's philosophy, the idea of the laws themselves that govern the movement of social relations is the independent product of K. Marx. He set himself the task of describing the historical development of the contemporary mode of production which is called capitalist and of explaining the laws governing it. Step by step, Marx explains the process of the transition of the mediaeval feudal economy into a handicraft economy, and the latter into the contemporary factory economy. A characteristic of the contemporary economy, in Marx's opinion, is the dominance of exchange relations. Every individual economic unit produces commodities for the satisfaction not of its own but of others' demands. The law of exchange value of commodities is determined by the socially necessary labor time expended on their production. This same law determines the exchange value of labor power which is a special kind of commodity in our society; the value of labor power is determined by the amount of labor required for the production of the means of the worker's subsistence. The capitalist purchases labor power on the market at its exchange value and then enjoys all of its usefulness, i.e. all the products that this labor power produces. Out of the discrepancy between the exchange value of labor power and the value of the product it produces emerges a value surplus (profit) which accrues to the capitalist. This surplus is created because the worker works longer than the time which covers the value of the means of his subsistence, or—which is the same thing—it is the result of unpaid labor. By lengthening the work day, by improving the combination and division of labor, and, most of all, by employing machines, the capitalist can increase the productivity of labor and thereby increase his profit. The surplus of the result of labor over the cost of subsistence in all fairness should belong not to capital but to the labor power itself and this can be achieved through the transition of the necessary conditions of production (land and the tools of labor) from private property to ownership by the entire society. Marx assumes that the very development of today's production is preparing the ground for such a transition. Under the pressure of competition, petty production gives way to big production which employs the most advanced methods of production and brings the workers together. The gradual concentration of capital consolidates markets and brings them closer together. When this concentration reaches an extreme, the hour will have struck for capitalist production and the era will dawn for the transfer of the means of production from the hands of the few where they are concentrated into the hands of society itself. Workers of all countries, moreover, in line with this movement and development of the relations of capitalist production should recognize the solidarity of their interests in the face of capital and should extend their hands to one another.

Hence arises the idea behind the founding of the "International Working Men's Association." But since in K. Marx's doctrine this transition has to occur by virtue of the development of the inherent relations of capitalist production itself, then "force", as he puts it, "is midwife to the old society only when it is pregnant with the new." He has been therefore, an ardent foe of doctrines that regard violence as the only means of altering economic relations. This is the source of his protest against anarchist tendencies, a protest expressed with particular force in a letter he sent to one of his friends in Vienna only four days before his death. Marx was no longer in any condition to write it himself and he dictated it to his friend Thomas Sanders; he signed it himself, however, with a trembling hand. This letter, which was published after his death in the *Vorstadt Zeitung*, says the following:

Friend! My letter, that of an old, sick exile, will of course surprise you. But the desire to unburden my heart to one who shares my ideas gives me no peace. A lot is being said about us in Vienna nowadays: the irrational criminal actions of a few scoundrels or blinded individuals are being used to . . .O, God! Have I lived this long only to see the majority of my countrymen less than ever understanding true social-democracy? A Paris newspaper recently printed an item taken from a Vienna paper: "The robbery assault on the well known Merschtallinger was perpetrated, it is alleged, by Viennese social-democrats." This is an invention! The very principle of the thing is such that the perpetrators of the crime cannot be social-democrats. But can well-meaning people really confuse anarchism with my theories? As deplorable as this is, I am afraid that it is so. Anyone who knows me knows that from the days of my youth I have shunned and fought the anarchists. Yet in that same Paris newspaper I read, among other things, the odd phrase: "anarchist social-democracy." I laughed very hard over this. It struck me that this was just like someone's talking about a republican monarchy. . . . My warmest regards to your countrymen. I am weary. Karl Marx.

Thus does Karl Marx in this letter hasten once more before his death to draw a sharp distinction between anarchism and socialism.

Besides the above-noted fundamental principles of K. Marx's theory, there is scattered throughout his *Capital* a multitude of other valuable pieces of research, among which of special importance are the following: the significance and origin of the cooperative movement, English factory legislation, the accumulation of capital, and the law of population in the capitalist economy.

For statisticians, the works of Marx are important because of his masterful way of employing statistical data to verify and illuminate economic laws.

Among Russian scholars, the best interpreter of K. Marx's theory is N. Ziber,[47] whose book *The Theory of Value and Capital* establishes the relationship between K. Marx's theory of value and the theories of his forerunners, a book that won the approval of the author of *Capital* himself in the second edition of his work.

LOSS OF A POWERFUL FORCE

Kalendar' "Narodnoi Voli" na 1883 god
[Calendar of The People's Will for 1883][48]
Geneva, 1883, 177–180.

. . . Marx died in London on 11 March 1883. Countless declarations from all sides have shown how vividly socialist-revolutionaries feel the loss of this powerful force. Adding our voice to these declarations, we Russians must also recall the sympathy with which Marx viewed our social-revolutionary movement and the fact that he decided in the last year of his life "on the instructions of the St. Petersburg Committee" (as Marx put it in his letter to Vera Zasulich) to write a pamphlet especially for Russia on the question of the possible development of our commune—a question that is of such burning interest for the Russian socialist. We have no information, unfortunately, whether Marx succeeded in completing this work.

HIS IDEAS HAVE FAILED

Grazhdanin (The Citizen),[49]
St. Petersburg, 13 March 1883, No. 11, 13–14.

, . . The method of Marx's principal work, *Capital,* is purely deductive. Stating a few axioms, which in fact and for anyone else are no more than fantastic hypotheses, he deduces from them idiosyncratic solutions to social questions which he considers to be incontrovertible truths. In point of fact, it doesn't take a very strongly developed critical apparatus to analyze them easily.

The basic idea of *Capital* is Proudhon's aphorism, reworked by Marx, that "La propriété — c'ést le vol." "Capital," says Marx, "is necessarily the result of plunder."

He adds to the above: "individuals matter only to the extent that they personify economic categories. My point of view, which sees the development of socio-economic formations as a natural, historical process, can less than any other make the individual responsible for those relations of which he himself from the social aspect is the product no matter how powerfully he may have transcended them subjectively."

In practice Marx did not follow his view to its conclusion. It is true that in 1870, when the Commune was proclaimed in Paris, Marx proposed to the then members of the International that they not take part in insurrections and that they respect the laws "until the power of reason and the yoke of injustice and persecution grant us victory."[50] But in the very next year in his pamphlet entitled *The Civil War in France*, Marx changed his attitude and began to preach struggle, which in turn brought about persecution of the International.

Marx's entire doctrine is based on the extremely widespread theory of value of Smith,[51] Ricardo,[52] Bastiat[53] and Carey.[54]

The sole source of value, according to *Capital*, is labor. In terms of value, commodities designed for exchange are nothing more than crystalized labor. The unit of measure for labor is the average workday. The amount of value a product represents is measured by its duration, i.e., in hours and days. The measure of value for an object is the labor time it requires at an average rate and with an average degree of skill under normal conditions of production at a given time.

All this is the same amended theory of A. Smith and Ricardo![55] One may boldly assert that there is no scientific rigor either in any of these average units (*moyennes*) or in any of these scientific abstractions. In actuality, every kind of labor has its own kind of value. Is the work day of the mason worth exactly as much as the day of the joiner, the artist, the goldsmith, the brazier, or the common unskilled laborer? Obviously, the answer is no. But then is it not necessary to admit that every worker's wage is exactly proportional to the value of the labor expended, since how else are comparisons made, if not according to the wages paid?

But this is just what Marx denies. And, in reality, if labor valued by its duration is the sole source of value, then commodities made in great quantity in the course of the same period of time do not, when taken all together, represent great values. Following a strictly logical course in the development of these abstractions, we arrive at the astounding conclusion that all scientific discoveries and all the advances of industry, even if they make it possible to produce more of life's necessities, do not, nevertheless, increase the sum of these products' values!

Marx's theory of the origin of capital similarly does not withstand criticism. In his opinion, capital arises not from savings and abstention from superfluous luxury, not from the exchange of commodities, but, as he puts it, from the use of labor power (*Arbeitskraft*). In other words, the same theory that we have just refuted is developed still further. In the end, this theory necessarily leads to the conclusion that the capitalist is obliged to give back all the hours of work (i.e., the wages paid for them) to the worker, without receiving any advantage at all for himself. In other words, this comes down to the notorious free credit (*crédit gratuit*) that has been refuted and ridiculed so many times over.

Marx's major and basic delusion is the idea he developed of value which, in his opinion, is always and everywhere proportional to labor. Furthermore, nowhere in his book does Marx discuss competition. He overlooks this important factor in economic relations. Capital, he thinks, is dead labor; the personal initiative of the capitalist counts for nothing. And so on, with a whole series of similar delusions.

This is not the time or the place over the fresh grave to undertake a summing up of his deplorable activity. But it can and must be said that Marx's audacious attempt to destroy the bases of contemporary society with the aid of what would seem to be the cardinal principles of political economy has utterly failed because he threw together heaps of abstract formulae that are not applicable to real life and are not justified by real life, and he did not clearly comprehend the essence of the matter, or, for that matter, even delve into it very deeply.

Science is a vital organism through which truth is developed. This would appear to be indisputable. But people, so far have regarded science with mistrust, and this mistrust is good. An accurate though vague feeling convinces people that science must hold the solution to the great problems of life, but, in the meantime, they see before their eyes learned men who are preoccupied for the most part with trivia and empty disputes, and even more with problems lacking any life, and who talk about the great problems in an incomprehensible and barbaric tongue. Most of all, people see that what these learned men offer for the future of society is a vague, mysterious, colorless, and purely materialistic communal life . . . And people become disillusioned in science, just as learned men become disillusioned in people and in life. . . .

One such learned man was Karl Marx.

K.

AS A SCHOLAR HE HAD FEW EQUALS

Moskovskii Telegraf[56] (Moscow Telegraph)
March 19, 1883

Economic science has suffered an extraordinarily great and irreplaceable loss. As a scholar, Karl Marx had few equals. Possessed of enormous erudition, Marx did not, however, lose his way in the mass of raw material which he collected (as, for instance, Rochet did).[57] For he was always master of this material, and illuminated it with his ingenious insights. Having sharpened his dialectical thinking, even while studying Hegel, Marx achieved a virtuousity in the art of logical construction of scientific scholarship by the deductive method, and, at the same time, every deduction is supported with a mass of historical inductions. The trenchant, expressive, utterly original language of Marx can be imitated only with difficulty. . . .

The pessimism of those to whom the interests of humanity are dear, and who have followed, along with Marx, the inhuman history of capitalism, is dissipated by Marx himself who points out that the capitalist system itself, by uniting the working masses, creates the ferment for its own destruction, and the creation, on the basis of the technological advances of the capitalist era, a new system.

ONE OF THE MOST GIFTED SONS
OF THE JEWISH PEOPLE

(Nedel'naia Khronika Voskhoda[58] (The Voskhod Weekly Chronicle, St. Petersburg, No.11, 1883, pp. 270, 272)

Death, which has reaped such a rich harvest of lives this year among the world's most prominent figures, has now overtaken *Karl Marx,* too. One of the most influential writers and public figures of our era, Marx was also one of the most gifted sons of the Jewish people.

As is well known, Marx was the originator and life-long source of the most recent social doctrines, the inspirer and guide of the workers' movement. Karl Marx dedicated his entire life, with all the power of his profound mind and all the strength of his iron will, to the struggle of the *fourth* estate against the domination of the *third,* the struggle of the poor against the rich, of the workers against the bourgeoisie and capital. He focused all his efforts on the task of making one solidly united class out of the workers, who have scarcely any political influence in the state. Upon their rebellious discontent and vaguely articulated needs, he endeavored to build the firm basis for a new society, a new order where there would be no disharmony, no class distinctions of rich and poor, no privileges for some and privations for others, but where there would be, rather, the establishment on earth of the kingdom of real equality and universal labor, the brotherhood of all men and nations. Before attaining the promised land of peace and happiness, however, one had, so Marx taught, to pass through the long and hard school of the class struggle. Herein lay the main practical task of Marx and his followers: the organization of the proletariat, getting it—so to speak—into fighting order.

Marx, of course, was nowhere near seeing the realization of his dreams during his own lifetime, but Marx's spirit has unquestionably made an enormous impression on the European workers' movement. The German Socialist Workers' Party owes its strength and influence, in part, directly to Marx, although primarily to his brilliant follower and interpreter Ferdinand Lassalle.

Besides the direct and tremendous influence of Marx on the popular masses, on the European working class, his scholarly works have had, if possible, an even greater influence on the contemporary direction of political economics (the study of the national economy). As is well known, modern political economics, particularly in Germany, differs substantially from the earlier discipline - the school of Adam Smith and his successors.

The hitherto dominant school of economics, the so-called Manchester school, held that the essential economic structure of society consisted in large scale production; the division of gross revenue into capital, profits, and wages; free competition; and the non-intervention of the state in economic activity. If these principal features of the contemporary economic structure have been considered the inviolable and eternal conditions of social life, then one can say that the latest German scholarship has appropriated a great many socialist doctrines, in a more or less modified form. This can be seen in the rise of the school of the so-called University socialists,[59] A school which has numerous shadings, but which is now dominant in Europe. The University socialists are now demanding the *participation of the workers in profits*, the withdrawal of some goods from private ownership, state aid to petty production, state supervision over factories or so-called factory legislation, etc. A substantial amount of the credit for this scientific revolution belongs to Karl Marx and his school, which is to say, primarily to Engels his collaborator and Lassalle his follower. Even legislation and the actions of contemporary politicians have to a remarkable degree reflected Marx's theory and teaching. This is especially noticeable in Germany where almost all the so-called socio-economic reforms and projects of Prince Bismarck are merely reworkings of socialist conclusions with (to be sure) a certain Bismarckian "flavor". Such are the projects of the state's purchase of the railroads, the state's subsidization of workers' insurance, various factory laws, etc. In this respect, Bismarck was influenced directly by Ferdinand Lassalle who had several conversations with the chancellor of the German Empire. Everyone remembers how Prince Bismarck, in a parliamentary session, lavished praise on Lassalle's unusual talents and his love for the fatherland. Thus Bismarck, the very same Bismarck who rendered such assistance (on the sly to be sure) to anti-Semitic agitation, learned a great deal from two Semite-Jews: Karl Marx and Ferdinand Lassalle. In the same way, the Prussian conservative party, the main carrier of anti-Semitism, was reared on and is even today nourished by the thoughts and programs of a Jew: *F. J. Stahl.* Nearly all who during Marx's lifetime tirelessly fought and persecuted him now acknowledge his tremendous importance and influence. Even the *Kölnische Zeitung*, a newspaper that follows a rather moderate line and that is at the same time close to the government and one of the most influential and widely read papers in Germany, candidly states that nearly all of modern German life is founded on the modified ideas of Marx![60]

One hardly needs to add that Marx, the founder of scientific socialism and the advocate of the regular and gradual development of mankind, has nothing in common with those numerous "shakers of the foundations" who also call themselves socialists but who all too frequently lack any understanding of what the term means. Thus, the name of Karl Marx will forever remain in the history of Germany as one of the most glorious and most cherished by posterity. Along with the names of Heinrich Heine,[61] Ludwig Börne,[62] and Ferdinand Lassalle, the name of Karl Marx is part of that splendid constellation which has shone and will continue to shine so brilliantly and long in the dark sky of Germany; these gifted *Jews*, by general consensus, have breathed a new spirit into the life of the *German nation* and contributed a great deal to its national revival.

As far removed as Marx was in his life and work from the Jews and the Jewish question, it is obvious that such is the irresistable force of that fate which hangs over even the most distant descendants of Abraham, that sooner or later, one way or another, they become involved in the Jewish question. The socialist emigré Karl Marx did not escape this fate. At the very beginning of his career, when he was already in exile in Paris, Marx published the article "Zur Judenfrage" in his *Deutsch-Französische Jahrbücher* of 1844. The well-known German writer Bruno Bauer had at that time attacked the "pretensions" of the Jews to civil rights, an attack based on the Jews' religious and national apartness. Marx's article was a reply to Bruno Bauer. Marx's views on the Jews have already been discussed in Mr. Morgulis' article (*Voskhod*, 1881, No. 1)[63] and we can therefore limit ourselves here to a brief mention of them. Proceeding from the premise that political and civil freedom in modern states is in no way bound to estate or class division in society, Marx finds odd the refusal of citizenship to the Jews, since citizenship has nothing in common with religious profession. Marx then moves from the question of the political and civil emancipation of the Jews to what he calls the question of their *human* emancipation, which means, apparently, the absolute abolition of Jewry as a *peculiar economic* and *social element,* which is to say as an acute expression of the contemporary bourgeois structure of society. Marx considers this possible only when society succeeds in destroying the *essence* of *Judaism*—commercialism and its elements. To put it another way, the failings specifically ascribed to the Jews are really failings of our time and our society in general; the Jews, as a result of the peculiar historical circumstances weighing upon them, are merely more sharply defined exponents of these failings. The final solution of the Jewish question, therefore, is possible only with the radical transformation of the present social structure. This is the view of the Jewish question held by the greatest socialist of our time.

Without entering upon an analysis and critique of Marx's ideas, let us merely note that, if the Jews are frequently accused of being the main representatives of capital and the bourgeoisie, they might point out the fact that the greatest opponent of the bourgeoisie—Marx (and in part Lassalle, too)—arose from the ranks of that same Israel. . . .[64]

FOR A WREATH FOR MARX

Studenchestvo, (The Student Body), illegal organ of the St. Petersburg Central University Circle, No. 4, April, 1883

Socialist dreams, ideas, and theories are, as is well known, a very old story. Let us take, for instance, the first case to come to mind. As early as some year like 1693, the Catholic monk Gabrielle Fugli fantasized about a nation whose entire way of life was based on the communality of property with the complete absence of authority. We'll pass over the eminent Thomas More and Campanella. A lot of water has passed over the dam since those times, of course. The body of scientific knowledge has grown tremendously and scientific methods in various fields of intellectual curiosity have been developed to a remarkable perfection. But the social sciences even now have not yet been granted complete legalization, so to speak. Thanks to their extreme complexity and to the interference of one or another kind of subjectivism, the bitterest fate of all in this case has befallen theories of economics. Here full scope has been given to one-sided enthusiasms. "Man shall not live by bread alone," but you won't live without if either. And this bread is not usually eaten by man in equal and identical amounts.

Everyone is interested in economic questions, but everyone decides them in different ways. As though swollen with pride over its first serious successes in the field of economic science (where such a prominent role has been played by great minds like Adam Smith and Ricardo), the European Areopagus has apparently decided to rest on its laurels in one way or another. The French economic school, in its objections to the "classic" (the English political-economists) has disputed really only one or another editorial version of general economic formulas, and it has not gone beyond the favorite fascination with the production of capital! Socialist attempts—the most multifarious-—seemed to the above-mentioned, solid Areopagus[65] like so many frivolous attacks on the integrity of the "truly scientific" world view. The truth has to be told: the voices so urgently needed from the side of the socialist opposition were not yet heard. At times there was heard Fourier's ardent sermon, overflowing with the most gorgeous ideas and opening up the most gorgeous horizons. But unfortunately, Fourier's socialist materials were more like splendid stuff for the philosophy of economics than anything else. In addition, they harbored romanticism. Some of Fourier's ideas are edifying: the passionate attractions that prompt man to produce, the harmonic significance of diversity and of noble emulation in the production, union, and division of labor, and so on. None of them, however, is tied together or informed by a definite, scientific world view. At other times, the peace of the (Areopagus) dwellers was disturbed by the noisy exclamations of the noble P. J. Proudhon who subjected orthodox economics to brilliant criticism. But even Proudhon is dear to us primarily for his negative attitude to economic reality. He did not have a structured economic system, either.

For the full force of the anti-capitalist protest to be felt, one prime point had to be hit, one sick spot had to be struck and with a fanaticism of logic, if one may use such an expression, aimed at a given series of phenomena. A man worthy of such a feat was finally found. This, of course, was Karl Marx. His iron logic, the force of which is acknowledged by friend and foe alike, his colossal erudition in the literature of the subject, his philosophical tenacity—proved all the more powerful since Marx did not go off in all directions at once. He proceeded along a very straight road. Orthodox economists were diligently concerned with production; destitution was ascribed to the will of "economic harmony." Marx collected a whole pile of facts that illustrated the condition of the [66] classes, which served as the basis for the luxuriant flowers and fruits of capitalism. Various lovers of economic freedom have been carried away by the contemporary formula of capitalism and they have stretched it this way and that way, projecting it into the distant past and making one think that it will account for virtually all the blessings of the future, too. Karl Marx, with the precision and the objectivity of the historian, isolated capitalism as the product of a particular era. The defenders of the alleged fundamentals of economics have wept abundant tears of tender emotion over the universally human significance of capital. Karl Marx, with the callousness of the mathematician, established the famous formula of *surplus value.* . . .[67]

This formula summarizes the entire, peculiar capitalist phenomena of the present, without which you will find it difficult to analyze the economic past. Only with the help of this formula will you, on the basis of a strict syllogism, *identify* all the abnormality of the contemporary economic system. I say *identify*, for you have already sensed this, of course, for a very long time.

Marx is reproached for one-sidedness. But, indeed, he never claimed to be an innovator-philosopher, from whom one can legitimately demand full sociological generalizations and all-encompassing ideals. Is the scientific orientation of his economic theories really one-sidedness? Science, which raises our standard of living and nips in the bud all the mirages that dull the mind and confuse the feelings is naturally not our enemy. Marx was even less one-sided when in 1848, at the very height of those pretty romantic enthusiasms of socialism, he and Engels published their glorious *Manifesto.* We have just recently read this *Manifesto* in Russian and were struck by the keenness of the characterizations, the force of the generalizations, the scientific dispassion and somehow prophetic novelty of the views. The *Manifesto's* author, who attributes such great importance to the economic side of things and at the same time in no way holds aloof from politics, cannot be called one-sided. Of course, if a man who energetically pursues a great task he has taken upon himself is one-sided, then Marx was one-sided.

Let us touch briefly on his biography. He was the son of a high-placed official and he married the sister of a minister. What could be more favorable to the establishment of a "career?" But Marx, of course, was not tempted by external blessings. He devoted himself to philosophical and politico-economic labors. As a German author has expressed it (in general, trying to cast a certain shadow over Marx's image), "even in his early years, he dedicated himself with selfless fanaticism to the struggle for the social emancipation of the proletariat, a struggle he has not interrupted during the course of his entire life." (The author was writing in 1877.) One can only envy such one-sidedness as Marx's.

The high-priests of "pure science" must, if you will, envy Marx, too. Marx's erudition and diligence are uncommon things! The author of one brief "historical essay" on German social-democracy—Mehring,[68] we think—quite rightly remarked that not a single civilized country of Europe (other than Germany, that is) has given birth to such first-rate socialists as measured by the value of their world view and their learning as Lassalle and Marx. The learned political economist Marx, however, was not content with armchair activity. Hitherto, the representatives of the most diverse schools have made decisions one way or the other between their public duties and the obligations of the scholar. Marx loved his ideal in word and deed. When the great meeting of the workers of all nations took place on September 28, 1864, the inspirer of the gathering, according to Lavel, was Marx. According to Mehring, the absorption of national socialism by international communism is a logical necessity which nothing can stop, and as early as 1847, Marx uttered his word communism with uncommon firmness and, "for the time, remarkable sobriety." And many, many "scholarly" heads have tried and are trying to figure out why this real vitality has been imparted to the social movement by a socialist with the most radical "schemes." And how could it be that this socialist turns out to be a scholar? A scholar and socialism! in and of itself this is something frivolous, illusory, baseless. An astounding sign of the times! The learned author of *Capital* with his wonted conscientiousness and earnestness gave himself to politics, too. He, without doubt, did not for a single minute let fall his sacred banner of struggle for the oppressed. At the most difficult moment in the life of the International, in 1872, when discord arose at the Hague Congress among the members of the Association, Marx made a spirited declaration of his motto. "As far as I am concerned," he said in his speech, "I shall continue to work at the same task. I shall not waver from the International. I have devoted all my working days to the cause of the triumph of socialist ideas and I shall continue to serve that cause now and until my dying day. And we are convinced that the hour of triumph and the reign of the proletariat will come."

Yet, Marx, too, was familiar with political compromises. We shall give an example. At a conference of International delegates in London in 1871, the means necessary for conducting propaganda were being debated. Among other things, it was even recommended that the workers join the political movement and not shun an alliance with bourgeois radicals. According to reports, this conference was directed in the main by Marx. Thus, Marx did not mind joining the bourgeois radicals, which is a compromise, isn't it? But this is a compromise, so to speak, of political tactics. The social cause itself was not involved here, for no serious political activity can put aside for a single moment its principles and guiding ideals.

Lavel, making use of certain circumstances, and not without a sense of triumph, calls Marx a representative of the economic history school. Without stopping to analyze the exactness of such a term, we shall only say that Marx, because of the *realism* of his views could only seem to some people to be insufficiently *radical*. And yet, this same Marx split with Lassalle. As early as 1862 at the meeting of Marx and Lassalle in London, a certain estrangement was beginning to be noticeable. The republican cosmopolite Marx did not like the nationalism of Lassalle's universal German workers' union! This same Marx, nevertheless, as early as 1847 had proclaimed himself a conscious, serious communist! All this is clear and instructive! Indeed, the social movement shows its *vitality* only so constantly and unalterably guided and inspired by broad, resolute, and definite goals, even while making at times *productive concessions* for the sake of labor tactics. Therefore (let us note incidentally), in our Russian life, too, only a genuinely *socialist* movement has a future.

We have tried in the foregoing lines to give some general indication of the significance of the recently deceased Marx as a scholarly political economist and as a social activist. Thanks, perhaps, to purely accidental circumstances, we have a translation of Marx's monumental work, *Capital*. And anyone who wishes to study seriously the economic issues agitating us must, it must be said, become familiar with this work of the extremely talented socialist. But since the contents of *Capital* are intimately connected, of course, with Marx's social ideas, we can only hope for the widest possible circulation and the greatest popularity of this work. In pondering over *Capital*, the reader will understand for himself what an integrated, solid and lasting substantiation of the need for the reconstruction of the contemporary social system Marx has provided in his book!

In conclusion, we shall say a few words about the subscription drive to collect money for the purchase of a wreath for Marx's grave. This idea, without doubt, deserves the greatest sympathy and, besides, it characterizes the well-known responsiveness of Russians—those who are alive and thinking. Marx's attitude to the Russian social movement is well known. He saw a vital and progressive chord where others among his compatriots and cultured persons of other countries see only the blood-thirstiness of Eastern fanatical cretins or, at best, the self-interested protest of a certain group of barbarians acting against their enlightened government. The German philosopher Dühring, whose ideas are extremely appealing, treated Russian protesters with inexplicable ill will. It has been said of some German social-democrats, that they disown the Russian progressives with zeal, even. Marx, however, showed great kindness to the citizens of the great Eastern despotism. Marx, called, G. Chernyshevskii an eminent Russian critic and scholar!

It has not been given to us Russians to see here anything like the Lassallean workers' union, let alone the International whose "living spirit" was Karl Marx! But the future is in no way closed for us! And the memory of Marx will not die here. Let us honor as best we can Marx who worked so hard to eradicate harmful socio-economic prejudices and to establish sound socialist concepts. As a scholar, Marx did not reject social action. May his life serve as a reproach to some of our learned men, who have too firmly esconced themselves in the armchairs, and to those of them who gave up too soon at the sight of danger.

All Russian forces who are awake! All who sincerely suffer from the anomaly of our hard reality! All who wish to fight as hard as possible for socialist ideals! Let us unite and say from our hearts: May your memory live forever, friend of the oppressed, brother in spirit, noble teacher! May the memory of Karl Marx live forever!

Contribute gentlemen, to the Purchase of a Wreath for K. Marx!

The groups conducting the subscription drive in the various educational institutions may send the money collected to the editors of *Studenchestvo*, who will take the responsibility of forwarding it to the appropriate persons.

7

CONTEMPORARY ESSAYS
AND ARTICLES
ON KARL MARX

INTRODUCTION

Most of the material in the preceding sections was published as part of obituaries or as editorials. But there were also, in the weeks following Marx's death, discussions of aspects of his life and work which were somewhat different in nature. I thought it best to include such material in a separate section even though it is part of the reaction to the death in the countries where it appeared.

The three articles that open the section are by leaders of the Socialist Labor Party in the United States and are self-explanatory. The fourth is actually a continuation of an earlier editorial tribute to Marx by the Dutch Socialist, Ferdinand Domela Nieuwenhuis, parts of which appear above. The fifth, "Marx and the Dynamite Policy," is noteworthy for its ignorance of the subject it discusses and as an indication of the sheer nonsense which appeared alongside serious articles in the weeks following Marx's death.

The long article by Professor Achille Loria (1857–1943) is in a different category. It has, to be sure, its full share of superficial rhetoric and errors. Moreover, Professor Loria concedes that while others had previously advanced concepts which appear in Marx's economic theories, they did not make any serious attempt to develop them or offer substantial proof of their statements. But he still clings to the view that there was not much original in Marx's thought. In his biographical sketch of Marx—not included here—Loria advanced the thesis that Marx himself was conscious of the weakness of his economic theories, and that he sought to answer his critics by promising to develop his ideas in the second volume of *Capital* even though he never really planned to write such a volume. ("If you allow me to say," Loria wrote, "I do not think that Marx ever entertained the idea of giving a second brother to his *Capital*.") Engels, to whom Loria sent his article, was annoyed by the Italian economist's obvious effort to prove his erudition even though he did not know too much of the subjects he discussed, but he was enraged by the underhand assault upon Marx's integrity. He wrote coldly to Loria:

> It seems to me that you appear to want to let the public know about the so-called famous sophism which dominates all of Marx's doctrines. But I can't find it. What kind of imbecile could image that a man like Marx would have threatened his critics with a second volume which he had never even considered writing, even if only for an instant, and that this second volume was nothing but an ingenious expedient thought up by Marx as a substitute for scientific arguments. *This second volume exists,* and will be published shortly, and it will teach you the difference between value and profit. I have the honor to treat it with proper respect.

Loria later mentioned Engels' "haughty response" in his autobiography, though he praised him as "a grand fighter for Socialism," and when volume II of Capital, was published, he acknowledged his error in having questioned whether the work even existed. However, he still clung to the view that Marx had done his best work before 1867 after which he began his improductive decadence which lasted until his death."[1]

Loria advanced a set of theories to which he gave the name "historical economism." It enjoyed an influence in Italy for a number of years, but the profound Italian Communist leader, Antonio Gramsci, dismissed it as a mixture of vulgar economy and vulgar Marxism. To Gramsci, Loria's ideas exemplified "certain degenerate and bizarre aspects of the mentality of a group of Italian intellectuals and therefore of the national culture. . . ." To this Gramsci gave the name "lorianismo."[2]

Nevertheless, Loria's article on Marx is of historical importance. It was published in *Nuova Antologia,* the most prestigious cultural review of Italian conservatism, and the most widely distributed journal in Italy. The article helped to make Marx's ideas better known in Italy, and thus was an important factor in the publication three years later of an Italian edition of *Poverty of Philosophy and Capital.* Professor Loria was one of the few Italians of the period who was familiar with the works of Marx, even though he misunderstood many of Marx's fundamental theories, he must be given credit for feeling that it was necessary to observe Marx's death with a discussion of his life and work. Mistaken and malicious though he was, he, at least, was more of an honest scholar than his colleagues in other countries who simply ignored the event.

The last article is the second of two by Eleanor Marx published in *Progress*. (The first, a biographical sketch of Marx, appears above.) It is a clear concise exposition of the theory of surplus value. In her scholarly and brilliant biography of Eleanor Marx, Yvonne Kapp says of the articles in *Progress*:

> The two articles taken together reflect Eleanor's grasp of the essentials of Marxism and her power to convey them in the simplest and most telling manner. Without any pretensions to great intellect, she demonstrated here that, by temperament and ability, she was peculiarly fitted to wield in practice with style and vitality the weapons Marx had forged, combining to a rare degree an understanding of theory with deep human feeling, uncommon in the world of politics.[3]

THE ESTATE OF KARL MARX

By Adolf Douai, *New Yorker Volkszeitung*, March 18, 1883

When the will of a millionaire is opened in probate court, one is often astounded at the size of his legacy and at the amount of wealth collected during his lifetime. One cannot but wonder at how it is possible that one person can amass so much wealth. The astonishment, though mixed with completely different feelings, will be just as great when the will of our deceased friend Karl Marx is opened. He leaves behind for us not only his known works but two further volumes of his major work *Capital* which will be edited by his friend and co-worker Frederick Engels. Marx had already informed some of his friends of the contents of the volumes. In his mind the two volumes were finished sixteen years ago, when the documentary material which would announce the new teaching was already collected, although the whole work was not completed by Marx because he continually wanted to enrich it with further statistics and polish the style. The completion of this work was hindered by deaths in his family, his own sickness and his untimely death. But his friend Engels is exactly the right person to complete it in his spirit. When the abundance of this treasure is bequeathed and handed to us, only then will we be astounded at the spiritual wealth which *one* man in a short lifetime could amass. But what a contrast to the will of the millionaire! The latter leaves behind *stolen* goods—our friend only that which he created himself. The one made the world poorer through his accumulation—this one *enriches* it even after his death. The millionaire is one of many of his kind because it takes no extraordinary characteristics to become a millionaire—this one *has no equals* except in particular aspects of his accomplishments. From the one, few inherit— from this one, all inherit.

How great the still unearthed treasure of Marx's estate is can be seen in the preface of the first volume of *Capital.* The first volume makes clear the origins of capital in the smallest detail; the two expected volumes will pursue the rest of the life story of the parvenue Mammon into its darkest corners. They will handle the "circulation process of capital and the formation of the total process of capital", then the last volume will deal with the "history of the theory of political economy." There we will find shown in its entirety how the monstrous, the unbelievable, became reality, how the century of discoveries and inventions crushed mankind to fetish worship, stripped it of almost all of its human dignity and how this, by historical necessity, was the essential prerequisite for the great revolution which will remove all kinds of idolatry.

The study of this imperishable work becomes more absorbing the more one reads it. It is such a strictly scientific work that a first understanding of it is a hard task. But from time to time a highly appropriate comparison, or an example, or a biting satire, a striking joke, a shining spotlight on known relationships inspires the reader to advance courageously. When one has studied the whole work through, a second wind comes enabling one to read it a second time, a third time, and so on, with less and less exertion, and the reading becomes more and more pleasurable. One finds with each new reading new truths which one missed before, real beauties of narrative and style which one did not appreciate the first time, inner relationships of all the individual parts. In short, the book—though like all human creations it has its mistakes—from the viewpoint of strict science and sharpness of logic is a masterpiece which one always sincerely admires with growing trust.

But what more could one say in praise of it than that innumerable wage-earning workers, with little or no higher education, have made this book their own, to the point of total understanding, have digested it into their flesh and blood? The obscure, learned method of expression, the many incomprehensible citations in a half dozen foreign languages, the similarly incomprehensible references to people and things which can only be familiar to well-read people—all this has not frightened away thousands of workers from fathoming the author's breadth of thought. And they have understood the content of the book and can explain it in their own language. Already that alone explains the secret magic the book exudes. We are convinced that an English translation of it would have had a great effect if Marx had decided upon it before the French translation, i.e., published the English first. That it is not finished, not even available, we sincerely lament.

MARX AND THE COMMUNE

By a German Socialist,
New Yorker Volkszeitung, March 18, 1883

Our pious forebearers thought it a particular concession by providence when someone died on a national, social or religious holiday because in this way his death received a part of the consecration connected with these days, and the memory of the deceased would be reinforced by its identification with the celebration of general holiday.

We, however, who have detached ourselves from the belief in this tradition and who see such occurances only as chance cannot fight off the feeling that, even if death inexorably makes its inevitable claim on a giant spirit like Marx, it is at least a satisfaction for the victim to die in such a way that death is a worthy close to an action-filled life. A man who devoted his entire strength uninterruptedly to the service of the workers' cause, who was the spiritual planner of two March 18ths, 1848 and 1871, who worked on their occurrence and who remained their most persuasive defender, such a man may—if he must die—lay claim to the weeks of March as his honorary date.

As the celebration of the Paris Commune is international so also is the honoring of the memory of Karl Marx, the creator of the International Workingmen's Association; as the rising of the Parisian workers in 1871 had the sympathies of workers of all nations, so the mourning for the great deceased who, like no other man guided and led the common cause, will be shared by the thinking proletariat of all nations. The scope of his freedom-bringing actions, transcending the boundaries of language, stretched over almost all the civilized world, even though the sword of his scientific research at first benefited only his German colleagues, since he wrote his major work in his mother language and he was only able to control the later translations as far as practicable. France, which had received the French edition of *Capital* in 1872, translated by Marx's sons-in-laws—Larfargue and Longuet, who in association with other partisans, had already spread the Marxist doctrine for years in the French workers' newspapers, can especially thank Marxist theory for dispelling by scientific concepts the unclear ideas about socialism, which the local *fantasy-ridden* systems had created. This schooling through a scientific system originated in the 1871 commune uprisings in a form greatly altered from previous Paris Revolution. In 1871 the workers refused to be led around by the bourgeoisie. Rather, they went staunchly toward their goal by grabbing the reins of government themselves and deciding to transfer provisionally all the closed shops and factories to the labor organizations. All practical measures taken by the Commune in its short existence originated with members of the International. This memorial to Marx should inspire us to continue to keep the atmosphere of socialism free from the fog of phrases and let our actions speak for us; and the memory of the commune, whose heroes fell having subordinated their individual wills to the total will of the revolution, should remind us that when the revolution breaks out, it will sweep away all artificial sectarian differences.

Only in this sense can the 18th of March continue to be a double holiday for the supporters of the International cause on which day the memory of the heroes and martyrs of the Commune is simultaneously celebrated with that of Marx, who was their most persuasive advocate. Among the numberless works about the historic tragedy of 1871 which have appeared in France and elsewhere which can measure up to Marx's in depth and sharpness of view, in spirit and knowledge of the facts, none contains such a shining justification of the Commune and such a devastating description of its destroyers, as Marx's own "Address of the General Council of the International on the "Civil War in France," which closes with the words:

"The Paris of the worker with its Commune will be eternally celebrated as the glorious precurser of a new society. Its members are burned into the great heart of the working class. History has already nailed its destruction to that pillory from which all the prayers of its priests are powerless to redeem it."

MARX AND THE RUSSIAN SOCIALISTS

By Sergius E. Schewitsch
New Yorker Volkszeitung March 18, 1883

I hope not to be accused of national vanity, of Pan-Slavic prejudice, if I make the assertion that it was the Russian youth, the intelligent Russian proletariat, which was among the first, perhaps the first outside of Germany, to take as its own the basic ideas of Marxist teachings about capital and labor. Already as far back as the 1850's, it was the thinker and martyr of Russian Socialism, N. G. Chernishevsky, who became acquainted with the first major work of Marx, *A Critique of Political Economy.* Applying Marx's critical method, Chernishevsky developed outlines that still belong to the classic literature of Socialism in which he dissected orthodox national economics as set forth by its foremost representative, John Stuart Mill.[4] The great noble scholar was worthy of the great master. What Marx was for the Socialist thought of Western Europe, Chernishevsky represented for the dark, enslaved East of the Continent.

Our readers know well from various sketches which the *Volkszeitung* has published in the last few years, how the seed spread by the noble thinker blossomed in the heart of the Russian revolutionary youth movement, and I do not have to refer to it here. Let me only make the passing remarks about the lively mental connection which existed at that time between Marx and the Socialist Party and which gave proof of how all-encompassing, and literally, international—that is common to humanity—the teachings and ideas of the great man truly were. When in the middle of the 1860's, the easing of the press laws on the part of the Czar, made publication of free thinking writings possible, at least in the area of science, the Russian Socialists acted at once to attain a translation of Marx's *Capital.* That such a "dangerous" book could be published at all was only because (due to the circumstances that) the censor in question, by his own admission could not understand a word of its intent. A work as difficult as this, he thought, could not possibly become dangerous. Here, of course, he was completely wrong. Not only was the book greedily absorbed by Russian student youth—who, unlike their fraternity brothers in Germany are more concerned with social questions than with drinking beer and carousing—but also it was printed in many free thinking publications. It appeared in the currently suppressed *Delo* and in the *Otechestvennye Zapiski* (Fatherland Chronicle) in the form of a series of articles which, under the pretext of reviews, actually contained a systematic and readily understandable exposition of Marxist teachings bringing them to the widest circles of the population. it may therefore be asserted without qualification that Marxist ideas were popularized in Russia even before they were in Germany.

At that time there existed a basic split in the ranks of the Russian revolutionaries which, of course, as happens everywhere stemmed mainly from tactical and temperamental differences, but which, nevertheless, often interfered with the movement's progress. It was the split between Anarchists and Socialists or, as they were called, between Marxists and Bakuninists. The more developed the movement became, the more the vanguard learned to differentiate between means and principles. The more completely these differences were delimited, the more decisively all thinking leaders of the movement inclined to the thoughts of Marx so that finally the most resolute terrorists, who certainly are more "anarchistic" in the ways in which they fight than many of these who have lately and loudly become self-proclaimed "anarchists", became the most convinced exponents of Marx's ideas. Was it not the same "executive committee" which ordered the execution of Alexander II and which addressed the famous letter to Karl Marx in which they completely endorsed his teachings?[5] This lively, spiritual contact existed on Marx's part as well as on the part of the "Nihilists." Marx did not belong to the type of thinkers who sit at their desks and destroy the world but cringe if they step on a fire-cracker in the street. The deeds of violence to which the relentless social struggle drove the Russian revolutionaries did not frighten him. On the contrary, he received with great joy every bit of news of every new resolute action of the "Nihilists." Marx welcomed every one of the group as if he were a member of the family. In his last years, he often said that he expected the first initiative toward the great social revolution to come from the Russian youth.

Yes, in Russia too, Marx was not a foreigner. He was "one of us." There, too, in many a humble study, in many a small village lost in the steppes, in many a heart languishing in a Siberian mine, the news of Marx's death will be felt as a harsh, irreplaceable loss. All of humanity stands sorrowing at the graveside of one of its greatest thinkers.

KARL MARX: IN MEMORIAM

By Ferdinand Domela Nieuwenhuis
De Dageraad (Dawn), Amsterdam
vol. IV (1882–1883), part V, pp. 321–29

Great Men Are The Cement of Society

Again one of those great men who leave inextinguishable imprints on the "sands of time" has left the world stage.

Karl Marx is no more!

What Darwin was in the field of natural science, Marx was in the field of economics. Both were stars of the first magnitude. With their rare sparkle, they are in the true sense of the word, tokens which have become omens. The names of both arouse among some people a feeling of hatred and contempt, among others, however, a feeling of gratitude and appreciation.

Endowed with rare gifts—as even now his opponents must concede—and with a keen sense of judgment, Marx was not afraid of any consequence, and no matter what the position of the men of official science, he acted mercilessly to destroy them whenever they erred or deviated from the path of logic.

Marx was the man who gave a scientific foundation to Socialism, who, possessing "the full armor of the total culture of his century," discovered the laws of economic development, and thereby made known the true source of capitalism.

Born in 1818 at Treves, he studied law at Bonn and Berlin. But he also threw himself with full vigor into the study of history and philosophy, and settled in 1842 as a lecturer (Privatdozent) in philosophy. But the political movement had destined him for another career. Becoming editor of the *Rheinische Zeitung*, he challenged the government, and despite all all censorship, he knew how to maintain this paper, until the government, powerless to prevent the publication legally, applied the usual government solution—prohibiting it summarily through violence.*

---

*How able the censors were is shown by the fact that one of them, the policeman Dollschall, erased the advertisement in the *Kölnische Zeitung* of the translation of

Married to the sister of Von Westphal, later a reactionary minister, Marx now went to Paris and there published, with Arnold Ruge, the *Deutsch-Französische Jahrbücher*. But the Prussian government did not allow him any rest, and succeeded in influencing Guizot to remove Marx from France in 1845. And who let himself be used for this dirty deed? The famous Mr. Alexander von Humboldt! Marx then settled in Brussels where, in 1847, he published an answer to Proudhon's *Economic Contradictions or The Philosophy of Poverty*, his *The Poverty of Philosophy*, with a devastating critique of the French sophist.

In association with his faithful friend, Friedrich Engels, Marx hurled the *Manifesto* of the Communist Party into the face of Europe shortly before the February Revolution of 1848. This remarkable document even now deserves our attention because of the sharp as well as correct analysis of economic development. After the February Revolution, Marx was expelled from Belgium but he was able to return to Paris and soon afterwards to Germany where he founded the *Neue Rheinische Zeitung, organ of democracy*. This journal, which existed about a year, was the finest paper ever published because of the soundness of its argument as well as the audacity of its actions. It was an independent press, and was neither the flunky of the powerful nor the paid servant of capital. This generated hatred against the paper which of course was suppressed when reaction increased. Its last issue, printed in red, carried that beautiful poem by Freiligrath, the poet of liberty (who alas later sold himself for money), of which I am able to give a translation through the aid of one of my friends.[6] It is a good thing that such verse is not forgotten.

Again Marx went to Paris but he was faced with the choice of going either to Britanny or leaving France, and so decided to go

Dante's *Divine Comedy* by Philalethes (the later king John of Saxony) with the remark that comedy may not be played with things divine.

How little progress we have made in this respect we can see from the fact that not long ago somebody was sentenced to a prison term because he had said: "The stomach of the church is strong as iron. It has without ever overeating, eaten up whole countries. And it has also, without suffering harm, eaten dishonest things with gusto." It did not help that the accused pleaded that this was a quotation from Goethe, the classical and honored poet, for whom statues have been erected. The man was sentenced.—*Footnote in original.*

to London where he stayed until his death. There he indulged in his love of science and dedicated himself exclusively to his economic studies. The result was his book, *Critique of Political Economy* which appeared in 1859. Here we already find Marx's theory of value, which he later elaborated in *Capital*. Marx did not hesitate to unmask the false brethren, as we see in his denunciation of Carl Vogt, the well-known free-thinking natural scientist, as a bought hireling of Louis Napoleon. Vogt slandered Marx in all possible ways because of this accusation, but the truth of the charge came to light later. On the list of Bonapartist hirelings under the letter V, an entry reads: "Vogt—in August, 1859, he received ten thousand francs." This list was found in the *Tuileries* and was published by the September government. Do you now understand why some persons found it in their interest to burn the Tuileries? Later they could blame it on the Commune, and, in the meantime, the goal was reached because the compromising documents, still to be revealed, had disappeared. This is the bourgeois idea of decency!

When German, French, English, and Italian workers formed the plan to found the International Workingmen's Association, they called in Marx, and Marx knew how to acquire more influence than Mazzini, who was not very informed on economics. Thus Marx became the soul of the International and one of the great powers who repeatedly force governments to tear their hair in despair. This Association has awakened the consciousness of solidarity among workers of both continents and made the workers into a political party. Although there was great rejoicing when this Association was, as it were, destroyed in the presence of Marx himself on the occasion of the Congress of the International at the Hague in 1872, it had nonetheless accomplished its task and could abdicate without damage. Everywhere spirits have been awakened, and now if the Socialist movement in different countries has become more and more a power, then it can be ascribed to the International, which was its first impulse.

In 1867 the first part of Marx's work, *Capital*, appeared, establishing him permanently in the rank of the economists. Although the work was systematically ignored in the beginning—the usual tactics—it began to make its mark and slowly voices were raised in recognition of its merits. Professor Beesley, for instance, states that Marx has no equal in his knowledge of Europe. Albert Lange says that Marx, without doubt, is the most leaned and keenest economist of our time. And Rudolph Meijer asserts that Marx's work, *Capital,* is the greatest scientific achievement of modern German economics.

But now the tactics have changed, and people are made wary of that book. Laveleye says in his *Contemporary Socialism* that it is a painfully difficult work.[7] And the lawyer Mr. Kerdijk, in his biography of Marx, one in a series of "Men of Importance," calls it "indigestible"—that word itself is supposedly digestible—and furthermore: "clumsy in its representation of ideas," also "an example of the desire to obfuscate the presentation," with a "terminology which for an ordinary mortal is a veritable torture." Nobody can say that these descriptions are an encouragement to read the book; on the contrary, they will deter many a person, and the book will not be read. Hence the goal is achieved. Of course, nobody can claim that the book should be read for relaxation, but it was not written for that purpose. It is a book for study. And I must say that reading it seems to me less complicated than, for instance, reading the works of Schaffle which are not mentioned in such an unfavorable way.

Both because of the size and complexity of the book, I believed that a synopsis of it could be of much service, and I communicated my idea to Marx with the request that he read the proofs of my version, since he understood Dutch as well as many other languages. I was very pleased when I heard from him that he endorsed my plan, and added: "To judge by the essays I read of you in the *Jahrbüch für Sozialwissenschaft,* I have not the least doubt that you are certainly the most appropriate person to give the Dutch a resumé of *Capital.*" I carried out my task. It was not very easy, but I was pleased that Marx wrote to me, after having received a copy: "The principle, the spirit of the thing, you have captured." Marx thanked me for the friendly dedication, with which he said, "you have personally thrown the gauntlet into the face of the bourgeois antagonists."[8] Those who therefore wish to study the theories of Marx should study that little book.* In that event, many so-called free thinkers would be able to speak and write less superficially about Socialism than is now the case among people who never trouble to inform themselves about it. Indeed, some believe they have already acted like heroes by joining the free thinkers, for which nothing is required, not even resigning their church membership. But as Marx said correctly: "The Anglican Church more easily forgives when attacked on thirty-eight of its thirty-nine articles of faith, than when attacked on one thirty-ninth of its financial income. Even atheism in these days is a small offense when compared to criticism of traditional property concepts."

And so it is indeed. I experienced it personally. A short time ago a so-called free thinker wrote to me: "What you produce in the field of free thought is so well reasoned." Or: "Where you present yourself as a free thinker, I feel friendly to you, in common with many other people." To be a free thinker is acceptable. To be a socialist . . . it makes you shudder. Truly, free thinking is an innocent hobby, especially when it is not accompanied by or is something quite different from free acting!! Besides, you should never forget that thinking is one of the integral parts of free thinking, and it can not be said of many free thinkers that they are very far advanced in thinking!

Only the first part of *Capital* has appeared, but we foster the hope that Marx advanced far enough in the elaboration of the second part, that his friend Engels can tend to its publication.

In that first part Marx shows that capital is nothing but robbery committed on the labor of others. "Capital is dead labor that comes to life again by absorbing live labor and the more it absorbs, the more it thrives." Here Marx attacks the system not the persons because in capitalist society it cannot be done otherwise. He also believes that society is in the process of disintegration, and that, for instance, England has already economically reached a point at which the transition from the capitalist to the Socialist means of production could occur without difficulty. Through this work, Marx has rendered a benefit even though he discovered a truth that many would have

*Obtainable at all booksellers and at the publisher Lieberg at The Hague.—*Footnote in original.*

like to have kept hidden. But truth breaks through despite all opposition and persecution!

In 1879 Mr. A. Kerdijk wrote a biographical sketch of Marx in his *Men of Importance* in which you can find all sorts of things. At one place he calls Marx "a rarely gifted man, whose goals and works I deplore sincerely, but whose importance cannot be denied." At another point, Kerdijk refers to the *Communist Manifesto* as "the language of a demagogue without conscience." At another place we hear that "the revolutionary German working class movement has predecessors who are quite different from mad zealots and hollow Phraseologists." At still another place he says that Marx is not "deterred by a falsification of historical truth, difficult to reconcile with the position of high priest of a new gospel of salvation." Or he describes Marx as "coolly calculating, rarely or never losing sight of his personal safety, and only showing himself where he need expect no danger."

Marx himself wrote to me about this biography. "The author of *Men of Importance,* a school superintendent or something of that sort, wrote me a letter to obtain material for my biography. Moreover, he asked his bookseller to address my brother-in-law to persuade me to cooperate with this request since I usually decline. This gentleman wrote me that he does not share my convictions but recognizes their importance, and declared his respects, etc. The same individual later was shameless enough to insert in his pamphlet a scandalous fabrication of the infamous Prussian spy, Stieber. Moreover—probably under the inspiration of an Academy-Socialist from Bonn—he intentionally ascribed falsified quotations to me. Furthermore this honorable gentleman has not even taken the trouble to read my polemic against the worthy Brentano himself in the *Volkstast.* There he could have seen that Brentano who, in the beginning accused me in *Concordia,* a paper of industrialists, of 'formal and material falsification,' later brushed it off with the lie that he had meant something different. A Dutch journal was willing to open its columns to me for the castigation of the "school superintendent," but *on principle* I do not reply to such stings of vermin. Even in London I have never taken the least notice of such literary yelping. If I had acted otherwise, then I would have wasted the best part of my time with notices from Moscow to California. In my younger days I often acted in this way, but now that I am older I am at least wise enough to avoid such useless dissipation of energy."

Indeed, the majority of authors and scribblers are of the opinion that socialists believe all means are permitted. This is specially contemptible since socialists, as is often the case in this country, have been denied the opportunity to answer. These authors mean to elevate themselves by thundering vigorously against the socialists, and when the latter defend themselves, then these thunderers do not busy themselves with the contents but only object to the tone and form. It is to this that the fool refers in *King Lear:*

> Truth's a dog must to kennel; he must be whipped out, when Lady the brach may stand by the fire and stink.

These words inspired an author to write: "It is an age-old trick to go all out in condemning the form when conscience tells one to avoid carefully the impossible struggle against the truth of the *content.*" With Multatuli we must ask such people: Where is your camel's hide that you wore out in the desert?

We have only roughly outlined the importance of Marx in order not to be overlong. But these words "In Memoriam" could not be avoided even though we only recently stood at the open grave of the great deceased.

On March 14 death laid its hand on him after his health had long suffered. The death of his faithful wife and not long afterwards of one of his beloved daughters, undermined his already weak constitution. He worked as few, and for that reason, earned the right to our respect. He strove and struggled with zeal and perseverance, and even if he erred, it is fitting to honor him. In a period when so many people are saying what they do not believe, a word of appreciation is due him who had the courage of his convictions. But more than a thinker, more than a fighter, he was *a man.* His heart beat so warmly for the oppressed and mistreated workers. His life's work was to call them to the struggle, so that they could liberate themselves from the house of bondage in which they find themselves through the power of capital. Always he was on the side of the oppressed! He showed this in that masterful manifesto that he proclaimed after the bloody suppression of the Commune, an event of which the nineteenth century can be as proud as the sixteenth was of its night of St. Bartholomew.[9] We can see progress in the fact that at that time only the clericalists had the honor of perpetrating the massacre but now clericalists and liberals together share the honor? In this manifesto Marx represented the true state of things as correctly as had ever been done.* Yes, his heart beat for the proletariat. Not for his own advantage but from a feeling of justice, he took up the gauntlet for the oppressed people. That is his honor, and also the cause for the curse inflicted upon him.

Let us weave a wreath of imperishable flowers on the temples of his head, not for his sake, but for our sake, for we have the need to honor our great dead. And even if for the time being no image in metal or stone will proclaim his glory, he has erected for himself a better monument in the hearts of grateful humanity. All cult of person be far from us, but honor to whom honor is due. This is a recognition of the only right to property that may be called sacred. And if persons die, the principles continue to live. Yes, "if I am no more here, may an avenger arise from my bones!"[10]

Honor to the memory of truly free thought, to Marx who not only had broken with religious but also with social prejudices. He has not only "merited the esteem of the fatherland," which is often true even for butchers like Thiers. No, the phrase that fits him is not associated only with nationality or boundary. He has merited the esteem of humanity.

*This manifesto has been entirely reprinted, because of the importance of its contents, in my history of the French Civil War of 1871, published by W. C. de Graaff. *Footnote in original.*

MARX AND THE DYNAMITE POLICY

By R. Macalester Loup,
De Gids, **Rotterdam, LXVII, 1883, part 2, pp. 341-54**

It is difficult when one looks at this serious German with benevolent mien, and the well-fed face, to think of the *hateful smile* and *fleshless bones* characteristic of Voltaire according to Russet's famous lines, but apart from this, the apostrophe in which the poet rebukes this philosopher for the downfall of the world of faith, could, in our days, be pointed with justification in the direction of Karl Marx, now that the practical fruits of the dynamite policy seems to announce to anxious souls, the downfall of the world of our economic relationships. While Voltaire's century was too young to read him, even faster than at we could call at Marx, *"your men are born."* Already when the German exile was stretched on his death-bed on English soil, there seemed to be cause to wail, *"He will fall on us, this immense edifice, which with your big hands you undermined day and night."* Indeed, if not immediately in the thunder of dynamite explosions and smoking flames of burning ruins occurred an apotheosis worthy of him, it has not been due to the good intentions of his disciples. And not only in England rages this hurricane, but it is as if an atmosphere pregnant with electricity sweeps over the different countries, and provokes explosions everywhere that sound as a warning for those who believed to enjoy in quiet rest the fruits of the times. In France the anniversary of the Commune has been commemorated with enthusiasm and in ever greater numbers, the meetings haunted by the memories of the Commune; beginnings have been made to place again the decision concerning the interest of the people into the rough hands of the multitude streaming together on the street. In Spain the proletariat in the southern agricultural districts spread death and ruin all around it, in the popular ways of Spain, wrapping itself through their society *The Black Hand* into more secretive and romantic garb than is customary for the populace in more northern countries.[11] In Russia the fear of the increase and power of the never ceasing machinations of the Nihilists weighs heavily on the festive mood into which the nation is being excited in behalf of the repeatedly postponed and at least definitely prepared imperial coronation. Even Austria had its socialist trial whose importance should not be underestimated, even if we are inclined to bestow a smile of pity on the cosiness, yes naivety typical of the doctrines of those overthrowers of society. And the plants of socialism grow luxuriously on the hospitable soil of America when the worried European governments try to exterminate them as obnoxious weeds, and from there they send again their shoots out into Europe to take roots anew and to grow up with fresh vitality.

But is it right to hold the German thinker responsible for all these acts of despair! We do not want to go deeply into the doctrine of responsibility for unwanted results from the criminal point of view, yet we believe that in last instance all these manifestations of wild passions and uncontrolled desire can be traced back to the theories and doctrines of two thinkers, the apostles of communism and anarchy, Karl Marx and Proudhon. It is not that the collectivists and nihilists of our day swear by these two names. The contrary is true, they are hardly known any more and their works were too abstract to be understood even by the elite of the proletariat. Moreover, the agitational power of both men was small, or at any rate, was soon exhausted: they were sitting in their study-cells while a Lassalle electrified the masses and an ignorant scatterbrain as Bakunin, succeeded in dethroning Marx. But they have scattered the seeds, which carried by the winds to all sides, found a fertile soil for their development in the hearts of the disinherited. And above all they have announced the paradoxes which, half understood, sounded to the untutored as a gospel of liberation, and in their turn, gave birth to the most audacious theories which probably have been denied by their original authors in their heart of hearts. With the one you find the paradoxical thesis: property is theft, and government is anarchy, with the other, the false principle that all labor is equal and its value is exclusively measured by time—where such theories were promoted, the terrible results of the war cry, "Proletarians, gird yourselves," can easily be imagined.

Karl Marx, however, has certainly in one respect not yet seen his ideal realized. His grandiose scheme of an international association of all proletarians has remained a chimera. Whether, for this reason, the fear of a general social revolution if no preventive and repressive means are taken, may be unfounded, we shall not decide here. But it is fact that the social movements in every country are determined and modified in such a way by the history and specific conditions in that country, that for the time being they are everywhere entirely different and a general understanding is absent.

It is true, of course, that there exists among all who are oppressed, or feel themselves oppressed, a feeling of sympathy that often shows itself in moral or material support, but this does not include community of ideals or goals, if at a former occasion we could observe how desperately divided in France, inside the limits of one country, were the revolutionaries, we find a greater division on a larger scale. And if once upon a time it will come to a unity of the dispersed powers, then it will be perhaps on another theoretical foundation than that of Karl Marx's theory of capital. Indeed, a younger school of more or less socialist writers has pointed to the deficiency in this theory, in that it makes too little difference between the capitalist-industrialist and the capitalist-landowner, and has observed that it is primarily the ever-increasing ground rent by which, on the one side, wealth is accumulated, and on the other, the wages of the proletarian is restricted. In this light the people get accustomed to seeing the great enemy in landed property, and if we look closer at the social movements of our day, then we see at their background, more or less clearly, also a struggle for the gound rent. This may not be true for France, where, as in no other country, small landed property has become the rule with the agrarian population, and the big cities are crowded with a workers proletariat; but in Spain, it is certainly an understandable hatred against landed property that arms *the black hands* to take revenge on the millionaires who, in the big cities, spend the fruits of the labor of the miserable peasants on their *latifundia*. For the Russian nihilists, in so far as their program aims at social reforms, the demand—the soil for the people—also stands in the foreground. And it is not doubtful that in Ireland the operation of the dynamite party are born exclusively out of the struggle against *landlordism*.[12]

With the volcanic shocks which everywhere make the soil tremble, the rulers show a certain hesitancy in how to fight these explosions in the best ways. It is a fact that they have become much more dangerous than in former times, now that science, advancing with giant steps, is just as servile to the works of darkness as to those of light. Not satisfied with the honorable name of century of steam and electricity, the nineteenth century also likes to adorn itself with that of being the century of dynamite. But who knows the horror with which posterity will remember that name! How can you arm yourself against this stuff so easily made and hidden, a small quantity of which in the hands of an enemy of the social order is sufficient to destroy half a city? . . .

KARL MARX

By Achille Loria
Nuova Antologia di Scienze, Lettere ed Arti
Seconda Serie, Volume Trentesimottavo Della
Raccolta Volume LXVIII, Roma, 1883

. . . Nothing is more difficult than to judge a man impartially, especially if he's a man around whose name has gathered the most different judgment, that was too often dictated by personal prejudices, party or class interest. Karl Marx has been the object of feverish enthusiasm and unforgiving hatred, immeasurable praise and terrible accusation. History will decide whether he really was responsible for the brutal exaggerations of his followers, and whether he was the mysterious inspirer of the dreadful deeds of the Paris Commune, the authors of which he himself severely criticized. Karl Marx will have his Sainte-Beuve[13] like Proudhon, his Brandes[14] like Lassalle. We, here, want to judge the man of thought rather than the rebellious agitator.

Those who have considered the development of his adventurous and fertile existence, probably have noted an analogy between the lives of Karl Marx and Dante Alighieri.[15] Both were aristocrats, both had that proud, persistent and indomitable spirit of men of belief, both were exiled from their native soil and driven in poverty to a strange land, and in both such exile laid the foundation for the final outburst of one hundred songs or 860 pages of pitiless irony. For Dante the exile stimulated his rebellious genius and made of him, once a Florentine prior and scholar, the prophet of the Middle Ages. In Karl Marx exile stimulated the hidden strength of his genius and made of him, once a professor of philosophy, relative of a minister and son of a counselor, the philosopher of social negation. What else is the *Divine Comedy* if not a criticism of the medieval society, just as *Capital* is a criticism of our present-day society. Dante sees the "great expansion of the boroughs as nothing other than anarchy, and the exuberance of the economic and commercial life as nothing more than corruption."* By the same token, Marx sees the free development of economic activities as nothing more than the pathological production of a dying, anarchistic era. Dante directs his rage against the "subtle provisions" of his city; Marx criticizes the regulations of his mother country and Europe. The *Divine Comedy* can be seen as a universal judgment, where Popes like Boniface VIII[16] Bourgeois like Ciacco,[17] and scholars like Brunetto Latini,[18] are all on trial. Marx's *Capital* is the supreme judgment of men of our century, where many are condemned, capitalists like the Sandersons, politicians like Thiers,[19] or philosophers like Bentham[20] and Mill. Dante railed at the medieval outbursts of

*Carducci, *Studi letterari, seconda edizione*, Livorno, 1880, 64. (Footnote in original.)

economic egotism, like the lending at high interest rates, and the buying of offices (simony). He fights against the medieval aspects of capital, usury, arguing that by natural law, and as it is written in *Genesis*, only labor produces, and any form of buying which does not spring from labor, is immoral. And such, more or less, is Marx's doctrine. Isn't Dante, perhaps, a socialist of the middle ages? He saw the errors of his age, its crimes, its robberies, its wars, and criticizes them all. To find a solution, he plunged into the study of philosophy and physics, theology and astronomy, philology and history. At the same time, though, he went to the people, to study their superstitions and their legends, becoming thus more aware of the mysteries of life. After eighteen years of meditation, he finally collected the ideas and the wandering notions of his era and reunited them in a symmetrical monumental masterpiece. So Marx, too, outraged by modern society, in which he sees only corruption and pain, conceived a scientific and popular criticism of it.

Thus, after having studied philosophy, physics, mathematics, Marx trained himself in religion, art, economics, statistics, technology and law. At the same time, he does not forget to study living things, so he visits offices, banks, London factories, always questioning, observing, weighing reality. From this accurate knowledge of science and life, he deduced the idea of his time, and, after eighteen years of meditations, he concentrated it in his economics. Yes, Marx is the Alighieri of Socialism, and his *Capital* is indeed the sacred poem of society's claim.

In judging Karl Marx's writings, it is best to distinguish the philosopher from the economist. Marx's philosophical beliefs are evidently an offshoot of Hegel's.[21] From Hegel he, in fact, took the concept of the thesis, antithesis, and synthesis of social epochs. The Hegelian character of Marx's doctrine becomes all the more evident when he affirms in the last pages of his *Capital* that the economy of the Middle Ages developed later into the capitalist economy in which property is individually held and labor is socially produced, and this because of mechanization. From this he concludes dialectically that another form of economy must emerge in which "social" labor and collective property are joined.*

*Marx. *Zur Kritik*, Verrede, X-XI. *Footnote in original.*

Yet, while Marx's doctrine is founded on the Hegelian historical systhesis, which is called by Lange one of the greatest anthropological discoveries, it differs from Hegel's doctrine in one fundamental characteristic. For Hegel, in fact, the beginning of history is formed in that nebulous reign of metaphysics, the universal spirit, which progressively through history defines itself. In Marx's system, on the other hand, the secret of human evolution lies in the evolution of the forces of production which, while developing, determine several economic forms and thus the superstructure. Marx therefore looks for the basis of history in the phenomena, and he sees thought itself as an output of the phenomena, its necessary reflection.

We thus see that the basic Hegelian philosophical concepts are turned upside down. For Marx, the Idea is no longer the creator of reality; it is rather reality which creates the Idea. Marx's innovation, or modification of Hegel's theory, will become clearer if we compare it with the philosophical concepts of another writer who applied Hegel's doctrine to the philosophy of law. The writer is Ferdinand Lassalle, and his major work is *The System of Acquired Rights.*[22] for Lassalle, as for Hegel, the universal spirit is the beginning of the historical evolution, and the varied manifestations of human activity in the different historical eras are nothing more than the product of the different phases of the Idea. Consequently, the Legal Code of a certain era is but the output of a specific moment in the evolution of the human spirit.

Lassalle uses such principles largely in his conception of law and particularly of inheritance. He affirms that the legality of a will consists in its direct relation with a period in the evolution of the Idea. Now, since the intimate conditions of the human spirit in a specific era are truly and honestly portrayed only in the religious concepts, such religious concepts of a specific era must be linked to the juridical phenomena which the era represents. The will, hence, becomes logical only if we trace its origin to the religious beliefs of the Etruscans and Pelasgi, at the center of which is the myth of the Lare, who symbolized the immortality of the will.[23] From this myth came the will, accepted in the Roman era, when the concept of the immortality of will was the byproduct of the historical conditions of the Idea. Today, though, the will has become illogical, unacceptable and unnatural, since we no longer believe in the immortality of will disposing of terrestial things.*

If we now compare Lassalle's beliefs with Marx's, we realize that the antithesis between the two philosophers could not be deeper. Lassalle, in fact, deduces his juridical forms, or the phenomena of reality, from abstract thought and from the most spontaneous manifestation of reality itself, i.e., religion. Marx, on the other hand, deduces the categories of thought, whether artistic, philosophical or religious, from the real phenomena, and more specifically, from the economic phenomena. For both fathers of Socialism, though, the identity of the object and the subject is central to their philosophies. But, while Lassalle obsequiously respects the unintelligible Hegelian identity, which was rightly called by Lange[24] "an enormous nonsense," Marx turns that identity upside down, making it rational and nearer to the Kantian identity and positivistic monism.[25]

Another difference between Marx's and Lassalle's theories is that Lassalle believes that the juridical forms determine the social system, and that, thus, a criticism of the social system is, in reality, a criticism of its juridical aspects (property, inheritance, etc.). Marx, on the other hand, sees political economy as "the anatomy of human society," and considers the juridical forms as a superstructure of the economy. As derivative and superficial forms, against which a criticism cannot be directed fruitfully, in the name of society. Thus, to the criticism of property Marx counterposes the critique of capital, and he substitutes the critical inquiries on the juridical forms with the critical inquiries on the economic form: wages, profits, etc.

Lassalle's book can be really considered as the last intellectual product of a specific phase of human thought, one in which the social interactions are seen as the product of civil institutions. Such an intellectual phase has lasted a long time and has included writers of that most varied tendencies, from Montesquieu to Vico,[26] from Hobbes[27] to Bentham, and from Troplong[28] to Rousseau.[29] Marx's *Capital,* on the other hand, can be considered the most significant scientific product of a

*Lassalle, *System der erworbenen Rechte.* 2d edizione, Leipzig, 1880, Volume II.

later phase in human thought, one which analyzes the aspects of society more deeply and sees in the economy the basis of human behavior. Lassalle closes one cycle of philosophical thought; Marx opens up a new one. The work of the first ends where the work of the latter begins.

Marx's attempt to take the principle of human history from the nebulous regions of the Idea to those of real phenomenon is indeed a notable one. But, while it is true that Marx has somewhat modified Hegel's historical metaphysics, it is also true that such modification is more apparent than real. Indeed, Marx sees the modes of production as the cause of human evolution, but the modes of production themselves are not born spontaneously. When they are considered in terms of their immediate derivation, they are merely the expression of the human intellect in the technological field. They are, thus, but a product of human thought.[30] Now, if industrialization is a product of man's intellect, to assume that the modes of production are the causes and the beginning of human evolution, is like assuming that thought itself is the real cause, since it is the originator of the modes of production. But in this case the basis of historical evolution is found again in Hegel's "Spirit," or in Buckle's "intelligence," returning thus to those doctrines which derive reality from thought.

It is precisely here that we find the great contradiction in Marx. When Hegel considers history as the developing of the Idea, he is being logical since the Hegelian Idea is the absolute which consists in itself. But for Marx to assume intellect as the basis of the social phenomena is a vicious circle. Indeed, while Marx repeats constantly that "the way we think derives from the way we are, rather than the other way around," he sees the social phenomena as the product of technological conditions, which is the same as saying the conditions of the human intellect. Thus, the intellect determines the social phenomena, which, in turn, determine the intellect, and thought becomes the product of its own result. It is evident that this is an enormous contradiction from which Marx's followers will find it difficult to escape.*

---

*A more extended criticism of the sociological system of Marx will be found in my book, *La rendita fondiaria e la sua elisione naturale*, 1880. Chapter VI. *Footnote in original.*

At this point we have to consider an issue which has caused great discussion and contradictions, i.e., the relationship between Marxism and Darwinism. As a disciple of Hegel and a believer in evolution, Marx greets Darwin's theory as a masterful demonstration of the "dialectics of nature." He affirms that the development of society is like that of nature, an evolution from one organic formation to a superior one. Marx is pleased to point out the analogy between his own doctrine and that of the great English naturalist. In fact, if Darwin's theory holds that the history of the species is nothing more than the history of a "natural technology" (of the formation of plants' and animals' organisms which are considered as their life's "means of production"), so also for Marx the history of mankind is but the history of industrial technology. Marx's work is thus meant to illustrate the laws which regulate the genesis, the development and the death of one of those social organisms, that which stemmed from the decomposition of the feudal system, the so-called "capitalist system." This capitalist system, Marx announces, is governed by laws which are enacted by strict necessity, but which are effective in respect to it alone. Nor will they govern the newer social formations to come.

In thus expressing the economic life and the laws of social biology, Marx follows the most correct historical method and applies to society the morphogenic theory. For this reason, Marx's social application of the theory of evolution is more scientific and meaningful than that of Spencer. Spencer, in fact, because of his limited knowledge of history and political economy, gathers under the same law the most diverse social systems without even suspecting that the structure of such systems is deeply diverse and that a generalization meant to enclose all of them is but a sterile emptiness.

Besides the before-mentioned analogies between Marx's and Darwin's theories, there are no others to be found. The other similarities discovered are more between Marx and Darwin as they have been interpreted by their followers, than between Darwin and Marx themselves. Among those theories, the "theory of the three revolutions" of Leopold Jacoby[31] is most famous. This ingenious writer argues that three revolutions are necessary in the biological process. The first revolution is that in which inorganic matter is transformed into organic matter from which the inferior animal species developed. In the second revolution, man, the higher animal, follows the creation of the lower animals. Finally, the third revolution will bring about a change as a result of which man will pass from an animalistic stage in which he suffers because of inequality, is ruled by the instruments of production, and is weakened by the daily struggle for survival, into a new stage in which he will be a social man, comforted by equality of living conditions, freed from the struggle for survival and arbitrator of the economic and productive forces. Lamarck[32] was the theoretician of the first revolution, Darwin of the second, and Marx, supposedly, of the third. We must point out, though, that at the basis of such a construction, lies the assumption that the evolution will ultimately end, a valid point by Hegel's standard,* but an invalid one by Darwin's.

On the other hand, Marx's theory differs for Darwin's in many respects. Marx considers society as we know it today, as a perverted and corrupted organism from which a new, healthy organism will derive, since "in history, as in nature, putrifaction is the laboratory of life." Darwin, though, does not talk of perverted organisms, but rather of imperfect ones, which will ameliorate through the struggle for survival. In asserting that human evolution has an aim and that such evolution will ultimately find its final determination in Socialism, Marx is not a follower of the ancient teleological concept, completely excluded from the modern theory of evolution.[33] And yet I do not find absolutely unfair Dühring's criticism that Marx wants to make history dance to the rhythm of Hegelian logic,[34] nor do Engels' arguments in response seem to me too effective. Marx, moreover, rejects Darwin's theory on the law of population.[35] In his attempt to disassociate misery from nature, to tie it to history, he negates the fact that at the basis of the modifications in the industrial technology is that imbalance between beings and subsistence which Darwin points to as the cause of the modifications in the "animal technology." Marx affirms that the

*Der unendliche Progress überhaupt der begrifflosen Reflexion angehört; die absolute Methode, die den Begriff zu ihrer Seele und Inhalt hat, kann nicht in denselben führen," *Logik*, II, Nürnberg 1816, p. 302. *Footnote in original in German.*

human struggle for survival has nothing to do with the physical law of population. Finally, Darwin does not, like Marx, believe that an organism must develop into another and a better one by means of a revolution. In this aspect Marx, more so than Darwin, is linked to Lyell,[36] who teaches how great telluric revolutions, produced by actual causes, put an end to geological eras.

Karl Marx's economic theories can be gathered under three headings: value, machines, and primitive accumulations. The first aims to explain the nature of profit, the second to establish the capitalist law of population, and the third to reveal the origin of bourgeois property. . . .The center of Marx's entire scientific theory is the theory of value, i.e., the belief that the value of goods is determined by the amount of labor needed to produce them. This is the principal means by which Marx condemned the whole social order. He even points out that "ancient" English economists, like William Petty[37] and James Stewart[38] believed in this economic principle. But what good does this do? An orthodox person could always argue that theories must be strengthened with arguments, not with citations or quotations. Now, Marx has only one argument with which to uphold his doctrine, and that is that value expresses an equation. To have an equation two terms are needed, and there must be something in common with both. Thus when goods are equated to value they must have something in common. This common something is, in fact, (the) utility since it is tied to the quality of things. Thus besides utility, goods have only one thing in common, namely, labor, the production of man's labor. Finally, the substratum of the equation of value is labor.

Now, economists do agree with Marx that at the basis of the equation of value is a common "something," but they argue that this something is not the sole, but rather a twofold one; not only labor, but labor and abstinence, two necessary efforts of production. Marx's argument thus has no weight, until it is proved that abstinence is not an effort, nor is it a factor of production, which Marx himself sought to prove. Marx, though, was very conscious of the fact that he had given no demonstration of his principle. He was so conscious of it that in his answer to Professor Sieber,[39] he admitted that in exposing his theory, he had followed an "a priori" method, which is but an artistic way to express something arrived at through a realistic method. Here everyone sees the comfortable expedient, where a discussion of scientific method is changed into a judgment *"ex informata conscientia."* And there is no more. The theory which reduces value to labor could be compared to the many hypotheses of physics which, because they give a complete explanation of phenomena, become laws. But what can we say when Marx's fundamental theory not only does not explain, but even contradicts the phenomena of reality?

Marx distinguishes between fixed and variable capital, and maintains that capital which is used other than to aliment labor reproduces its own value spontaneously in that of the finished product. However, that capital which is used for wages reappears augmented in the value of the product. The workers who are supported by this capital spend part of their working day producing goods and the rest to produce an extra wealth which, in turn, constitutes the profit. Thus the capital not used for wages is "constant", does not produce profit; and consequently, profit is produced only by that capital used for wages, which is thus "variable."

We see here that Marx's own dialectics plunge him into contradiction with reality's phenomena. Since if in reality, that capital not used for wages is "fixed capital," i.e., gives no profit, those industries which, for technical needs, employ a greater amount of constant capital, should register accordingly a lower profit. This is clearly absurd, since it is in contradiction with an economy based on free competition and makes those industries in which the fixed capital predominates, almost an economic impossibility.[40] Now Marx is aware of such contradiction, and he admits (Kap. XI) that in reality, profit may be the same in different industries, and that this fact is "apparently" a contradiction of his theory. But how does he solve the conflict? Merely by sending the reader to a second volume still to come, in which he will explore the theory of competition! It is thus not without reasons that I affirmed that this famous second volume, always threatened against his opponents and never published, might have been an ingenious expedient used by Marx to withstand scientific arguments.

From his postulate, Marx deduces the profit theory. He asks, if value is determined by labor, how can capital produce a profit? The capitalist buys raw materials and machines; he also hires workers. The value of the goods he produces is given by the amount of labor employed to process them, the raw materials plus the amount of labor directly employed by the workers. Now if the workers attain that part of the value which is produced by their labor, the capitalist is left with the equivalent of the machines and the raw materials. How can he thus produce a profit? By not paying the workers the equivalent of their labor. While the worker produces in a day's work the value of a day's work, his wage is (for example) the product of half a working day. Thus the product of half a day is left to the capitalist and constitutes his profit. This is how the prolific quality of the capital can be explained; it is, in fact, nothing more than "unpaid labor."

From this we can further deduce that since a day's labor is paid by the product of half a day's work, the wage is not equated to the value of labor; it is nothing else than the value of the strength of labor (labor power), i.e., the value of the products necessary to restore the worker's strength. The capitalist thus pays with the salary the exchange value of the ability to work, and consumes its "usage value." In this the capitalist is much like any buyer who pays the exchange value and consumes the "usage value" (consumer value). But the strength of labor (while it is consumed by the capitalist) creates a new value which is partly a restoration of the value of its strength, and partly an additional value left to the capitalist gratuitously.

This is briefly the "static" of Marx's system. It is meant to demonstrate that in an economic system based on wages, labor will never attain its just value; it also demonstrates that poverty is the final result of the capitalist economy. Marx's proof of this "reality" is based on his theory of machines which he wants, audaciously, to substitute for Malthus's population theory. He argues that the technical demands of industry require that capital be used in ever large proportions as "fixed capital." Thus, with the process of accumulation, the "variable capital," from which the lot of the worker derives, becomes a decreasing fraction of the total capital. Often, though, the "relative" decrease in the variable capital becomes an "absolute" decrease.

This happens when those phenomena occur which the capitalists call "conversion of flowing capital into fixed capital." This relative or absolute decrease of the "wage" capital brings about overproduction. This phenomena occurs not because of an absolute increase in the population as related (and in excess) to the capital, but because of a decrease in the amount of that capital to be distributed as wages. This influence of the machine in creating overpopulation is a strong ally of the capitalist, since it allows him to increase suddenly production and to free himself of the extra workers in periods of decreased production demands. This influence deprives the request of work of any bilateral character, since it allows the capitalist to regulate the offers for work, leaving a constant surplus labor to bring down wages.[41]

The length of this article does not permit us to give an extensive criticism of this particular Marxist doctrine.- . . . Thus we will limit ourselves to pointing out merely that Marx's population theory is based on the erroneous assumption that the introduction of machines will not determine the creation of. a new capital which will reabsorb those workers discharged by other capitalists. Economics shows that the machine, by allowing great emphasis on accumulation of production, tends to rehire those previously discharged. The machines do not dismiss workers irrevocably, unless they are introduced by the capitalist with the intention of meeting the increase in labor costs, since, in this way, they do not stimulate the accumulation of capital, and those workers, not needed in production, are definitely excluded from work. We have thus come to the "territorial law of the relative surplus population."

It must here be observed that with his new theory of population, Marx created a new difference between his system and that of Lassalle. For Lassalle, as for Ricardo, it is the absolute increase in the population which reduces wages to the minimum necessary for survival. For Marx, on the other hand, such decrease in wages is the result of the relative decrease of capital, and would thus occur even with a stable population, as long as the capitalist system of production survives. And while Lassalle affirms that the increase in wages produces an increase in population, Marx affirms that such doctrine is incompatible with the needs of capitalist production. He believes that the increase in wages tends to bring its own negation, producing thus a conversion of floating capital into fixed capital, and with it an artificial increase of the offers of work. Lassalle is a follower of Ricardo and Malthus and their physical laws. Marx is the originator of the social laws which tend to separate society from nature's influence.

Finally, after having demonstrated how the mechanism itself of the capitalist system generates an increasing misery, Marx deals with an ultimate problem. Profit, he argues, results from the acquisition of labor and from its exploitation. But this process presupposes the existence of a "primitive" capital which cannot be the result of capitalistic accumulation, since it constitutes its genesis. How does the capitalist become the owner of his initial wealth? How does he find in the market miserable people who must sell themselves? All this is explained in the celebrated study on "the secret of primitive accumulation." It's the old story over again:

"Criminibus debent hortes, praetoria, mensas, Argentum vetus et stantem extra pocula caprum,"[42] sang Giovenale[43]* about Roman property. In the first years of the seventeenth century, Loyseau[44] wrote a satire in which he demonstrated that the feudal properties were the result of violent acquisition. Marx, too, develops a theory on the origins of capitalist property. He wants to show that it developed from the expropriation of the independent colonizers in the seventeenth and eighteenth centuries. By accumulating the riches of the expropriated ones, and by throwing them on the labor market, the colonizers created the two poles of the bourgeois economic system. Capitalist property thus originated from the exploitation of workers.

Professor Chicherin points out that the weak side of this theory lies in the following consideration by Marx: "Leaving aside the purely economic influence, we will here deal with the means applied to precipitate violently the process of expropriation." Actually, the scientific analysis should have dealt with the economic causes which formed the basis of that historical

---

*Satira prima. *Footnote in original.*

period, rather than with the form that process took. The analysis of the economic causes of the expropriation of the farmers demonstrates hów it was the product of the increased population which made impossible the separationist system of the unrelated farmers. Thus any criticism of property which wants to demonstrate how property originated from exploitation is, from the scientific point of view, totally unfounded. Also, if we demonstrate that the origins of property are illegal, we must also demonstrate that the property of today was also generated illegally. Marx demonstrates that in England capitalist property originated from illegal occurrences, but he does not show how it could have not developed otherwise.

Other writers, Malthus,[45] for example, have dealt with the origins of modern property with a logical method, making it develop from the progress of population and, ultimately, from human nature. Marx could have proved that such logical presentation is unfounded and could have challenged it with a general demonstration of the illegal origins of property. But he just points to the brutal, bare fact, thus leaving the economists a bit disappointed. Hence this man, who for so long based his doctrines on the logical method, suddenly departs from it, bases his thesis on the sole historical index. Such balancing between two opposite methods, such unstable equilibrium between logic and history, evident in Marx, has often been criticized.

Thus closes this great book which Meyer called the most significant work ever written by a German author.[46] Of course, it is not difficult to prove that several of Marx's theories originated with other writers—indeed, he himself points this out.[47] The theory which affirms that economic evolution is based on the technical evolution, can be found in Fourier; the value theory can be found in a number of writings by English scholars; the money theory in Fullerton[48] and Tooke;[49] the distinction between constant and variable capital was hinted at by Ramsay;[50] the theory of surplus value was developed by Bernhardi;[51] the wage theory was developed by Hodgskin[52] and Bray,[53] that of the machine by Burton,[54] Ricardo and Sismondi.[55] Finally, the

Russkii dilettantizm i votchinnoe zemlevladenie; Moscow, 1878, 164. *Footnote in original.*

theory of primitive accumulation was first developed by Thornton,[56] Rogers[57] and several other British writers. Marx developed all of these theories, he backed them up with statistics, and finally, he coordinated them into a compact system. Because of this, his book was original and has a high intellectual value. It proves how the intellect may reflect nature's work, and, like nature, give life to a new creation based on already existing seeds.

In the acuteness of his economic laws, Marx can be compared with Ricardo. . . . In the depth of his thought, he reminds us of Thunen.[58] Marx, in total, had such a versatile intellect that he could equally produce high philosophical theories and entertain precise technical researches. Many of his theoretical ideas are real and true, but too often he used knowledge as his sole base of argument. He was an objective scientist, but also too often a sophist who wanted to negate the actual society even at the price of truth. . . .

By observing Marx's works and his life we can realize what great inspirations they later gave, and also what great failures they produced. Marx gave an energetic shake to scientific optimism by inspiring the economic writings of his disciple Lassalle, and he exercised a powerful influence on the social discussions in Germany. With the publication of *Capital*, he awoke the sleeping politics of his time. "Scholastic Socialism" is thus a product of Marx's revitalization of economic index. With his brief history of British legislation on the factories, Marx pointed out to the continental government the necessity for providing for the working class. The German government no longer conceals the fact that Marx exercised a powerful influence on its economic policy. Two years ago, in fact, Bamberger[59] pointed out to the German Reichstag that the bill presented by the Chancellor concerning insurance on the job, seemed written by Marx because of its terminology and content. Marx's doctrine of historical evolution destroyed anarchical Socialism and detached democratic Socialism from mob riots for which Marx had a deep dislike. Marx had illustrated the economics and the economic relations of England in an unchallengeable way. He has succeeded in awakening in the fourth estate a feeling of independence and dignity, in educating its intellectual virtues, and in ameliorating its economic conditions. These are the best and indisputable results of Marx's work.

But his atttempt to create an "algebra of the revolution" and to form an international workers' union, his desire to theorize on, and at the same time, to organize the social revolution, did not achieve much success. His algebra seemed sophistic. The association he founded collapsed under his very eyes. The impartial economists saw the mistakes of his doctrines and refuted them. The workers whom he wanted to rally around the banner of revolution did not respond to his call. As a result he lived a lonely life and died abandoned. His works won the admiration of more and more people, but the idea that was at its foundation was shattered. He appeared to many as supernatural; but tested with cold scientific analysis, his doctrines fell. His admirers worshipped him, but did not accept all of his dogmas. He fascinated people with his mystical appeal, but, at the same time, his works could not survive criticism.[60]

In his doctrines as in his life, Karl Marx was the fatal product of the age in which they developed. It was 1840. The old metaphysics was dying, the new positivism had not yet been born. It was thus too late to be a metaphysicist and too early to be a positivist. A student of Hegelian philosophy, Marx tried to rejuvenate it by associating it with historical research. Later, when the new science had become established, he dedicated himself to empirical investigations. He studied the social life, and tried to renew Hegel's philosophical theories with the new positivistic notions he had acquired. Yet, in spite of his awareness of the real life, he remained a metaphysicist in a crowd of positivists, dreaming of the realization of the Idea in the midst of people who did not understand him.[61]

His life, like his thoughts, underwent much the same developments. He was born in a period in which reactionary ideas were dying and freedom was not yet born. It was too late to be reactionary, too early to be openly liberal. He became a revolutionary, a conspirator, a fighter against any existing institution, be it political, social or economic. When the period of reaction had ended, and with it conspiracy, Marx tried to reconcile his revolutionary propaganda with the new mood. He called for legal, free and parliamentarian agitations, and condemned secret conspiracies. He remained a revolutionary in an era and in countries in which revolution was neither normal nor opportune. He continued criticizing the Prussia of 1870 as if it were still that of 1844. Thus Marx's life proceeded, like his thought, amidst permanent contradictions.

But those who believe that these contradictions have reduced Marx's greatness are much mistaken. It was they who created it. Society often undergoes periods in which an old order is in the process of dying, but will not die until the new order, which will follow it, is strong enough to substitute itself. Critical periods produce great men, men whose work will shake the dying form of society to allow the new one to bloom. These men reflect the age which brings them about, and the antagonism which dominates it. It is from this antagonism that they derive their greatness since it gives them power. It is also this same opposition which, when their mission is accomplished, will turn against them. It was this contradiction which created Marx's greatness. He was a metaphysicist amidst a crowd of positivists. But his metaphysics invigorated a whole generation, and hastened a social development in the face of which any positivistic idea was useless. His economics exercised such an influence as no great positivist method could ever have done. He was a conspirator when the age of conspiracy was over. But he stood up proud and strong. The very contradiction of his life and thought places Marx in an abnormal condition. But it was this abnormal condition which made of him a revolutionary and shook the old form of society.

But if this contradiction made his work great, it also made it precarious. As the result of this contradiction developed, it became less and less efficacious. His criticisms shook science, and his economic criticism developed not metaphysics but rather positivism. His continuous agitations shook governments and societies. His was not a conspiratorial, regulation action, but rather a conservative one. Marx thus saw himself being put aside by his own works. That great evolution he so proudly asked for finally developed, but against him, thus signalling the end of his mission. He was still worshipped by, and dear to, many, but he was abandoned by the younger generations who, even though they recognized him as the Prometheus of sacred revindications,[62] renewed the myth of the three thousand Oceanides who came one day to console the eternal martyr, but left him in the evening.[63]

MARX'S THEORY OF VALUE

By Eleanor Marx,
Progress, London, June, 1883, pp. 362–66

David Ricardo begins his great work, *Principles of Political Economy and Taxation*, with these words: "The value of a commodity, or the quantity of any other commodity for which it will exchange, depends upon the relative quantity of *labor* necessary for its production, and not on the greater or less *compensation* which is paid for that labor." This great discovery of Ricardo's, that there is but "one" real standard of value, *labor* forms the starting-point of Marx's *Capital*. I cannot enter here into a detailed account of the way in which Marx completes, and partly corrects, Ricardo's theory of value, and develops, out of it, a theory of that fearfully contested subject, "currency," which by its clearness, simplicity, and logical force, has carried conviction even into the heads of many political economists of the ordinary stamp. I must confine myself to the mode, based upon his theory of value, by which Marx explains the origin and the continued accumulation of capital in the hands of a, thereby, privileged class.

Suppose all exchanges of commodities to be entirely fair; suppose that every buyer gets the full value in goods for his money, and that every seller receives in money the full value of the necessary labor invested in his produce. If, then, as political economists are in the habit of assuming, every producer sells that which he does not want, and buys with the money thus obtained that which he does want, but which he does not himself produce, then all things are for the best in this best of economical worlds; but the formation of Capital—this word taken, for the present, in its usual meaning—is possible. A man may save money, or store up goods, but he cannot, as yet, use them as Capital, except perhaps by lending the money on interest. But that is, though a very ancient, yet a very subordinate and primitive form of Capital. The making of profits is impossible on the basis supposed above.

And yet, we see every day that profits, and very large profits, are made by some people. In order to account for this, let us begin by looking at the "form" of the transaction which produces profits. Hitherto we have dealt with independent producers, who, under a system of social division of labor, sell what they do not want, and buy what they do want for their own use. But now the producer appears as a man who enters the market, not with produce, but with money, and who buys, not what he wants, but what he does "not" want for his own use. He buys, in one word, in order to re-sell what he has bought. But to buy 20 tons of pig-iron, or 10 bales of cotton for £100, and to re-sell them for £100 would be an absurdity. And indeed we find our businessman does not commit such an absurdity. He buys his commodities, say for £100, and re-sells them, on an average, say for £110. But how is this possible? We still assume that all commodities are bought and sold at this full labor-value. Then no profit can come out of any amount of such buying and selling. A change in the value of the commodity bought and sold, for instance, the rise in cotton in consequence of the American Civil War, may explain how profits arise in a few solitary instances. But commodities do not always rise in value, they generally fluctuate about a certain average value and price. What is gained now is lost hereafter. With our supposition of equal exchanges, profits are impossible.

Very well. Suppose now, exchanges were not equal—suppose every seller to be able to sell his article 10 per cent above its real value. Then, what every one of them gains as a seller, he loses again as a buyer. Again, let every buyer buy at 10 per cent below the value of the article bought. What he gains as a buyer, leaves his hand again as soon as he turns seller.

Suppose, finally, profits to be the result of cheating. I sell you a ton of iron for £5, while it is worth no more than £3. In that case, I am £ 2 richer, and you are £ 2 poorer. Before the bargain you had £ 5 in money and I £ 3 in value of iron—together £ 8. After the bargain you hold £ 3 in iron and I £ 5 in gold—together again £ 8. Value has changed hands, but it has not been created, and profits to be real must be value newly created. It is self-evident that the totality of the capitalist class of a country cannot cheat itself.

Thus if equivalents are exchanged, profits are impossible; and if non-equivalents are exchanged, profits are equally impossible. Yet they exist. How is this economical enigma to be solved?

Now it is evident that the increase of value which appears in the re-sale as profits, and which transforms money into capital, cannot arise from that money, for both in the buying and in the selling the money merely represents the value of the commodity bought and sold (we assume here again all exchanges to be exchanges of equivalents). Nor can it arise from the value of the commodity which is supposed to be bought and sold at its full value, neither more nor less. The increase of value can therefore, arise only out of the "actual use" of the commodity in question. But how can new value arise from the use, the consumption of a commodity? This would only be possible if our businessmen had the good luck to find in the market a commodity endowed with the special quality that its consumption would be, "ipso facto," a creation of wealth.

And that commodity exists in the market. That commodity is called by economists *Labor,* but Marx, more correctly, calls it *Labor-power,* and this expression I shall use here.

The existence of Labor-power as a commodity in the market, presupposes that it is sold by its owner, and, therefore, that the latter is a free agent, who sells his Labor-power to another free agent, both dealing with each other voluntarily and on an equal footing. It presupposes, moreover, that the sale is for a limited time only, as otherwise the seller, from a free agent, would become a slave. And, finally, it presupposes that the owner of the labor-power, the future laborer, is not in a position to sell commodities, the produce of his own labor, but that he is compelled to sell, instead, his capacity of labor. Thus, our business-man lives in a society where he meets the free laborer in the market—free not only to dispose as a free agent of his labor-power, but free also from the possession of all means by which he himself could transform the labor-power into actual labor, into work. A free man—but free also from the ownership of victuals, of raw material, and of tools, unless, perhaps, the simplest and cheapest.

That our two "free agents" are enabled to meet each other in the market, is evidently not a phenomenon produced by simple nature. It is the result of a long historical process, the result of many previous revolutions of society. And, indeed, it is only since the latter half of the fifteenth century that we find the mass of the population being gradually turned into such "free" sellers of their own labor-power.

Now labor-power, as a saleable commodity, has a value and a price like other commodities. Its value is determined, as in all other cases, by the labor necessary for its production, and therefore its reproduction. The value of labor-power is the value of the necessaries of life required to keep the laborer in a state fit for his work, and, as he is subject to natural decay and death, to reproduce and to continue the race of sellers of labor-power. The extent and composition of these necessaries of life varying very much for different epochs and countries, are yet more or less fixed for a single country, and a given period. The standard of life established there among the working class settles it.

Let us now see how our business-man consumes the labor-power he has bought. Suppose the work to be done is cotton-spinning. The hired laborer is introduced into the factory and there finds all the requisites for his work: cotton in the state of preparation which renders it fit for spinning into yarn, machinery, etc. Suppose the normal production of a spinner per hour to be one and two-third pounds of yarn, for which one and two-thirds pounds of cotton are required (leaving unavoidable waste out of the question). Then in six hours our spinner will turn 10 lbs. of cotton into 10 lbs. of yarn. If the value of the cotton be 1s. per lb. the 10 lbs. of yarn will represent in value of cotton 10s. Assuming the wear and tear of machinery, oil, coal, etc., during these six hours to represent a value of 2s., that will raise the value of the yarn to 12s. There remains to be known how much is added to its value by the labor of the spinner.

Suppose the value of labor-power for one day, that is to say the value of the necessaries of life required to maintain the laborer for one day to be 3s. Suppose, again, that this sum of necessaries, or the 3s. representing it in money, are equivalent to, or embody the labor of one worker for six hours. Our spinner, then, at the end of six hours work has added a value of 3s. to the yarn, so that its total value is 15s. Our business-man, now a master cotton-spinner, has in his yarn the full equivalent of his outlay: 10s. for cotton, 2s. for wear and tear, etc., 3s. for labor-power employed—total 15s. He is repaid in the value of his yarn for every fraction of a farthing he has advanced. But there is no margin for any profits. But our master cotton-spinner or would-be capitalist very soon informs us that this is not the way at all in which *he* understood his bargain. If six hours' labor suffice to *keep* the laborer for a full day, including the night, that is no reason why the laborer should not "work" a whole day. He, the master, has hired the man's labor-power for a day. He, therefore, is entitled to have a full day's work out of him. The value of the labor-power and the value of the labor it is capable of performing may be different things. If they are, then the worker is entitled to have the first and the employer is equally entitled to pocket the second. Labor is not only the source of wealth, and of value, but it is also the source of more value than that of the labor-power required to perform that labor. And that is the very reason why the employer has hired the laborer.

Instead of discharging his workman after the six hours he makes him work say another six hours, twelve in all (we will not at present mind the Factory Acts). Then after twelve hours' work we have the following result:

20 lbs. of cotton at 1s.	£ 1	0	0
Wear and tear twelve hours, twice 2s., ...	0	4	0
Labour added in twelve hours	0	6	0
Value of 20 lbs. of yarn	£ 1	10	0

OUTLAY OF EMPLOYER:

20 lbs. of cotton, as above, ...	£ 1	0	0
Wear and tear as above	0	4	0
Wages paid to spinner	0	3	0
	£ 1	7	0

Margin for profit ....3s.

The enigma is solved, the possibility of profits explained. Money has been transformed into capital.

The above simple transaction between employer and workman not only explains the genesis of capital, but it forms the groundwork of our whole system of production (called by Marx *capitalist production*). It forms the gist of Marx's whole book, and is at this moment perfectly understood by the Socialists of the Continent, especially by those of Germany and Russia.

I said the 3s. were not profit, but *margin* for profit. The sum thus entering the pocket of the capitalist Marx calls *surplus value*. It is not all profit, but it includes the employer's profit. He has to share it with others: with the Government in the shape of rates and taxes, with the landlord for rent, with the merchant, etc. The laws that regulate this repartition will be explained in the third book (2nd volume) of *Capital* which, together with the second, the author has left in manuscript. It will be published in German as soon as possible.

Thus, all classes of society not composed of actual and immediate producers of wealth (and these, in England at least, are almost exclusively wages-laborers), all classes, from kings and queens to music-masters and greengrocers, live upon their respective shares of this surplus-value. In other words, they live upon the net produce of the surplus labor which the capitalist extracts from his work people, but for which he does not pay. It matters not whether the share of surplus-labor falling to each member of society not actually a producer is granted as a gift by Act of Parliament from the public revenue, or whether it has to be earned by performing some function not actually productive. There is no other fund out of which they can be paid, but the sum total of the surplus value created by the immediate producers, for which they are *not paid*.

APPENDICES

INTRODUCTION

Of all the reports of Marx's premature death, the one in the fall of 1871 is of special interest since Marx, who usually ignored the reports, wrote a denial of it. The report of Marx's death caused a stir among radicals and reformers in the United States and led to adoption of resolutions of grief by the Cosmopolitan Club of New York, a forum organized by a group of radicals and reformers with connections to sections of the First International in the United States.[1] The resolutions were published in *Woodhull's & Claflin's Weekly*, issued by Victoria C. Woodhull and her sister Tennessee C. Claflin. The sisters had created a sensation in 1870 by starting a banking and brokerage business with the help of Cornelius Vanderbilt, the railroad and financial tycoon, and rapidly became known as the "Bewitching Bankers of Wall Street." An advocate of woman's rights and an opponent of the existing institution of marriage, Victoria Woodhull was also in favor of proportional representation, dissolution of corporate monopolies, control of national banks, direct taxation, national education, labor reform including an eight-hour day, and abolition of standing armies. In short, Victoria Woodhull was an advanced thinker for her day. She and her sister became leaders of Section 12 of the International in the United States.[2] Her *Weekly* was the first American periodical to publish *The Communist Manifesto*.

Marx must have read the resolutions adopted on the report of his death, for he wrote to the sisters denying the report, and accompanying it with a long account by Jenny Marx of her arrest (along with Eleanor Marx) in France. The letter was published in *Woodhull & Claflin's Weekly* along with the following comment:

KARL MARX

This active friend of freedom is not dead but lives, and speaks, to the confusion of despots and pseudo-Republicans. A brief letter from him and a long one from his daughter, showing the sound liberalism of the Versaillists, will be found elsewhere in our columns.[3]

The interview with Karl Marx written by John Swinton has already been mentioned. We have also noted that some of Swinton's ideas are inaccurate. But it remains an interesting and valuable document, and appearing on the front page of the New York *Sun* of September 6, 1880, it helped introduce Marx to many American readers.

In the November 29, 1885 issue of his journal, *John Swinton's Paper*, Swinton added an interesting note to his account of the interview with Marx. It dealt with the translation of *Capital* into English and quoted Marx's comment on this question during his original report of the interview.

Swinton was often accused by the reactionary press of being a socialist and/or communist. But those who knew him well rejected these labels. In honoring Swinton at a reception in 1890, the Socialist Labor Party greeted Swinton as "Labor's champion and friend," rather than as a fellow member of the movement.[4] Marx best characterized Swinton when he called him (in a letter to Sorge) a "well-meaning bourgeois."[5]

APPENDIX I

AN EARLIER REPORT OF THE DEATH OF KARL MARX

Woodhull & Claflin's Weekly,
New York, September 23, October 21, 1871

The sudden and unexpected death of Karl Marx will exert a very powerful influence upon the movements of the Internationals everywhere, and will probably accelerate the transfer of the central organization to the United States, where alone the objects of this powerful organization can be accomplished within the law and without violence. At a very full meeting of the Council of the Cosmopolitan Conference, held on Wednesday evening a very interesting discussion on the life of the great reformer took place and the following resolutions were adopted unanimously.

Whereas, The Atlantic Cable has surprised us with the news of the sudden and unexpected death of Karl Marx; and

Whereas, We recognize in Karl Marx one of the truest, most fearless and most unselfish defenders of all classes and all peoples suffering from oppression: therefore

Resolved, That we profoundly deplore the loss of so powerful an advocate of the people's cause, which is likewise our own.

Resolved, That the oppressed toilers not of Europe only, but of all countries, claim the right to share in the grief which his family and more immediate associates must feel at this sudden bereavement.

Resolved, That the Cosmopolitan Conference of New York tenders to the family of Karl Marx, and to the International Workingmen's Association, their profound sympathy.

Resolved, That the loss of Karl Marx devolves upon every member of the Cosmopolitan Conference, and upon every friend of the despoiled and down-trodden working classes everywhere the duty of laboring with redoubled zeal for the vindication of those rights which he so boldly, so generously, and so steadfastly defended.

Resolved, That while we feel a personal grief at the death of this great fellow-soldier in the battle of reform, and cannot but recognize the severity of our loss, yet are we not dismayed, but are impelled by the sacredness of our cause to fight on unhesitatingly and to struggle with even more determined courage for the full accomplishment of that victory of universal justice whose approaching triumph he so clearly foresaw, but was not permitted to share.

Resolved, That the secretary he instructed to forward a copy of these resolutions to the family of the deceased.

London, N.W. September 23, 1871

Mesdames: I have the honor to send you, for insertion in your WEEKLY, if you judge the contribution sufficiently interesting for your readers—a short relation of my daughter Jenny on the persecutions she and her sisters, during their stay at Begneres de Luchon (Pyrenees), had to undergo at the hands of the French Government. This tragico-comical episode seems to me characteristic of the Republic Thiers.

The news of my death was concocted at Paris by the *Acenic Liberal*, a Bonapartist paper.

Since Sunday last a private Conference of the delegates of the International Workingmen's Association is sitting at London. The proceedings will terminate today.

With my best thanks for the highly interesting papers you had the kindness send me,

I have the honor, Mesdames, to remain,

Yours most sincerely,

Karl Marx

APPENDIX II

JOHN SWINTON'S TRAVELS

Current Views and Notes of Forty Days in France and England.

Karl Marx

One of the most remarkable men of the day, who has played an inscrutable but puissant part in the revolutionary politics of the past 40 years, is Karl Marx. A man without desire for show or fame, caring nothing for the fanfaronade of life or the pretense of power, without haste and without rest, a man of strong, broad, elevated mind, full of far-reaching projects, logical methods and practical aims, he has stood and yet stands behind more of the earthquakes which have convulsed nations and destroyed thrones, and do now menace and appall crowned heads and established frauds, than any other man in Europe, not excepting Joseph Mazzini himself. The student of Berlin, the critic of Hegelianism, the editor of papers and the old-time correspondent of the *New York Tribune,* he showed his qualities and his spirit; the founder and master spirit of the once dreaded International, and the author of *Capital,* he has been expelled from half the countries of Europe, prescribed in nearly all of them, and for 30 years past has found refuge in London. He was at Ramsgate, the great seashore resort of the Londoners, while I was in London, and there I found him in his cottage, with his family of two generations. The saintly-faced, sweet-voiced, graceful woman of suavity, who welcomed me at the door, was evidently the mistress of the house and the wife of Karl Marx. And is this massive-headed, generous featured, courtly, kindly man of 60, with the bushy masses of long revelling gray hair

Karl Marx? His dialogue reminded me of that of Socrates—so free, so sweeping, so creative, so incisive, so genuine—with its sardonic touches, its gleams of humor, and its sportive merriment. He spoke of the political forces and popular movements of the various countries of Europe—the vast current of the spirit of Russia, the motions of the German mind, the action of France, the immobility of England. He spoke hopefully of Russia, philosophically of Germany, cheerfully of France, and sombrely of England—referring contemptuously to the "atomistic reforms" over which the Liberals of the British Parliament spend their time. Surveying the European world, country after country, indicating the features and the developments and the personages of the surface and under the surface, he showed that things were working toward ends which will assuredly be realized. I was often surprised as he spoke. It was evident that this man, of whom so little is seen or heard, is deep in the times; and that, from the Neva to the Seine, from the Urals to the Pyrenees, his hand is at work preparing the way for the new advent. Nor is his work wasted now any more than it has been in the past, during which so many desirable changes have been brought about, so many heroic struggles have been seen, and the French Republic has been set up on the heights. As he spoke, the question I had put, "Why are you doing nothing now?" was seen to be a question of the unlearned, and one to which he could not make direct answer. Inquiring why his great work, *Capital*, the seed field of so many crops, had not been put into Russian and French from the original German, he seemed unable to tell, but said that a proposition for an English translation had come to him from New York. He said that that book was but a fragment, a single part of a work in three parts, two of the parts being yet unpublished, the full trilogy being "Land," "Capital," "Credit," the last part, he said, being largely illustrated from the United States, where credit has had such an amazing development. Mr. Marx is an observer of American action, and his remarks upon some of the formative and substantive forces of American life were full of suggestiveness. By the way, in referring to his *Capital*, he said that anyone who might want to read it would find the French translation superior in many ways to the German original. Mr. Marx referred to Henri Rochefort, the

Frenchman, and in his talk of some of his dead disciples, the stormy Bakunin, the brillant Lassalle and others, I could see how deeply his genius had taken hold of men who, under the circumstances, might have directed the course of history.

The afternoon is waning toward the long twilight of an English summer evening as Mr. Marx discourses, and he proposes a walk through the seaside town and along the shore to the beach, upon which we see many thousand people, largely children disporting themselves. Here we find on the sands his family party—the wife, who had already welcomed me, his two daughters with their children, and his two sons-in-law, one of whom is professor in Kings College, London, and the other, I believe, a man of letters. It was a delightful party—about ten in all—the father of the two young wives, who were happy with their children, and the grandmother of the children, rich in the joysomeness and serenity of her wifely nature. Not less finely than Victor Hugo himself does Karl Marx understand the art of being a grandfather; but more fortunate than Hugo, the married children of Marx live to make jocund his years. Toward nightfall, he and his sons-in-law part from their families to pass an hour with their American guest. And the talk was of the world, and of man, and of time, and of ideas, as our glasses tinkled over the sea. The railway train waits for no man, and night is at hand. Over the thought of the babblement and rack of the age and the ages, over the talk of the day and the scenes of the evening, arose in my mind one question touching upon the final law of being, for which I would seek answer from this sage. Going down to the depths of language and rising to the height of emphasis, during an interspace of silence, I interrupted the revolutionist and philosopher in these fateful words: "What is?"

And it seemed as though his mind were inverted for a moment while he looked upon the roaring sea in front and the restless multitude upon the beach. "What is?" I had inquired, to which in deep and solemn tone, he replied: "Struggle!" At first it seemed as though I had heard the echo of despair: but peradventure it was the law of life.

New York Sun, September 6, 1880

APPENDIX III

WHAT KARL MARX HIMSELF SAID ABOUT THE TRANSLATING OF "CAPITAL"

by John Swinton
(*John Swinton's Paper*. November 29, 1885)

There is a rumpus among the disciples of Karl Marx in London about the translating from German into English of his masterpiece, "Capital." It has just been translated by John Broadhouse, and is now being published piecemeal, in the London magazine, *The Day*. But Frederick Engels, one of Mr. Marx's literary executors, has fired a broadside into Broadhouse's translation. He shows that Broadhouse has an imperfect knowledge of German, with a feeble command of English, and that he is wholly unfitted to translate this most untranslatable of German prose writers.

This squabble recalls to my mind the remarks made to me about the translation of *Capital* by Karl Marx himself, when I spent an afternoon with him at the English town of Ramsgate five years ago. Asking him why it had not been put in English, as it had been put in French and Russian, from the original German, he replied that a proposition for an English translation had come to him from New York,[6] and then he went on to make other remarks that ought to be of interest to both Broadhouse and Engels. He said that his German text was often obscure and that it would be found exceedingly difficult to turn it into English. "But look at the translation into French," he said as he presented me with a copy of the Paris edition of "Le Capital." "That," he continued, "is far clearer, and the style better than the German original. It is from this that the translation into English ought to be made, and I wish you would say so to any one in New York who may try to put the book into English. I really took great pain in revising this French translation which was made by J. Roy; I went over every word of the French manuscript and much of the language and many of the passages so hard to turn from German into English can be easily translated from the French version. "When it is put into English," he repeated, "let the French version be used."

These are the words of Karl Marx himself which are now for the first time put in print.

A few days ago in taking up the first chapter of Mr. Broadhouses's translation, my eye fell on a sentence so obscure as to be unintelligible, but in turning to the French version, the meaning of the sentence was plain.

It would seem as though Mr. Marx's literary executors must have heard from his own lips what he said to me in August of 1880.

NOTES

INTRODUCTION

1. Der Sozialdemokrat, Zürich, March 29, 1883.
2. New York, 1933.
3. Zeitschrift fur Geschichtswissenschaft, XVI, Jahrgang, 1968, Heft 4, 471–92.
An earlier effort to present contemporary reaction to Marx's death is the article, "The Turinese Press on the Death of Marx," a survey of the editorial comment in newspapers of Turin, Italy, published in Avanti, Rome, May 7, 1962. See below 164.
4. Voice of the People, March 25, 1883.
5. Atlantic Monthly, LII, August, 1883, 200-10; North American Review, CXXVI, May, 1883, 454-66; The Contemporary Review, April, 1883, 570–80.
The following monthly or quarterly journals contained no mention of Marx's death or discussion of his life and work in issues of 1883; British Quarterly Review; Fortnightly Review, London; Westminster Review, London; Quarterly Review, London; La Nouvelle Revue, Paris; Revue des Deux Mondes, Paris; Journal des Savants, Paris; Revue Critique d'Historie et de Literature, Paris; Revue de Belgique, Brussels; Deutsche Rundschau, Berlin. The only monthly journal in the United States to note Marx's death was Harper's Monthly Magazine. In its May, 1883 issue, under "Obituary," there is the entry: "March 16—At Argentuil, Karl Marx, aged sixty-five years." (LI, 966.) There are two errors in this single sentence: Marx died on March 14, and he died in London.
6. My research on reactions of the press in the Middle East was conducted in libraries in Cairo and Jerusalem.

7. The Library of Congress has microfilm copies of a few papers published in Latin America during March-May, 1883. However, I also consulted newspapers of this period in Havana, Cuba, Lima, Peru, and Mexico City, Mexico. Mr. Stephen Fogg assisted by consulting newspapers in the libraries of Santiago, Chile.

The absence of comment in the Latin American press is perhaps understandable when one realizes that the Socialist movement did not emerge in these countries until after Marx's death.

8. Except for short trips to Mexico, Central America, Santo Domingo, and Jamaica, José Martí lived in the United States from 1881 to 1895. Most of these years were spent in New York. For nearly all of the fifteen years, Martí was the North American correspondent of important newspapers in Latin America.

9. Copies of a number of labor and Socialist papers published in the United States in 1883 are missing, including the *Paterson Labor Standard,* edited by J.P. McDonnell, who was associated with Marx and the First International, and joined the Socialist movement in the United States after he came to this country.

Issues of the New York *Globe,* edited by T. Thomas Fortune, for March, 1883 are no longer in existence. Fortune, a radical black American, was greatly influenced by Henry George, but he was also impressed with Marx's theory of value. He wrote in his 1884 book, *Black and White: Land, Labor and Politics in the United States:* ". . . capital is the offspring of labor, not labor the offspring of capital. Capital can produce nothing. Left to itself, it is as valueless as the countless millions of gold, silver, copper, lead and iron that lie buried in the unexplored womb of Nature. This stored wealth counts for nothing in its crude, undeveloped state. As it is to-day, so it was a thousand years ago. Years may add to the bulk, and, therefore, the richness of its value; but until man, by his labor of muscle and brain, has brought it forth, it has no value whatever. To have value, it must become an object of barter, of circulation, in short of exchange. As its value depends upon its utility, so when it can longer be used it again becomes a useless mass of perishable wealth. It is the product of labor, pure and simple. . . . Labor is the one paramount force which develops the resources of the world. It produces all the wealth. . . ." (New York, 1884, 147–52.) We do have Fortune's comment on Marx, but this was almost two years after Marx's death. Reviewing several books on socialism and anarchism (*The Conventional Lies of Our Civilization* by Max Nordau, a work on Anarchism translated from the German; *Co-Operative Commonwealth* by Laurence Gronlund, and *Contemporary Socialism* by James Rae), Fortune wrote: "Karl Marx is now the great Magus of the socialistic agitators. They turn to him and his system as embodied in *Capital,* as the mariner turns to the North star. Circumstances made him an exile for some thirty years in England, where he wrote his great work. He was a born agitator, and found his first outlet in newspapers; but this means being cut off by the interdict of the German government he sought a less restricted atmosphere. He was, however, active in all the socialist movements on the continent. He believed in political power to relieve the burdens of the proletariat." (New York *Freeman,* February 14, 1885.) The *Freeman* was a continuation of the *Globe* under a different name, and was also edited by Fortune.

10. A good example is *La Igualdad* of Santiago, Chile which was considered mildly pro-working class.

11. Frederick Engels wrote to Laura Lafargue that the obituary notices that appeared in English and German were "inexact and badly informed, but upon the whole decent." (Engels to Laura, March 25, 1883, *Frederick Engels Paul and Laura Lafargue: Correspondence,* London, 1959–1963, I, 212).

1. FREDERICK ENGELS REPORTS THE DEATH OF KARL MARX

1. Many newspapers received the news of Marx's death from their Paris correspondents, and published that he had died in France.

2. Friedrich Adolph Sorge (1827–1906), German-American communist, music teacher by profession, who fought in the Baden uprising of 1849, and emigrated to the United States in 1852, joined the New York Communist Club in 1858, and actively corresponded with Marx and Engels. Sorge was one of the leaders of the local sections of the First International in the United States. After the General Council of the International was transferred to New York in 1876, Sorge became General Secretary. He was active in the formation of the Socialist Labor Party of the United States, and helped organize the International Labor Union in 1878.

3. Wilhelm Liebknecht (1826–1900) was one of the founders and leaders of the German Social-Democratic Party, and became editor of the party paper, *Vorwärts*. Liebknecht was one of the first to enter the Reichstag as a Socialist, and during the Franco-Prussian War (1870-71) voted against war credits and protested against the annexation of Alsace-Lorraine for which he was imprisoned by Bismark. He published a book about the life of Marx in 1896 which included personal reminiscences of his relations with Marx.

4. Julia Bebel (1843–1910) was the wife of August Bebel (1840–1913), founder and leader of the German Social-Democratic Party.

5. Helene Demuth ("Lenchen") (1823–1890) was the housekeeper for the Marx family from 1837, and a very close family friend. After Marx's death, she kept house for Engels.

6. Jenny von Westphalen Marx (1814–1881) was the daughter of the Prussian State Councillor, Ludwig von Westphalen. She married Karl Marx in 1843. Jenny Marx died of cancer on December 2, 1881. Marx was not well enough to attend the funeral. At the Highgate graveside Engels said: "If ever there was a woman whose greatest happiness was to make others happy, it was this woman."

7. Jenny Marx Longuet (1844–1833) was Marx's eldest daughter. She married the French Socialist, Charles Longuet. Her death on January 11, 1883 was a terrible blow to her father.

8. Eduard Bernstein (1850–1932) was a leader of German Social-Democracy, and editor of the German *Sozialdemokrat*. He became a chief exponent of German revisionism, abandoning Marxism.

9. Johann Phillip Becker (1809–1886), a brushmaker by trade who became a German Communist, and participated in the 1848 Revolution in Germany. While in exile in Switzerland, he was one of the organizers of and active workers in the First International, and edited *Vorbote* and *Precurseur* in Geneva. Becker was a close friend of Marx and Engels.

10. Carl Schorlemmer (1834–1892) was a noted German chemist and Communist who became a close friend of Marx and Engels. He fought in the Baden uprising of 1849, and later became professor of chemistry in Manchester and Fellow of the Royal Society.

11. Eleanor Marx-Aveling ("Tussy") (1856-1898) was the youngest daughter of Karl Marx. She was born and lived all her life in England; married Edward Aveling, and during the last fifteen years of her life, she played a significant part in the British labor movement and women's Socialist movement. She made standard English translations of several of Henrik Ibsen's plays.

12. Sir Edwin Ray Lankester (1847–1929) was a British naturalist and

Professor at the University of London and later at Oxford. He was a friend of Marx.

13. According to the recollections of Mrs. Marrian Comyn, Eleanor Marx, Marx's daughter, commented while Marx was lying-in-state: "I want no condolence. If he had lingered during a long illness, and I had seen his mind and body decaying before my eyes, I should have stood in need of consolation. But it was not so. He died in harness, his intellect untouched. He has earned his rest. Let us be grateful for so much." (Yvonne Karp, *Eleanor Marx*, London, 1972, I, 247.) While this report, written 39 years later, may have been accurate, it should be contrasted with Engel's observation in his letter to Sorge.

14. Epicurus (341–270B.C.) was the famous Greek materialist philosopher.

15. Friedrich Lessner (1825–1910), a tailor by trade, was a leading German Communist. He was sentenced to three years in prison in the Cologne Communist trial. Later he became active in the British trade unions and was a member of the General Council of the First International.

16. The second volume of Capital, subtitled, "The Process of Capitalist Circulation," was published in Hamburg in 1885.

In his preface to the 1893 edition, Engels wrote: "It was no easy task to put the second book of *Capital* in shape. . . . The great number of available, mostly fragmentary, texts worked on added to the difficulties of this task. . . . The bulk of the material was not finally polished in point of language. . . . Thoughts were jotted down as they developed in the brain of the author. Some parts of the argument would be fully treated, others of equal importance only indicated. . . . At conclusions of chapters, in the author's anxiety to get to the next, there would often be only a few disjointed sentences. . . . This is the material for Book II, out of which I was supposed 'to make something,' as Marx remarked to his daughter Eleanor shortly before his death. . . ." (For a discussion of Engels' work on *Captial* after Marx's death, *see* Heinrich Gemkow and associates, *Friedrich Engels: Eine Biographie*, Berlin, 1970, (Vollender des "Kapitals"), 503–16.

17. Laura Marx (Mrs. Paul Lafargue) was furious when she read this sentence in the *Sozialdemodrat*, and wrote to Engels: "Will you oblige me by telling me whether Papa told you that he desired Tussy to be, with you, his literary executrix? Not having been with my dear father at the end you will, I know, understand that I am desirous to learn what were his ultimate directions. What his wishes and intentions were at Vevey *I know.* " Later, she insisted that while in Switzerland Marx had told her that he wanted her to have the documents and papers required for a history of the International, and to undertake a translation of *Capital*. Engels replied that the expression "literary executors" was his own, and he apologized for having offended her. However, he made it clear that the work involved in completing *Capital* had to be done in England, and that the "real work . . . will mostly have to be done by me." (*Frederick Engels Paul and Laura Lafargue Correspondence*, I, 250–58.)

2. THE FUNERAL OF KARL MARX

1. Kapp, *op. cit.*, 246–47.

2. *Karl Marx: His Life and Work: Reminiscences by Paul Lafargue and Wilhelm Leibknecht*, New York, 1943, 62.

3. The Appeal was published in *The Worker*, October 7, 1922.

4. William Montgomery Brown (1855–1937), Protestant Episcopal Bishop, was a left-wing Socialist who joined the Communist movement, and was a close friend of Charles E. Ruthenberg, the first secretary of the Workers (Communist) Party of the United States. Accused of being a Bolshevik in the Post-World War I Red-Scare, he replied: "If to be a bolshevik is to be one who is in favor of turning the world upside down with those above who, though they produce everything have scraps for food, shoddy for clothing and shacks for shelter, and with those below who, though they do not produce anything have the choice of everything, the best foods, the finest clothes, the luxurious houses, I am indeed a bolshevist, yet not an anarchist." (*Ohio Socialist,* July 16, 1919.) Bishop Brown was unfrocked for heresy in 1925.

5. "A Monument for Marx?" *The Worker,* October 14, 1922.

6. Despite the pledges, Marx's grave continued to be neglected. Writing in the *New Masses* of May 8, 1940, William Blake reported: "The headstones are small. The plot is usually in a wretched condition. The lawn has not been renewed these many years. I visited the grave three times during my long residence in London, and only once did I see a wreath. It carried a Russian inscription on a faded satin red ribbon from a Workers' Study Circle in Moscow. . . ."

7. The London Communist Workers Education Association was the pioneer workers' education organization in England.

8. Marcel Deprez (1843–1918) was a French engineer and mathematician. He conducted the first experiments of long distance transmission of electric power.

9. Charles Longuet (1833–1903) married Marx's daughter Jenny. He was a French journalist and member of the General Council of the First International and of the Paris Commune.

10. Peter Lavrovich Lavrov (1823–1900) was a Russian Revolutionary-Narodnik, and a member of the First International.

11. The French Workers' Party (*Parti Ouvrier*) had split in September, 1882, when the National Committee, dominated by the Possibilists, expelled the Marxists from the Party. The Marxist minority, led by Jules Guesde and Paul La Fargue, organized a separate French Workers' Party. The message came from that party.

12. José Mesa, a Spanish Marxist, lived in Paris where he was a journalist. He was a close friend of Pablo Iglesias, the first secretary of the Socialist party of Spain.

13. George Lochner (born about 1824), was a German cabinet-maker who became an active German revolutionary, a member of the Communist League, and went into exile in London. He maintained close contact with Marx who nominated him to the General Council of the International Workingmen's Association (First International) to which post he was elected.

14. In 1837 Engels' father became a partner in a cotton manufacturing mill near Manchester, England, and five years later, the 22-year-old Frederick was sent to England to learn the business. After two years in the Victoria Mills, Engels completed the work through which he first acquired a European reputation: *Die Lage der arbeitenden Klasse in England* (Leipsic, 1845; 2nd edition, 1848; translated into English by Florence Kelley Wischnewtzky and published in New York in 1887 under the title, *The Condition of the Working-Class in England in 1844*). Engels dedicated the first edition of 1845 to "The Working Classes of Britain," and wrote in English in the German publication: "I have tried to lay before my German countrymen a faithful picture of your condition, of your suffering and struggles, of your hopes and prospects. . . . I have . . . devoted my leisure hours almost exclusively to intercourse with plain working men; I am

both glad and proud of having done so. . . . Having, at the same time, ample opportunity to observe the middle-classes, your opponents, I came to the conclusion that you are right, perfectly right in expecting no support whatever from them. . . . What have they done to prove their professed goodwill towards you? . . . Have they even done as much as compile from those rotting Blue Books a single readable book from which everybody might easily get some information on the condition of the great majority of 'freeborn Britons'? Not they. . . . They have left it to a foreigner to inform the civilized world of the degrading situation in which you have to live. A foreigner to *them*, not to *you*, I hope. Though my English may not be pure, yet I hope you will find it *plain* English. . . ."

Engels also published a series of articles on the British labor movement in the *Labour Standard*, May-August, 1881 which appeared as a book under the title, *The British Labour Movement* (London, 1934).

15. The translation of the telegram is from the original in Russian published in Abram Lazarevich Reuel, *Russkaya ekonomicheskaya mysl 60-70-kh godov XIX veka i marksizm* (*Russian Economic Thought of the 1860's and 1870's and Marxism*), Moscow, 1956, 365.)

For another effort to solicit funds for a wreath for Marx, *see* 184.

16. The reaction of the Slavic socialist student union in Zürich ("Slavia") was conveyed in a letter to Engels of March 19, 1883 from the President of the union, A. Mas'e, and the secretary, I. Teodorov. It read in part: "In accordance with the resolution of 18 March 1883 of the general assembly of the union 'Slavia', the union of youth from Slavic countries living in Zürich, we hasten to express our most profound sorrow over the untimely death of Karl Marx, citizen of the world and indefatigable champion of the rights of the proletariat of all nations. . . . We hope that the memory of Karl Marx will be perpetuated by the establishment of an international fund in his name for the granting of assistance to the victims of the great liberation struggle, as well as to the support of the struggle itself. For this purpose the union 'Slavia' will solicit continuous contributions among its members." (Reuel, *op. cit.*, 366n.2.)

3. KARL MARX: A Biographical Sketch

1. *New Yorker Volkszeitung*, March 15, 1883. The sketch was entitled, "The Founder of the International, His Life, His Work."

2. The quotation is from Shakespeare's *Julius Caesar* and is a comment on Brutus.

4. REACTION TO THE DEATH OF KARL MARX IN THE UNITED STATES

1. No daily papers in Washington, D.C., Baltimore, Denver, Cincinnati, Mobile, Atlanta, Savannah, and many other cities carried any news of Marx's death. The San Francisco *Chronicle* carried a dispatch from London in its March 19, 1883 issue but it contained nothing about Marx. The day before a dispatch from Paris carried news about the celebration in honor of the Paris Commune, but made no mention of Marx. An editorial on March 20 was devoted to the

death of Lady Florence Dixie in London, but the death a week before of a leading socialist thinker in the world passed unnoticed in the editorial page.

2. Morton Borden, "Some Notes on Horace Greeley, Charles Dana and Karl Marx," *Journalism Quarterly*, XXXIV, 1957, 457–65; William Harlan Hale, "When Karl Marx Worked for Horace Greeley, *American Heritage* VIII, April, 1957, 20–25. Thirty-two of the articles which appeared under Marx's authorship in the New York *Daily Tribune* (part of the total of 487 such articles which the *Tribune* published over the ten year period 1851–1861) are included in Henry M. Christman, editor, *The American Journalism of Marx and Engels, A Selection from* the New York *Daily Tribune*, New York, 1966. Though appearing over Marx's name, Engels was the author of many of them—eight of those in Christman's volume.

3. In 1873, following Horace Greeley's death, Whitelaw Reid, who had been associated with the paper since 1868, became head of the New York *Tribune*, then the most powerful newspaper in America. Under his direction, the *Tribune* became increasingly conservative. On December 4, 1878, the *Tribune* editorially urged deportation of "the (German) socialist element here." While Charles A. Dana, who had been instrumental in introducing Marx to the readers of the *Tribune*, also became increasingly conservative and bitterly hostile to labor unions after he acquired the New York *Sun* at the close of 1867, he never ceased to admire Marx, and his paper was one of the few in the United States which carried an editorial on Marx's death. No other newspaper in New York City, including the *New York Times*, had an editorial.

4. *Documents of the First International: The General Council of the First International, 1864–1866*, Moscow, n.d., 50, 53, 57, 60, 68, 69, 94, 96; *The Civil War in the United States by Karl Marx and Frederick Engels*, New York, 1937, 279–86.

5. Philip S. Foner, "Marx's *Capital* in the United States," *Science & Society*, XXXI, Fall, 1967, 461–66.

6. Samuel Bernstein, "American Labor and the Paris Commune," *Ibid.*, Spring, 1951, 154–60.

7. New York *Sun*, September 9, 1871.

8. *Woodhull & Claflin's Weekly*, August 12, 1871.

9. *First Annual Report of the U.S. Commissioner of Labor, 1886*, 60.

10. Meetings to protest the anti-Socialist laws in Germany were held in response to a call from the National Executive Committee of the Socialist Labor Party. In New York City five thousand gathered in Chickering Hall to hear John Swinton denounce "Bismarckism" and the reactionary drive against the German Socialists. (*Chicago Socialist*, January 4, 18, February 15, 22, 1879.)

11. *New Yorker Volkszeitung*, January 10, 1879; *The Socialist*, January 11, 1879; *Vorbote*, January 11, 1879.

The interviews with Marx in the New York *World* and Chicago *Tribune* are reprinted with an introduction and notes in Philip S. Foner, "Two Neglected Interviews with Karl Marx," *Science & Society*, XXXVI, Spring, 1972, 3–28.

12. For the text of John Swinton's article, *see* Appendix II.

In the same letter to Swinton in which he thanked him for his article, Marx spoke of the suffering of socialists in Bismarck's Germany, and urged Swinton to raise money on their behalf. "I believe," he wrote, "that a man of your influence might organize a subscription in the United States." He advised Swinton to contact Sorge, at that time a resident of Hoboken, New Jersey, and to work out details for holding public meetings to protest the German Chancellor's anti-socialist policy. Marx believed that the socialists of Europe would be encouraged and Bismarck hurt by the knowledge that the German situation was being publicized in America. Evidently Marx may not have known of the meeting protesting Bismarck's policy held in New York City in February, 1879 at which Swinton was the principal speaker.

The day after he wrote to Swinton, Marx sent a letter to Sorge in which he reiterated the needs for funds and that he had "written to *John Swinton* . . . and told him to apply to you for detailed information regarding German conditions." It was in this letter that Marx characterized Swinton as a friend of, but not one of, the socialist movement. He described Swinton as a "well-meaning bourgeois." (*Karl Marx and Frederick Engels, Letters to Americans 1848–1895*, 121, 124.) There is no evidence to show that Swinton and Sorge ever contacted one another.

13. For Marx's correspondence with Americans, *see Karl Marx and Frederick Engels, Letters to Americans 1848–1895*, New York, 1953.

14. Philip S. Foner, *History of the Labor Movement in the United States*, New York, 1947, I (From Colonial Times to the Founding of the American Federation of Labor), 448–50, 512–20; Marx to F. Bolte, Nov. 23, 1871, *Karl Marx and Frederick Engels, Letters to Americans*, pp. 93–94.

15. Samuel Gompers, *Seventy Years of Life and Labor*, New York, 1925, I, 38, 85. In a letter to Engels, January 9, 1891, Gompers described himself as "a student of your writings and those of Marx and others in the same line." Referring to the composition of the American Federation of Labor, he noted: "Some of our best men . . . are well-known and avowed socialists." (Philip S. Foner, "Samuel Gompers to Frederick Engels: A Letter," *Labor History*, XI, Spring, 1970, 207–11. *See also* John R. Commons, "Karl Marx and Samuel Gompers," *Political Science Quarterly*, XLI, June, 1926, 281–86.) As is well known, Gompers later became a bitter foe of socialism and socialists.

16. For a discussion of Powderly's hostility to socialists, *see* Philip S. Foner, *History of the Labor Movement in the United States*, New York, 1955, II, 89–91, 112–13, 162–63.

17. The editorial was headed "Karl Marx."

18. Ferdinand Lassalle (1825–1864) was the German lawyer and labor leader who founded the General German Workers Union in 1863, and was criticized by Marx as an advocate of opportunism in German Social-Democracy. For a detailed characterization of Lassalle by Marx, *see* his letter to Kugelmann, February 23, 1865, in *The Selected Correspondence of Karl Marx and Frederick Engels, 1846–1895*, New York, 1942, 193–97.

19. The *New Yorker Volkszeitung* was the daily organ of the Socialist Party. It was edited by Sergius E. Schewitsch.

20. *Freiheit* was edited by Johann Most, the acknowledged leader of the anarchists in the United States.

21. The *Irish World and Industrial Liberator* was primarily devoted to the Irish struggle for emancipation from British colonial domination, but also paid attention to labor activities in the United States, especially those of Irish-American workers. In noticing the death of Marx, the paper observed: "In 1880, Dr. Marx, through his daughter, sent a strong and ringing letter on the Irish question to the *Irish World*. In it he expressed the greatest love for Ireland and the Irish, and said that he had always looked upon their struggles with hope and sympathy—that in his great work on *Capital*, he had devoted two chapters to Ireland and her cause, and his hope in the closing days of his life that she would stand before the world in all the worthiness that the nature of her people and her soil warranted. He even spoke more strongly and looked with the most intense anxiety on the movement of the Land League, then growing to great

magnitude." (*Irish World and Industrial Liberator*, March 31, 1883; reprinted in *Truth* (San Francisco), April 7, 1883.) A search of the files of the *Irish World and Industrial Liberator* for 1880 and 1881 failed to turn up Marx's letter, evidently sent in his name by Eleanor Marx, and it is clear that the paper did not publish it. Yvonne Karp, biographer of Eleanor Marx, informs me that there is no record of such letter in the sources she has examined, and both the Institute of Marxism-Leninism in the Soviet Union and the Institute of Marxismus-Leninismus in the German Democratic Republic inform me that the letter is not in their archives.

For the two chapters in *Capital* referred to above and other writings of Marx on Ireland and the Irish question, *see Ireland and the Irish Question: A Collection of Writings by Karl Marx and Frederick Engels*, New York, 1972.

22. *The Carpenter* was the official organ of the Brotherhood of Carpenters and Joiners affiliated with the American Federation of Labor.

23. *Progress* was the official journal of the Cigarmakers' Progressive Union affiliated with the Knights of Labor.

24. The *Voice of the People* was published by the Workingmen's Co-operative Association and was the official organ of the Central Labor Union of Greater New York and Vicinity. It was also endorsed by the Central Trades and Labor Union of Boston which recommended it "to the working classes of this country." (*Voice of the People*, March 18, 1883.)

Denounced as a "Communist" publication by the conservative press—especially by the New York *Tribune*—the *Voice of the People* replied that since "workingmen are called communists because they want what they earn," the term was "not such a bad word after all," and that "if it is flung recklessly around much longer it will become an excellent synonym of justice and honest dealing." (March 18, 1883.)

25. The editorial carried no title. It was the only editorial on Marx's death in Boston newspapers.

26. The term nihilist was first used in the novel by Ivan S. Turgenev, *Fathers and Sons* (1862), and was identified with anarchist and terrorist thought in Russia.

27. Herbert Spencer (1820–1903) was the formulator of Social Darwinism, an effort to apply Darwinism to society, which saw the Anglo-Saxon civilization as a superior development out of previous civilizations, and the result of competition, and became a leading justification both for the unlimited power of the capitalist class and for imperialism. In *The Man Versus the State* (1884) Spencer expressed his great fear of socialism.

28. The Springfield *Republican* was an independent Republican paper edited by Samuel Bowles, eldest son of the founder of the paper, Samuel Bowles. Apart from the one in the Boston *Daily Advertiser*, this brief comment was the only editorial on Marx's death to appear in the New England Press.

29. The brief comment on Marx's death in *The American Israelite* was the only editorial to appear in the Jewish press either in the United States or England. However, in the article, "The Jewish Problem" published in *The Century* of February, 1883, Emma Lazarus, (1849–1887), best known for her sonnet, "The New Colossus," carved on the base of the Statue of Liberty, wrote that "the modern theory of socialism and humanitarianism, erroneously traced to the New Testament, has its root in the Mosaic Code," and observed that "we find the fathers of modern socialism to be three Jews—Ferdinand Lassalle, Karl Marx, and Johann Jacoby." (Reprinted in Morris U. Schappes, *Emma Lazarus, Selections from Her Poetry and Prose*, New York, 1967, 78.) Johann Jacoby

(1805–1877) was a Reichstag deputy, author of a widely translated speech, "The Social Question." Although he viewed him as bourgeois democrat, Marx respected Jacoby for being a consistent democrat.

30. The editorial was probably written by George Putnam Upton who was an editorial writer for the Chicago *Daily Tribune* from 1870 to his death in 1919, and who translated many works from the German. The previous day (March 16) the *Tribune* carried a long dispatch from New York reporting Marx's death which was followed by a selective biographical sketch, and included editorial commentary which was much less complimentary than the editorial of March 17. It stated: "He is the originator of Communism and the author of the idea that property is robbery, although Proudhon first give it those words in the French tongue. Lassalle was his first really powerful pupil, and he died nearly twenty years ago. Should the theories of Communism ever work any amelioration in society, Karl Marx would then stand in political economy where Darwin stands in natural history. Should society finally extirpate Communism, monopoly, consolidation, and all the levers with which social theorists have hoped to work, then Karl Marx must take his place as the arch-foe of humanity—a greater curse to the world than even Napoleon. . . . No Communist before Karl Marx was ever practical. Society became in the greatest of danger when he bent his great executive powers to the task of breaking it down, whether by fair means or foul." Neither in the March 16th or March 17th issues was mention made of the fact that in 1879 the *Tribune* had carried a long interview with Marx. Two other papers in Chicago, apart from *Vorbote,* carried a notice of Marx's death—the Chicago *Herald* and the Chicago *Interocean.* The one in the *Herald* appeared on March 17 under the heading, "A Great Labor Reformer Dead," and consisted of a dispatch from London, dated March 16 which while it reported that Marx had died in that city—and not in Argenteuil as many papers had it—spelled Engels' name "Engel," described him as the "son-in-law of Karl Marx," and noted: "The difficulty in getting details of his death was caused by the fact that, though Dr. Marx had been ill a long time, Professor Engel [sic] was the only person who was allowed to see him." The dispatch also reported: "From respect to the wishes of Dr. Marx, who always avoided any demonstration, his family has decided that his funeral shall be private. About eighteen persons are to be present, including a few friends, who are coming from the continent. The place of internment has not been announced. Professor Engel [sic] will probably speak at the grave." The Chicago *Inter-Ocean* of March 17 also carried a dispatch from London, dated March 16, but this one stated that Marx was reported to have died in Argenteuil, but that "Dr. Frederick Engel [sic], an intimate friend of Karl Marx, says Marx died at London, near Regent's Park." The dispatch also contained the same comment on "the difficulty" of getting facts about Marx's death and about the plans for the funeral, but added the sentence: "There will be no religious ceremony."

31. The *Arbeiterzeitung* was the weekly organ of the Socialist Labor Party.

32. The reference was undoubtedly to Henry Thomas Buckle (1821–1862) whose *History of Civilisation in England,* published in two volumes (London, 1857–61) is one of the most important works in the history of social science.

33. The *Labor Enquirer* was published by Joseph R. Buchanan, the militant socialist, and was the official organ of the Knights of Labor Assembly in Denver, Colorado. Buchanan was the author of an autobiography, *The Story of a Labor Agitator,* New York, 1903.

34. This is an excerpt from John Swinton's article published in the New York *Sun,* September 6, 1880.

35. Guiseppe Mazzini (1805–1872) was the founder of "Young Italy" and the European Democratic Committee with the objective of unifying Italy. His program demanded the independence and unity of Italy under the slogan, "God and the People." Marx frequently criticized the bourgeois character of Mazzini's program.

36. *Truth* was a weekly pro-socialist, pro-labor paper published in San Francisco by Burnette G. Haskell, leader of an independent socialist movement in the far west and the Rocky Mountain region. The paper was also the official organ of the Knights of Labor assemblies in San Francisco. For Haskell and his movement, *see* Charles McArthur Destler, *American Radicalism, 1865–1901*, New London, Conn., 1946, 79—103.

5. THE COOPER UNION MEMORIAL MEETING

1. *Karl Marx and Frederick Engels, Selected Correspondence, 1846–1895*, 404.

2. The meeting was addressed by Adolph Douai and Chr. Pattberg. Over the speaker's stand was the sign, "Proletarians of the World, Unite." (*New Yorker Volkszeitung*, March 19, 1883.)

3. *Ibid.*, March 16, 1883. The *Volkszeitung* commented that this was the only flag in the entire world which had been lowered in a show of sadness and honor of Marx.

4. Chicago *Vorbote*, March 24, 1883.

5. *Minute Book of the Chicago Socialist Labor Party, 1882–1885*, VII, March 19, 1883, 11–14, Thomas Morgan Collection, Illinois State Historical Society.

6. Chicago *Daily Tribune*, March 26, 1883. A briefer account appears in the Chicago *Inter-Ocean*, March 26, 1883.

The Chicago *Tribune* of March 26, 1883 also mentions a workingmen's meeting on March 25 at which August Spies, the German-American anarchist and later one of the Haymarket martyrs spoke, but there is nothing to indicate that Marx was mentioned at the gathering.

7. *Progress*, March 20, 1883.

8. *Karl Marx and Frederick Engels, Letters to Americans, 1848–1895*, 7, 142, 160–87, 289–90.

9. The New York *Herald* devoted most of a column to a report of the proceedings under the headlines, "Karl Marx. Socialistic Demonstration in Honor of His Memory. Red Banners and Red Speeches. Polyglot Tributes to the Achievements of the Social Reformers." (March 21, 1883.) The New York *World's* account was on its first page of March 21, 1883 under the heading: "In Memory of Carl Marx. The Tribute of the Workingmen of New York to the Founder of the International." The *New York Times'* report of the proceedings—briefer than that which appeared in other papers—was headed: "Communists in Mourning. Testifying Their Respect for Karl Marx and His Doctrines." The *Irish World and Industrial Liberator*, the Denver *Labor Enquirer*, and *Truth* of San Francisco were a few of the labor or pro-labor papers which reprinted the *Voice of the People's* detailed report of the meeting. *Truth* noted that the report of the meeting "deserves to be read by every poor man in the world." (April 7, 1883.)

10. *New Yorker Volkszeitung*, March 22, 1883; *Karl Marx-Friedrich Engels. Werke*, Berlin, 1967, Band 36, 45, 750.

11. Chicago *Vorbote*, March 31, 1883.

12. *Karl Marx and Frederick Engels. Letters to Americans, 1848–1895*, 137–38.

In 1876 Engels wrote to Marx: "This fellow, I mean Most, condensed the whole of *Capital* without understanding any of it." (Engels to Marx, May 24, 1876, *Karl Marx-Friedrich Engels, Historisch-Kritische Gesamtausgabe Werke/Schriften/Briefe*, Berlin, 1927–35, IV, Part III, ffl.(

Most's attempt to summarize Volume I of *Capital* was published in Chemnitz, Germany in 1873 under the title *Kapital und Arbeit. Auszug aus Karl Marx's "Kapital."* The second edition, with revisions by Marx, was used by Otto Weydemeyer for his English translation which when published in the *Labor Standard* and later as a pamphlet, offered Americans an introduction to the basic ideas set forth in Volume I of Capital. (*See*, Philip S. Foner, "Marx's *Capital* in the United States," *op.cit.*, 465–66.)

Morris Hillquit in his *History of Socialism in the United States* (New York, 1910) discusses the conflict between socialists and anarchists in 1883, but makes no mention of the Cooper Union meeting or the effect of Most's speech.

13. This is the headline in the *Voice of the People* over its account of the meeting.

14. Peter J. McGuire was born in 1852. Influenced by German-American Socialists, he joined the Lassallean movement. Later he supported the principles of pure-and-simple trade unionism. He organized the English-speaking branch of the Socialist Labor Party in 1876, and the Brotherhood of Carpenters and Joiners in 1881; drafted the call the convention that set up the American Federation of Labor in which he was an active figure. He is known as the father of Labor Day, but this is contended by those who favor Matthew MacGuire, a S.L.P. and trade unionists of New Jersey.

15. Edward King was President of the Linotypers' Union; John Ritter was President of the union of Zimmerlaite, and Philip Van Patten, a leader of the Socialist Labor Party, was the secretary of the Central Labor Union of Greater New York and Vicinity.

16. Victor Drury arrived in the United States from France in 1867, and became a leading figure in the French section of the International in America. He was greatly influenced by the ideas of producers' cooperatives set forth in the works of Proudhon and later became an active supporter of cooperation in the Knights of Labor.

17. Swinton who had been managing editor of the *New York Times* during the Civil War and chief editorial writer for the New York *Sun* in the 1870's founded *John Swinton's Paper* later in 1883, resigning his lucrative post as managing editor of the *Sun*. Until August 21, 1887, when it ceased publication, *John Swinton's Paper* was the outstanding labor paper in the United States, and was a significant force for militant trade unionism and independent working class political action. Swinton died in 1901 at the age of seventy-one. He published an autobiography, *Striking For Life*, New York, 1894.

18. In his account of the interview with Marx, published in the New York *Sun* of September 6, 1880, Swinton is inaccurate in describing Bakunin and Lassalle as "pupils of Marx." Michael A. Bakunin (1814–1876) the Russian ideologist of anarchism, was an inveterate enemy of Marx, and the latter led the move for his expulsion from the First International at the Hague Congress (1872) as a factional conspirator. Lassalle never represented Marxism; on the contrary, he distorted and falsified it.

19. Henri Rochefort (Marquis de Rochefort-Lucay) (1830–1913) was a French publicist and leader of Left Republicans under the Second Empire.

20. Marx was in frequent correspondence with American socialists and gained considerable knowledge from their letters about events in the United States. In

addition, they supplied him with American newspapers, books and official reports. (*See for example,* Marx to Sorge, October 19, 1877, *Karl Marx and Frederick Engels, Letters to Americans, 1848–1895,* 117.)

21. Wendell Phillips (1811–1884), one of the greatest of the abolitionists, who fought for the rights of women and of the labor movement as well as against Negro slavery.

22. John Brown (1800–1859) devoted most of his life to the overthrow of Negro slavery. He was hanged on December 2, 1859 for having led a small band of white and black followers in an attack on Harpers Ferry, Virginia and seized the United States armory. His aim was the building up of an insurrectionary movement among Negroes throughout the South. John Swinton had known John Brown in Kansas where the two were involved in the free-soil movement.

23. Giuseppe Garibaldi (1807–1882) was the Italian republican leader who led his "Red Shirts" in 1859 to battle for the unity of Italy. Garibaldi was one of the great leaders of the Italian independence movement.

24. Victor Maria Hugo (1802–1885) was the great French novelist, playwright, and poet, and leader of the romantic movement.

25. Nikolai Gavrilovich Chernyshevsky (1828–1888) was the Russian radical journalist and literary critic. He was author of the popular novel, *What is to be Done?* the title of which Lenin, who admired the author as a non-Marxist radical, used for his own pamphlet of the same name.

26. Francisco Pi y Margall (1824–1901) was the Spanish political leader of the movement for republicanism and federalism. A political and economic theorist, he translated Proudhon's writings into Spanish and was himself the author of a number of works on politics and economics.

27. Michael Davitt (1846–1906) was the Irish revolutionary democrat, and one of the organizers, in 1870, of the Land League. A Home Rule Advocate, he became a Member of Parliament in 1895 and served to 1899.

28. Dr. Adolphe Douai (1819–1888) was a German-American abolitionist, educator, and socialist. He had been active in the Revolution of 1848 in Germany, taught in Russia, and then emigrated to Texas in the United States where he established an anti-slavery paper, the *San Antonio Zeitung.* Driven out because of his anti-slavery views, he came to New York, helped launch the kindergarten movement in the United States, and edited *Die Arbeiter Union* until 1870. A confirmed and ardent Marxist after he had read *Capital,* Douai was co-editor of the S.L.P. paper, *New York Volkszeitung,* from 1878 to 1888.

29. Henry George (1839–1897) was the celebrated author of *Progress and Poverty,* published in 1879, which became one of the best-read books on political economy in the United States and influenced many in Europe. George argued that land belonged to society, which created its value and properly taxed, through the "Single Tax," poverty could be eliminated. On June 2, 1881 Marx wrote to John Swinton: "As to the book of Mr. Henry George, I consider it as a last attempt—to save the capitalistic regime." (*Karl Marx and Fred-Engels. Letters to Americans, 1848–1895,* 127.) In 1886 George ran for Mayor of New York City on the United Labor Party ticket and was almost elected.

30. J.P. McDonnell was active in the Irish Fenian movement, and represented Ireland at the Hague Congress of the First International in 1872. He emigrated to the United States where he joined the Workingmen's Party and then the Socialist Labor Party. He was editor of the socialist *Labor Standard* in which he published a number of articles by Engels. In 1883 he organized the New Jersey State Federation of Trades and Labor Unions and was its Chairman for fifteen years.

31. Sergius E. Schewitsch was a Russian-American socialist, leader of the Socialist Labor Party, and editor of the *New Yorker Volkszeitung*.

32. The New York *World's* brief obituary of Marx noted that he had few supporters in the United States. Even its account of the Cooper Union meeting was sneering in tone, stating: "The Socialist societies of this city and neighborhood united last evening in what they styled 'an international labor demonstration in honor of the late Karl Marx' at the Cooper Institute." (March 20, 1883.)

33. It is likely that Schewitsch referred to Chernyshevsky and the reporter wrote Tchernikoff instead.

34. Joseph Bunata had been a leader of the Bohemian section of the First International in the United States.

35. The reference is undoubtedly to Theodore Millot, a bookbinder, who had been secretary of Section 2 of the First International in the United States.

36. Johann Joseph Most (1846–1906), a bookbinder by trade, he was a socialist who become an anarchist. After having been expelled from the German Social-Democratic Party in 1880, Most went first to England and them in 1883 to the United States where he published *Freiheit*, and became the leading anarchist in the country.

37. Prince Alexander Mikhailovich Gorchakov was the Russian foreign minister who in 1870 promised Bismarck neutrality in a Prussian war against France—in exchange for a free hand in the east for Czar Alexander II.

38. William Ewart Gladstone (1809–1898), British statesman and leader of the Liberal Party who was Prime Minister during the years 1868–74, 1880–85, 1886, and 1892–94.

39. Otto Eduard Von Bismarck (1815–1898), the leading representative of Prussian Junkerism who was the first Chancellor of the German Empire (1871–90). He did encourage social reform where it contributed to national unity and strength, as in nationalizing the railroads, but he undertook an anti-socialist campaign in 1878.

40. Otto Lehmann assisted Bismarck in carrying out the anti-Socialist laws in Germany.

41. Although Martí was no socialist, he did recognize the valuable contributions the socialist working class leaders could make to the Cuban Revolution, and he welcomed their assistance and sought their advice in organizing the Cuban Revolutionary Party. Later, the Cuban *El Socialista* said that while Martí was not a socialist, it could be said truthfully that "in him we see a brother." (Philip S. Foner, *A History of Cuba and its Relations with the United States*, New York, 1963, II, 324.)

6. REACTION TO THE DEATH OF KARL MARX IN EUROPE

1. *Annual Register* (London), March, 1883, 137.

2. Henry Mayers Hyndeman (1842-1921) was an English lawyer, journalist and socialist. Ernest Belfort Bax (1854–1926) was a British socialist and idealist philosopher, and later an editor of *Justice* and *Today*. Both Hyndeman and Bax later became reformist leaders. The Democratic Federation later became the Social Democratic Federation.

3. Engels to Kautsky, July 19, 1884, *Karl Marx and Frederick Engels. Selected Correspondence. 1846–1895,* 425.

4. These are *Le Catholique, Dépêche de Paris,* and *L'Action Politique et Sociale.*

5. These are *L'Appel au Peuple de Paris, La Bien Public, La Citoyenne, Correspondance Havas, Correspondance Républicaine, Correspondance Universelle, Le Drapeau, des Deux Mondes, La France Nouvelle, L'Impartial, Le Jour, L'Opinion, La Patrie, La Reforme de Paris.*

6. These are *La Reveil, L'Opinion Nationale, Le Combat Par le Peuple et Pour le Peuple, Le Marseilles,* and *Moniteur Universel.*

7. Pradeep Bandyopadhyay, "The Many Faces of French Marxism," *Science & Society,* vol. XXXVI, Summer, 1972, p. 132.

8. Apart from those in this section, there were obituaries in the paper published by the Algemeen Hederlandsch Werklieder (General Dutch Workers League), *De Tyd,* a Catholic daily, and a brief account of the burial of Marx in *Algemeen Handelblad,* organ of the Amsterdam commercial bourgeoisie.

9. One of Nieuwenhuis' articles is in this section; the other will be found in the following section.

10. Engels to Cuno, January 24, 1872, *Karl Marx and Frederick Engels. Letters to Americans, 1848–1895,* 99.

For a discussion of the history of Anarchism and Socialism in Italy before the death of Marx, *see* Richard Hostetter, *The Italian Socialist Movement, I: Origins (1860–1882),* Princeton, New Jersey, 1958.

11. *L'Opinione* of Rome, and *La Perseveranza* of Milan, both conservative papers, and *Ill Diritto* of Rome, a pro-democratic paper, all carried the same single sentence on March 17, 1883: "Socialist Karl Marx died at Argentuil." They evidently obtained the same incorrect information from the same wire service.

12. *Cf.* Abram Lazaverich Reuel, *op.cit.,* Chapter 8, "The Russian Press of the 1880's on the Death of Karl Marx." *See also Vol'noe Slovo (la Parole Libre),* Geneva, April 1, 1883.

13. In this connection, the following comment by Marx on the conditions of Jews in Jerusalem, published in the New York Daily *Tribune,* of April 15, 1854, is significant: "Nothing equals the misery and the sufferings of the Jews of Jerusalem, inhabiting the most filthy quarter of the town, called *hareth el-yahouad,* in the quarter of dirt, between the Zion and the Moriah, where their synagogues are situated—the constant objects of Mussulman opposition and intolerance, insulted by the Greeks, persecuted by the Latins, and living only upon the scanty alms transmitted by their European brethren."

14. The journal first appeared in December, 1882 and published eight numbers in all. ("Na venok Marksu" ["A Wreath for Marx"], *Katorga i ssylka,* book 3 (100), Moscow, 1933, 166–67.

15. *Perepiska K. Marksa i F. Engel's s russkimi politicheskimi deiateliami* (Correspondence of K. Marx and F. Engels with Russian Political Figures, 263; reprinted in Reuel, *op.cit.,* 365–66 *n.3.*

16. Edward Spencer Beesley (1831–1915) was the distinguished radical Professor of history and political economy at University College, London. He supported the Union cause actively during the Civil War and later championed the Paris Commune. He was chairman at the meeting in St. Martin's Hall, London, September 28, 1864, at which the International Workingman's Association was founded. Marx differed with him but wrote that apart from his belief in the ideas of August Comte, he was "a very capable and courageous man." (*Karl Marx and Frederick Engels. Selected Correspondence, 1846–1895,* 306.)

17. "Blue Books" were the reports of British Commissions such as Factory Commission, Children's Employment Commission, and other government reports which Marx studied and incorporated his findings in *Capital.* However,

he did not confine himself to "Blue Books" of England alone. On October 19, 1877 Marx wrote to Sorge: "A few years ago (not many) a sort of Blue Book was published (I don't know whether official or not) on the conditions of the miners in Pennsylvania who live, as we know, in the most feudal dependence upon the moneylords. . . . It is of the greatest importance for me to have this publication, and if you can get it for me I will send you what it costs. . . ." (*Karl Marx and Frederick Engels, Letters to Americans, 1848–1895*, 117.)

18. *Progress* was edited at this time by Dr. Edward Aveling, and he appears to have conveniently placed himself at the graveside. He also claimed later to have paid his last respects to Marx as he lay in his coffin, but this was no more accurate than his report of having been present during the proceedings at the grave.

19. The same editorial appeared on the same day in *Der Sozialdemokrat* official organ of the exiled German Social Democratic Party and *Arbeiterstimme*, official organ of the Social Democratic Party of Switzerland and the General Workers' Organization. However, the last sentence appears only in *Arbeiterstimme*. Before that, in the *Sozialdemokrat* there is the sentence: "His thoughts will live forever," followed by "Editor, *Sozialdemokrat.*"

20. The exception was the nasty treatment Marx received at the hands of Paul Brousse (1854–1912), the French petty-bourgeois socialist and one of the leaders of the French Possibilists, in *Prolétaire* of Paris. In articles on April 5 and May 3, 1883, the *Sozialdemokrat* protested Brousse's denigrating article. (*See below*, pp. 148–9.)

21. During his lifetime Marx was repeatedly accused of having stolen his ideas, and especially of having purloined the theory of "surplus value" from Adam Smith, David Ricardo, or William Thompson.

22. The editor of the *Vossiche Zeitung* was obviously unaware of the comment Marx made to a question about Lassalle in the interview published in the Chicago *Tribune*, January 5, 1879: "Lassalle anticipated our general principles. When he commenced to move after the reaction of 1848, he fancied that he could more successfully revive the movement by advocating co-operation of the workingmen in industrial enterprises. It was to stir them into activity. He looked upon this merely as a means to the real end of the movement. I have letters from him to this effect.

"You would call it his nostrum."

"Exactly. He called upon Bismarck, told him what he designed and Bismarck encouraged Lassalle's course at that time in every way possible."

The charge that Lassalle worked secretly with Bismarck is well founded. It was confirmed in 1928 by the discovery of correspondence between Lassalle and Bismarck in which the former promised the latter the support of German workers.

23. In addition to the articles reprinted here, *Neue Zeit* also published, as part of its tribute to Marx, an extract from "A Remarkable Decade" by P.V. Annenkov which appeared originally in the Russian review, *Vestnik Evropy (European Messenger)* of 1880. The extract consisted of Annenkov's relationship with and correspondence with Marx, especially, in the latter case, on Marx's opinion of Proudhon's *The Philosophy of Poverty*. The piece in *Neue Zeit* is entitled "A Russian Voice on Karl Marx."(I, 1883, 236–41.) The complete text of Marx's letter to Annenkov on Proudhon dated Brussels, December 28, 1846, appears in *Karl Marx and Frederick Engels. Selected Correspondence, 1846–1895*, 5–19.

24. The death of Richard Wagner (1813–1883), the great German composer, occurred about the same time as Marx's and scores of papers which carried no news of Marx's death devoted columns to Wagner.

25. For a discussion of Marx's essay on the Jewish question, *see below*, 180.

26. Of all the distortions in this article, the statement that Marx "never looked need in the face" is the most blatant. Marx's life, after he left Germany, was one of continual hardship. "We were permanently hard up," his wife once recalled, "our debts mounted from day to day." Often during winters the family was without coal or money in the house to pay for fuel, and Marx's recurrent illness kept him from being able to work for long stretches.

27. The statement is inaccurate. Following the battle with Bakunin at the Hague Congress in 1872, to prevent the International from being captured by the Bakunists, Marx and Engels proposed that the General Council be moved to New York City. There it remained until it was formally dissolved in July, 1876. By that time, however, the International had ceased functioning as a viable organization, and most of the sections had disappeared.

28. Leo Frankel (1844–1896) was an Hungarian jewelry worker and socialist who, while living in France, was one of the founders of the Lyons section of the First International and one of the leaders of the Paris Commune, in which he served as Minister of Labor. After the fall of the Commune, Frankel lived in London, where he was Corresponding Secretary for Hungary on the General Council of the First International. Returning to Hungary, he was active in the Hungarian workers' movement and a founder of the Hungarian Social Democratic Party.

29. *Neuwe Rotterdamsche Courant* was the paper of the commercial bourgeoisie of Rotterdam.

30. For Marx's opinion of this book, *see below* 207.

31. The article is not signed but it is by Ferdinard Domela Nieuwenhuis. Parts were repeated in his fuller discussion of Marx which appears below and are eliminated here.

Ferdinand Domela Nieuwenhuis (born 1846) was originally a pastor but left the church in 1879 and travelled the path followed by a number of socialists in Europe—from freethinking to socialism. He was one of the leaders of the Social-Democratic Federation of Holland, formed in 1881 by a group of socialist societies. He was imprisoned for his radical activities but hailed as a hero by the Dutch working class and was triumphantly elected to Parliament in 1888. Here he became increasingly disillusioned with political action because of his inability to achieve social reform legislation, and when he lost his seat in the general election of 1892, he veered more and more to anarchism. Although a profound admirer of Marx with whom he corresponded, he finally broke with the Marxist workers' movement at the London Congress of the Second International in 1896.

32. *Rechts voor Allen* was a socialist paper.

33. In his *Socialism, Utopian and Scientific,* Frederick Engels defined as "Utopian Socialism," the doctrines of men like Robert Owen and Charles Fourier which were deficient in the understanding of actual historical and social process.

34. Daniele Manin (1857–1904) was the Italian statesman who fled to Paris after the fall of Venice in 1849, adopted monarchist views which involved him in controversy with Mazzini but won him the support of Garibaldi. He became the first president of the Societa Nazionale and was prominent in the successful struggle for the liberation of Italy which began in 1859.

35. Benjamin Disraeli (1804–1881) was the British statesman, author, and staunch advocate of imperialism. He was prime minister in 1868 and 1874–80.

36. The author is obviously José Mesa y Leompart who sent the telegram to be read at Marx's grave in the name of the Spanish Workers Party (Madrid Brotherhood).

37. *La Lega Democratica*, a daily paper, was edited by Alberto Mario, a leader of the Garibaldi Volunteers during the "Risorgimento," and at one time a follower of Bakunin. On March 20 the paper carried another article on Marx which contained biographical details and briefly discussed the differences between his ideas and those of Lassalle.

38. Most of the article was a biographical sketch.

39. Claude H. de R. Comte de Saint-Simon (1760–1825) was the pioneer French utopian socialist who advocated cooperation between industrialists and workers to achieve a better social order.

40. Francois Charles Marie Fourier (1772–1837) was the French utopian thinker who developed the concept of the Phalanx around which the new social order would grow. His followers included Horace Greeley and Albert Brisbane, and the adherents of Fourierism in the United States incorporated his principles in such colonies as Brook Farm and Hopedale.

41. Robert Owen (1771–1858) was the self-made British industrialist who became a leading figure in the utopian socialist movement and hoped to persuade the industrialists to join him in instituting communities in which labor and social relations would be rationally organized. He established a short-lived colony based on his principles in New Harmony, Indiana. Owen was a champion of the rights of labor and of other oppressed groups.

42. George V. Plekhanov (1856–1918), the founder of Russian Marxism who began as a Populist, but turned to Marxism. He organized the "Liberation of Labor" group in 1883, the first Russian Marxist organization which was formed in Switzerland by former members of the Populist "Black Repartition." Though regarded as the leading Russian theoretical contributors to Marxism before Lenin, he was viewed by Lenin, despite his contributions, as a man who had turned reformist and betrayed socialism.

43. Vera Ivanova Zasulich (1849–1919) was the Russian revolutionary who, on January 24, 1878, fired at and wounded the chief of the St. Petersburg police, Trepov, who had ordered the flogging of a political prisoner. The jury acquitted her. In 1880 she fled to Switzerland, and was one of the organizers of the "Red Cross of the People's Will," a movement to help political prisoners in Russia. Together with Plekhanov she was a founder of the "Liberation" group. She translated works of Marx and Engels into Russian.

44. Pavel Borisovich Akselrod (1850–1928) joined the Populist movement in 1872; in 1880 he was one of the founders of "Black Repartition" and in 1883, jointly with Plekhanov of the Marxist "Liberation of Labor."

45. This was the popular St. Petersburg weekly primarily devoted to illustrations, published by the German-born G.D. Goppe (Hermann Hoppe).

46. This was the monthly journal published by the Moscow Law Society and edited after 1880 by S. A. Muromtsev, jurist, law professor, and prominent Russian liberal who later became one of the leaders of the Constitutional Democratic Party (Kadets) and the President of the first State Duma. The journal's section on political economy frequently included articles on Marx's economic theories.

47. Nikolai Ivanovich Ziber (Sieber) (1844–1888) was a Russian political economist whose father was Swiss and who himself settled in Switzerland in the 1870's. He knew Marx and Engels personally from visits to London, and was a regular contributor to *Iuridischeskii Vestnik*. He was one of Russia's first "legal Marxists," so-called because they took advantage of the censorship's permission to discuss and defend Marxian economic ideas in scholarly journals.

48. This was a yearbook published in Geneva by the People's Will, the group of terrorists who carried out a number of assassinations of high government

officials in Russia, including and culminating in the assassination of Alexander II on March 1, 1881.

49. This was the conservative weekly published in St. Petersburg by Prince V.P. Meshcherskii, a notorious reactionary and anti-Semite who enjoyed the favor (and subsidies) of both Alexander III and Nicholas II. Dostoyevsky had edited the paper for Meshcherskii in the 1870's and published installments of his *Diary of a Writer* in its columns. Meshcherskii himself was editor at the time of Marx's death in 1883.

50. This is a reference to the *Second Address on the Franco-Prussian War* issued by the International and written by Marx. But it is inaccurate. It is true that in the *Second Address* the International cautioned the workers against premature Revolution, but it concluded: "Let the sections of the *International Workingmen's Association* in every country to action. If they forsake their duty, if they remain passive, the present tremendous war will be but the harbinger of still deadlier international feuds, and lead in every nation to a renewed triumph over the workman by the lords of the sword, of the soil, and of capital." *(Karl Marx and Frederick Engels, Writings on the Paris Commune, New York, 1971, 49.)*

51. Adam Smith (1723–1790) was the Scottish philosopher, founder of the classical school of political economy, and author of *The Wealth of Nations*. In a letter to Engels, April 30, 1868, Marx wrote of "A(dam) Smith's nonsense, which has become the main *pillar* of all economics hitherto. . . ." *(Karl Marx and Frederick Engels. Selected Correspondence, 1846–1895, 245.)*

52. David Ricardo (1772–1823) was the English banker and economist who was viewed as the outstanding representative of classical political economy. Marx called Ricardo's *On the Principles of Political Economy and Taxation* (1817) a "great work," but he considered Ricardo's theory of rent "senseless."

53. Frederic Bastiat (1801–1850) was the French economist, who popularized Adam Smith in France. Marx described him as "the shallowest and therefore the most successful representative of the apologists of vulgar economics."

54. Henry Charles Carey (1793–1879) was the American bookseller who became an economist, opposed Ricardo's theory of rent, and propounded a theory of the harmony of class interests. Marx viewed him as a shallow economist.

55. This was a frequent accusation of Marx's critics.

56. The *Moscow Telegraph* was a daily paper. It was non-political.

57. The reference is probably to Louis Rochet, French writer and scholar.

58. This was the weekly supplement to *Voskhod (The Dawn)*, monthly St. Petersburg journal of literary and political commentary devoted to the interests of the Russian Jews. It was published and edited by Adolf Landau, a Russian-Jewish journalist, who founded *Voskhod* in 1881 to replace his earlier *Evreiskaia Biblioteka (The Jewish Library)*, which he had brought out at irregular intervals in the 1870's.

59. This refers to *die Kathedersozialisten* or socialists of the University Chair, the rubric applied to such German political economists as A. Wagner, G. Schmoller, and others.

60. *See above* p. 130.

61. Heinrich Heine (1796–1856) was the German-Jewish poet and radical whose verses and prose writings dealt with romantic, humanitarian, and libertarian ideas. An expatriate who lived much of his life in Paris, he became a bitter critic of Prussian authoritarianism. His poem, "The Weavers," inspired many revolutionaries.

62. Ludwig Börne (1786–1837) was the German-Jewish author, journalist and

precursor of the Young Germany movement. He moved to Paris in 1830 and spent the rest of his life there, fighting through his writings for the enlightenment of Germany, equal rights for Jews, and the general struggle for the liberation of humanity.

63. This was in the first issue of *Voskhod*. M.G. Morgulis was a regular contributor to *Voskhod*.

64. The rest of the article comments briefly on the death of Sir George Jessel (1824–March 23, 1883), a leading Jewish figure in England, and Aaron Levy Green (1821–March 11, 1883), the prominent London rabbi and public figure who was one of the founders of Jews' College, London.

65. Areopagus was the supreme council of ancient Athens.

66. A word is omitted here.

67. There follows a seven line explanation of surplus value.

68. Franz Mehring (1846–1919) was the noted biographer of Marx, theoretician and historian of the German Socialist Democratic Party, and a founder of the Communist Party of Germany.

7. CONTEMPORARY ESSAYS AND ARTICLES

1. Engels letter to Loria and Loria's response are quoted in Gian Mario Bravo, "Engels e Loria: relazioni e polemiche," *Estratto de Studi Storici*, XI, July-September, 1970, 539–40. The article notes that Loria must be credited with introducing Italians to Marx's work, pointing out that his weaknesses must be viewed in terms of the backwardness of philosophic and economic thought in the Italy of his day.

2. *Selections from the Prison Notebooks of Antonio Gramsci*, edited and translated by Quintin Hoare and Geoffrey Nowell Smith, New York, 1971, 13,162,163,164, 457–60.

In advancing his "frontier thesis" in 1893, the American historian Frederick Jackson Turner was influenced, among others, by Achille Loria's theory that human behavior was a product of the ratio of men to free land.

3. Yvonne Kapp, *Eleanor Marx*, London, 1972, I, 277.

4. John Stuart Mill (1806–1873), English historian, philosopher and classical economist who championed the rights of women and labor, and who in later years took socialist position.

5. Alexander II was assasinated on March 13, 1881.

6. Ferdinand Freiligrath (1810–1876), the German revolutionary poet who was an editor of *Neue Rheinische Zeitung* and a member of the Communist League. He later gave up radical principles and joined the bourgeoisie.

A translation by Professor Struik of part of Freiligrath's powerful poem, "A Word of Farewell from the *Neue Rheinische Zeitung*" (from Dirk J. Struik, *Birth of the Communist Manifesto*, New York, 1971, 83) follows:

No open blow in an open fight,
By tricks they are doing the slaying—
I am killed by the rascals that sneak in the night,
The knaves that the Tsar has been paying.

A translation of another stanza of the poem (from Heinrich Gemkow, *Karl Marx: A Biography*, Dresden, 1958, 182) reads as follows:

Now adieu, now adieu, you struggling world,
Now adieu, you fighting armies!

Now adieu, you powder-blackened fields,
Now adieu, you swords and spears!
Now adieu,—but not forever adieu!
They do not kill the spirit, you brothers!
Soon I will arise, shaking my chains,
Soon I will return with arms in hand.

7. Emile Louis Victor de Laveleye (1822–1892), Belgian economist, political scientist, and historian, viewed as a "socialist of the chair." *Le socialisme contemperain* was published in Brussels in 1880.

8. For another letter of Marx to Nieuwenhuis, February 22, 1881, *see Karl Marx and Frederick Engels. Selected Correspondence, 1846–1895*, 386–88.

9. The reference is to the massacre of many thousands of Hugenots which began in Paris on St. Bartholomew's day, August 24, 1572.

10. The quotation is from Vergil.

11. For Engels' critical discussion of anarchist secret societies in Spain, *see Karl Marx and Frederick Engels. Letters to Americans, 1848–1895*, 97,99,103–04.

12. A wave of peasant action against English landlords swept Ireland, led by the Land League and various secret societies. To suppress the mass action of Irish peasants, Parliament adopted, early in 1881, a series of laws suspending constitutional guarantees and introducing a state of siege in the country. But even the dispatch of troops to help landlords evict tenants did not halt the mass struggle which forced Gladstone to repeal the emergency measures of 1881.

13. The reference is to Charles August Saint-Beuve (1804–1869) the French literary critic.

14. The reference is to George Mons Brandes (1842–1877), the Danish literay critic.

15. Dante Alighieri (1265–1321) was the great Italian poet, author of *Divine Comedy*.

16. The reference is to Pope Boniface VIII (1294–1303).

17. The reference is probably to Pasquale di Cicco (1789–1865), the Italian writer and political theorist.

18. Brunetto Latini was an Italian scholar of the sixteenth century.

19. Louis Adolphe Thiers (1797–1877), the French politician and business man who became infamous as the "butcher of the Paris Commune," and whom Marx characterized in his *Civil War in France* as "the complete intellectual expression of the class corruption of the French bourgeoisie."

20. Jeremy Bentham (1748–1832) was the noted English philosopher and jurist, famous as a proponent of utilitarianism.

21. George Hegel (1770–1831) was the leading representative of classical German philosophy who investigated the laws of dialectics which created categories of reason and had an influence upon Marxian dialectics.

22. Lassalle's *System of Acquired Rights* was published in 1861.

23. The Pelasgi were the "sea-people," people who lived in the region of the Agean Sea before the coming of the Greeks. The Lares were Gods or spirits in Roman religion who were associated with the fields and the house and later as beneficent ancestral spirits.

24. Frederich Albert Lange (1828–1875) was the German scientist and political writer, author of *The Labour Question: Its Significance for the Present and Future*.

25. While Marx had some views in common with the positivists he also sharply

differed in some areas. Marx was not a monist; he regarded the question of what kind of substance exists (material, ideal, or both) as a scholastic one of no importance.

26. The reference is to Giovanni Battista Vico (1668–1744), the Italian philosopher.

27. Thomas Hobbes (1588–1679) was the English philosopher who wrote *Leviathan*.

28. The reference is to Raymond Theodore Troblong (1795–1869), the French jurist and politician.

29. Jean Jacques Rousseau (1712–1778) was, like Montesquieu one of the great figures of the French Enlightenment, author of works on political philosophy, education, and morality.

30. There is actually no contradiction here unless one is an idealist like Hegel. To think up a technological innovation is not the same thing as bringing that technological innovation into existence as a real element in production with its attendant changes in the relations of production. In Marx's view a technological change thought of, but not brought into action by labor (human action) would have no consequences on human evolution. Loria fails in this discussion to see that it is real human action that changes history and not just the logical unfolding of ideas by themselves.

31. Leopold Jacoby (1840–1895) was the author of *Die Idee der Entwickelung Einer Soziat Philosophische Darstellung*, Berlin, 1874–76.

32. The reference is to Jean Baptiste Pierre Antoine de Monet Lamarck (1744–1829), the French naturalist.

33. Marx was not a teleologist, a believer that natural processes are determined by their utility in an overall natural design.

34. Karl Eugen Dühring (1883–1921) was a philosopher and economist, and lecturer in Berlin, a violent opponent of dialectics and Marxism. Engels wrote his famous *Anti-Dühring* to combat Dühring's ideas on science.

35. In *Capital*, Marx wrote: "Darwin has interested us in the history of Nature's technology." For Engels' discussion of the similarity between Darwin's "account of plant and animal life and the Malthusian theory," *see* his letter to F.A. Lange, March 29, 1865, *Karl Marx and Frederick Engels, Selected Correspondence, 1846–1895*, 198.)

36. The reference is to Charles Lyell (1797–1875), the British geologist.

37. The reference is to William Petty (1623–1687), the English political scientist, author of *Essays in Political Arithmetick* (1655).

38. The reference is to James Steuart (1712–1780), known as "the last of the Mercantilists," the British author of *An Inquiry into the Principles of Political Economy*," in which the term "political economy" appears to have been used for the first time in an English work.

39. For Sieber, *see* above 175.

40. Loria overlooks the fact that the decline in the rate of profit is consistent with the absolute amount of profit increasing.

41. *See* Eleanor Marx's article on surplus value for a clear discussion of this issue.

42. The quotation is from Juvenal, *First Satire*, 1, 75–77. It changes the word hortos to hortes and omits the opening line. The whole reads:

"Honesty is praised and freezes; to their crimes do they (the wealthy, etc.) owe their pleasure, gardens, mansions, and goblets with goat standing outside." The goat was sacred to Bacchus.

43. Decimus Junius Juvenalis (Juvenal), the Roman satirist.

44. The reference is to Charles Loyseau (1564–1627), the French jurist and author of works on the feudal system.

45. Reverend Thomas R. Malthus (1766–1834), English clergyman whose *Essay on the Principles of Population* (1798), maintains that the production of food cannot keep up with the increase in population, and thus causes hunger and poverty.

46. The reference is probably to A. Meyer, the German economist.

47. Marx, of course, studied the writings of all of the classical economists, but he also pointed out the contradictions in their work. (*See*, for example, his letter to Engels, July 6, 1863, *Karl Marx and Frederick Engels. Selected Correspondence, 1846–1895*, 153–56.)

48. George S. Fullerton (1859–1925), philosopher and author of *A System of Metaphysics.*

49. The reference is to Thomas Tooke (1774–1858), English economist and author of *History of Prices . . . 1796–1856* in six volumes.

50. The reference is to Sir George Ramsay (1800–1871) English economist, author of *Essays of Distribution of Wealth* (1836) in which he argued that wages vary directly as the demand for, inversely, as the supply, of labor.

51. Theodore Van Bernhardi (1802–1887), German economist and historian.

52. The reference is to Thomas Hodgskin (1787–1869), English journalist and social theorist, author of *Labour Defended against the Claims of Capital* (1825) in which he declared that labor alone produces wealth and is therefore entitled to the whole produce of industry.

53. The reference is to John Francis Bray (1809–1895), early socialist writer and labor agitator and author of *Labour's Wrongs and Labour's Remedy* (1839) in which he asserted that labor is the essence and measure of value and receives only part of its production.

54. John Hall-Burton (1809–1881), Scottish author of *Political and Social Economy and its Practical Applications* (1849).

55. The reference is to Jean Charles Leonard Simonde de Sismondi (1733–1842), Swiss historian and economist.

56. The reference is to Henry Thornton, British economist, who developed the Thornton sequence of profit-margin theories in his *An Inquiry into the Nature and Effects of the Paper Credit of Great Britain* (1802).

57. The reference is to James Edwin Thorold Rogers (1823–1890), English economic historian, author of the seven-volume *History of Agriculture and Prices in England* and *Six Centuries of Work and Wages.*

58. The reference is to Johann Heinrich Van Thünen (1783–1850), German economist who developed a theory of natural wages and their relation to the rate of interest and rent.

59. Ludwig Bamberger (1823–1899), was the leader of the National Liberal Party in Germany.

60. This is one of Loria's most ridiculous comments.

61. Loria's interpretation that Marx sought to rejuvenate Hegel by applying the new positivist notions fails to acknowledge Marx's criticism of positivism.

62. Promethus was the Titan who, in Greek mythology, stole fire from Olympus and gave it to man.

63. Oceanides refers in Greek mythology to any of the ocean nymphs held to be the daughters of Oceanus and Tethys. Loria's purple passage only serves to emphasize the shallowness of his conclusion.

APPENDICES

1. Samuel Bernstein, *The First International in America*, New York, 1965, 74–75, 105–06.

2. The leaders of the International in the United States charged Miss Woodhull with using the organization for personal advancement, attracting all kinds of malcontents to the cause. The same issue of *Woodhull & Claflin's Weekly (September 23, 1871)* which published the resolutions of sorrow over the report of Marx's death, contained a cold letter to the sisters from the German Workingmen's Society, Section 1 of the I.W.A. in the United States, signed by F.A. Sorge, R. Starke, and Fred Bolte. It condemned them for having reprinted (in the September 2, 1871 issue) an article from *Grezboten* on "Karl Marx, the founder of the International" in which were interwoven "falsehoods and truths." It closed: " . . . we request you earnestly in the interest of our association, in the interest of truth—the cardinal principle of the association—not to give publicity in your *Weekly* to anything regarding the International Workingmen's Association except authentic information. . . ." Very likely, Sorge and his associates were not happy over the fact that Marx had written to the sisters and sent them Jenny Marx's long letter.

Section 12 was expelled from the International at the Hague Congress in 1872.

3. *Woodhull & Claflin's Weekly*, October 21, 1871.

4. *Workmen's Advocate* (New York), October 18, 1890.

5. *See* Leonard E. Mins, editor and translator, "Unpublished Letters of Karl Marx and Friedrich Engels to Americans," *Science & Society*, II, Summer, 1938, 223.

6* In 1887 two separate editions of the third German edition of Vol. I of *Capital*, translated by Samuel Moore and Edward Aveling, and edited by Frederick Engels, appeared in the United States. Both were originally published in London by Swan Sonneschein, Lowrey & Co., but one carried on its end papers an advertisement of Julius Bordellow, a New York bookseller, as agent for the edition, which read: "The Greatest Work of the Age on Political Economy *Capital: A Critical Analysis of Capitalist Production* by Karl Marx only authorized translation by the life-long friends of the author, Samuel Moore, assisted by Edward Aveling and edited by Frederick Engels. In 2 vols. Cloth $7.00. Julius Bordello (American Agent) 104–106 East Fourth Street." The other had an imprint tipped in, bearing the notice: "New York, Scribner & Wellford." Both editions had been imported into the United States from London, probably in sheets. Twenty years after its first publication in German, a complete English translation of the first volume of *Capital* was available in the United States."

INDEX